Notes from an Odin Actress

> As an actress I sit, speak, run, sweat and, simultaneously, I represent someone who sits, speaks, runs and sweats. As an actress, I am both myself and the character I am playing. I exist in the concreteness of the performance and, at the same time, I need to be alive in the minds and senses of the spectators. How can I speak of this double reality?
>
> Julia Varley

This is a book about the experience of being an actress from a professional and female perspective. Julia Varley has been a member of Odin Teatret for over thirty years, and *Notes from an Odin Actress* is a personal account of her work with Eugenio Barba and this world-renowned theatre company.

This is a unique window into the in-depth exercises and day-to-day processes of an Odin member. It is a journal to enlighten anyone interested in the performances, the discoveries and the hard physical work that accompany a life in theatre.

Julia Varley joined Odin Teatret in 1976. She is an active actor, director, teacher and writer. She is closely involved with ISTA (International School of Theatre Anthropology) and the Magdalena Project, a network of women in contemporary theatre. She is also artistic director of the Transit Festival in Holstebro and editor of *The Open Page*, a journal devoted to women's work in theatre. Her articles and essays have been published in journals such as *Mime Journal*, *New Theatre Quarterly*, *Teatro e Storia*, *Conjunto*, *Lapis* and *Máscara*.

Notes from an Odin Actress
Stones of Water

Julia Varley

LONDON AND NEW YORK

First published 2011
by Routledge
2 Park Square, Milton Park, Abingdon, Oxon OX14 4RN

Simultaneously published in the USA and Canada
by Routledge
270 Madison Ave, New York, NY 10016, USA

*Routledge is an imprint of the Taylor & Francis Group,
an informa business*

© 2011 Julia Varley

Typeset in Times New Roman by
Florence Production Ltd, Stoodleigh, Devon
Printed and bound in Great Britain by
TJ International Ltd, Padstow, Cornwall

All rights reserved. No part of this book may be reprinted or
reproduced or utilised in any form or by any electronic, mechanical,
or other means, now known or hereafter invented, including photocopying
and recording, or in any information storage or retrieval system,
without permission in writing from the publishers.

British Library Cataloguing in Publication Data
A catalogue record for this book is available from the British Library

Library of Congress Cataloging in Publication Data
Varley, Julia, 1954–
  [Pietre d'acqua. English]
  Notes from an Odin actress: stones of water/Julia Varley.
    p. cm.
  1. Varley, Julia, 1954–. 2. Actors – Great Britain – Biography.
  3. Acting. 4. Odin teatret. I. Title. II. Title: Stones of water.
  PN2598.V37A3 2010
  792.02′8092 – dc22
  [B]
  2010006455

ISBN10: 0–415–58628–3 (hbk)
ISBN10: 0–415–58629–1 (pbk)
ISBN10: 0–203–84704–0 (ebk)

ISBN13: 978–0–415–58628–3 (hbk)
ISBN13: 978–0–415–58629–0 (pbk)
ISBN13: 978–0–203–84704–6 (ebk)

To the editors of *The Open Page*:
Geddy, Gilly, Jill, Luciana, Maggie, Maria and Rina

Contents

Foreword ix
Preface by Maggie B. Gale xi
Acknowledgements xv

Introduction 1
Dancing history 1

1 First steps 7

Becoming an actress 7
Odin Teatret 13
Teachers 15

2 The dramaturgy of the actress 20

Personal terminology 20
The echo of silence 23
Stage presence 28
Pursuing oppositions 30
Rodin's torsos 33
Precision and decision: the whole body 36
Precision and decision: the whole voice 40

3 Training 43

Aspects of training 43
My own training 45
The purpose of training 48
Reduction 53

4 Improvisation and composition 56

The creation of material 56
Stimuli, strategies and procedures 62
Repetition, memory, fixing 66

Before, during and after improvisation 68
Elaboration: from the actress's point of view 71
Elaboration: from the director's point of view 74

5 Score and subscore   78

A useful but wrong word 78
The paper song 79
Thought 80
The subscore of creation 81
Chaotic order 83
The subscore of repetition 83
The subscore of performance 85

6 Text and subtext   86

Textual interpretation 86
Textual analysis 87
Physical actions as subtext 89
Vocal actions as subtext 92
Melodies and music as subtext 94

7 The character   96

Identities 96
Mr Peanut 102
Doña Musica 110
Dramaturgy according to Daedalus 114
The puppet character 126

8 The director   130

Meeting a director 130
Working with a director 133
The surgeon and the mountaineer 139
The peasant and the cook 148

9 The performance   153

Replica and difference 153

10 Faces, words, landscapes   159

Foreword

Actress or actor? She, he or s/he? I have had to choose from the start. Wanting to subvert the current habit of including the feminine in a universal masculine word, and in order to explicitly define myself as a woman, I decided to use actress, she and her, even when speaking of the craft in general. I would like to contribute to creating new rules and customs of vocabulary, following a logic of my own. I asked a friend of mine, Clara Bianchi, for advice. She is an Italian primary school teacher, a profession that is 98 per cent female, but which is still generally referred to in the masculine gender in her country. Clara suggested I use the term actress, giving to the word a manifest value by using it to denote both the women and the men who work in this profession. Perhaps male readers will feel excluded, as I have so often felt when men of theatre and letters, actors and directors are being spoken of. In making this choice I wish only to contribute to a more open recognition of the importance of women in theatre history.

    Memories, sensations, aspirations, visions, necessities and technical knowledge mix in me, in my body: they allow me to create actions for the stage. There is no need to know whether what inspires me is true, a wish or a flight of fancy. My actions – the performances – are what permit me to meet others. The most important experiences of my thirty years at Odin Teatret remain veiled, while history is composed of accounts of exercises, productions, journeys, books and meetings. The process is continuous and fluid: even the deepest mutations do not appear as clear and solid turning points, but as the rapids and cataracts of a twisting river. The stones that mark my path are stones of water; in them a process brought to conclusion merges with the next one that has already started.

The Castle of Holstebro
Julia Varley
Photo: Jan Rüsz

Preface

I am so pleased that this book – written by an English woman who has spent most of her life, when not travelling, in Italy and Denmark – already published in French, Italian and Spanish, is now available to English-speaking audiences. Julia Varley is an actress, director, teacher and writer. She is all of these things and yet none of them in any traditional sense. A long-term member of a theatre company whose original actors, mythically, were all rejected by theatre schools and conservatoires, Julia has also made a significant intervention into the professional lives of women working in the experimental and marginalised theatres of the late twentieth and early twenty-first centuries. She is a pioneering founder member of the Magdalena Project, an international network of women in contemporary theatre that began its practical life as a series of questions and working propositions in Wales in the mid-1980s. Julia has performed and taught all over the world for over thirty years, through workshops, work demonstrations and symposia. *Notes from an Odin Actress* is a book about all and none of these things: it is an autobiography, a lively patchwork documentation, a pedagogical text and a testimony. Moreover, it is a book that suggests a new model for writing about the intersections of everyday life and professional practice. I would like to propose that every student of theatre interested in going beyond the surface realities of a commercial industry, interested in the poetics of performance making, should read it.

I have seen many of Julia's performances over the years but I first knew of her through her work with the Magdalena Project. A group of us who had just finished university drove to Cardiff in Wales, to attend the closing performance of the first Magdalena Project festival – we witnessed the product, not the process, of this event. But it was the impulse and the process that underpinned the event that became foundational to my meetings with Julia over the years. Although from different generations and from very different professional perspectives, we share a project around the desire to find a way of articulating, investigating and documenting women's creative work in theatre. I am a cultural historian and Julia has often criticised me for only writing about dead women, while I always remind her to look to history for examples, to find resonances with the questions she poses about women's professional theatre practice in the present. She, on the other hand, has always tried to get me to engage with the present and the extraordinary range of women's theatre and performance work that the Magdalena network has hosted and nurtured over the years. This book is a way of bringing together these two timeframes and perspectives – as Julia says, an actress's work is very much in the present, but in order for it to leave traces and make connections from the present back to the past and into the future, she has had to choose the written form. She has had to use a historical framing for her professional engagement with theatre to, as she says, 'convert practical experience into concepts that transcend both the current moment and personal motivations'. Here, her work with the journal *The Open Page* is also important. Having created the journal from the Magdalena Project's newsletter, the editorial team stuck with the remit of trying to encourage and accommodate many different theatre women's voices in their attempts to articulate their own experiences and practices as actresses, directors, singers and so on.

For the dozen or so years we worked on the journal together with Geddy Aniksdal and Gilly Adams, we all argued about translation, about ownership of language, about how much intervention we could make as editors into other people's attempts to find expression through language. Julia always stuck to her principles and, as you can intimate from *Notes from an Odin Actress*, worked all the time – writing letters, translating articles, sending emails, bartering work demonstrations and performances in lieu of payment for our accommodation, placating administrators, flattering writers while changing what they had written, editing, proofing – and then, as soon as one issue went to press, starting work on the next. I have an arsenal of jokes about our collective images of Julia typing at five in the morning; translating from one language to another while speaking to someone in yet another language on the phone; cooking for ten people and running a meeting on scheduling a Transit Festival for one hundred women from twenty different countries; writing in between rehearsals, performances and meetings at Odin Teatret. Her life is both a hybrid form and a hive of activity. This energy and vitality breathes life into the writing of *Notes from an Odin Actress*. Julia has produced a vibrant book that crosses forms and purposes – an autobiography, a testimonial history and a book that provides a delicately woven, and yet deeply rigorous, exploration of the process of working as an actress and theatre maker. I know that, for Julia, the intent in writing was largely related to the need to find a way of articulating fine-tuned details about the processes of theatre making with which her professional life has been engaged. I know that these articulations speak, in some ways, to practitioners more than they do to academics. But the beauty of this book is that Julia has a remarkably scholarly way of finding a language to explore practice and this will be appreciated by all readers whether practitioners, scholars or students.

From the perspective of cultural history it is important to understand the significance of her starting place as an actress. Julia was a ski-racer and student, but she found a means of political activism through theatre. Part of the generation of European political agitators who prevailed in the countercultural milieu of the 1970s, Julia came to Odin and to the profession of actress bypassing the traditional routes that most actresses of her generation would have taken. Far more in tune with the apprenticeships actresses from previous generations have followed, Julia trained and performed simultaneously, working in the company as student, assistant and then performer. She documents the work of her teachers and mentors, and the dynamics of working in a company of performers who have trained and performed together for many, many years. Their techniques have developed through the performances they have made and have interfaced with those of many other performers and theatre makers globally. As such, this book is a welcome demystification of practice – training, improvisation, vocal technique, composition – and at the same time places the work of one of the most innovative and challenging European theatre companies of the last hundred years, in terms of those whose presence and creative energy the company represents. The book interweaves the personal – Julia's travels and her research, her frustrations with her vocal training – and the professional – her meetings with other companies and practitioners, such as Flora Lauten in Cuba or Patricia Ariza in Colombia whose work she has promoted and championed. It is a departure from many 'autobiographical' accounts by actresses who, often under commercial pressure or because perhaps they think no one is actually interested in the 'work' aspect of their careers, only talk of their star roles or the celebrities with whom their paths as actresses have crossed. Having said this, anyone interested in the work of Odin Teatret or of any of the 'Third Theatres' of the mid to late twentieth and early twenty-first centuries, will find a wealth of detail and insight in this book. Similarly, Julia's willingness to expose her own frailties and uncertainties as a performer and teacher, her research and practical processes in creating characters she has performed – and continues to perform – such as Mr Peanut or Doña Musica, her attitudes towards the complexities of articulating practice, all contribute to making this an extraordinarily inspiring book. She has worked in the gaps and fissures of theatre making, in places where practitioners from the mainstream may look for ideas, inspiration and an ethical stance, but rarely venture professionally. Julia has been central to the 'social theatre' work Odin Teatret have carried out, alongside making performances that challenge and push at the boundaries of aesthetic and cultural practices. Here we see echoes and manifestations of the political imperative in her early theatre work in the 1970s, feeding her theatre projects in and with communities. Julia works a lot with those who have no funding or no theatre building of their own, but who, for example, take theatre to villages and towns in countries ravaged by decades of war. It is this same political drive that has been so important in her work with the Magdalena Project and her unique Transit Festivals hosted by Odin Teatret in Denmark. Here she is tough but patient, tightly organised but fully embracing of spontaneity and the potential chaos that can ensue when an international group of women practitioners meet to exchange working practices. This is not the political drive of an actress like Judith Malina or Franca Rame from the generation that precedes Julia's; it is more subtle perhaps, less defined by political affiliations and more open to the dynamics of a world in which the certainties of black and white are less assured than the grey that lies somewhere between and in the margins. Many great artists work on such borderlines, and many who will be inspired by this book will find their assumptions about Odin Teatret and more particularly about the process of performing and performance making challenged in some way.

I like very much what Julia says about theatre in the closing pages of *Notes from an Odin Actress*: 'Theatre taught me to recognise paradox as the norm and to think differently, in a way often considered conservative by the revolutionary and revolutionary by the conservative.' For me, the ambiguity of paradox is part and parcel also of the ways in which we construct histories, and part of Julia Varley's intention in writing this book was to find a way of giving her work and the work of other women in theatre a visible presence – what I would call its own history. Like all good histories, it weaves together experience, theory, conjecture, analysis and observation. This book works on you as a reader; it takes you on a journey, not necessarily from not-knowing to knowing, but on a journey with a working actress and, more importantly, with an actress at work.

Maggie B. Gale
Manchester 2010

Acknowledgements

I should thank many people for having shown me the way, even if they were not always aware of doing so: political leaders and colleagues, actresses and critics, sports teachers and intellectuals, musicians and relatives. My apprenticeship took place within an environment of theatre groups, organisers and friends, and also historians and artists linked to ISTA (International School of Theatre Anthropology). A particular thank you goes to every member of Odin Teatret and to the women of the Magdalena Project.

To Eugenio Barba, Lorenzo Gleijeses and Ana Woolf a special acknowledgement for their comments after a first reading of this book; to Gilly Adams, Jill Greenhalgh and Leo Sykes for help in translating the original Italian version into English; and to my parents for their patience at seeing me always at my computer during my summer holidays.

Introduction

Dancing history

In 1992, in Mexico City, after my work demonstration *The Dead Brother*, a spectator asked me a recurrent question:

> As an actress, what do you think about when you are improvising? What happens to your original images when the fixed material of the improvisation undergoes transformation and is elaborated to become part of a performance? How do you work on your 'subscore', on your internal references?

I tried to reply:

> When I improvise, I do not think in images or frames as in a film. My senses, my body memory, my mind and my nervous system think, act and react as a whole. Without consciously identifying my points of departure, my actions remember the original information and this continues to be part of them even when the actions are transformed and acquire new meanings for the spectator. I do not use a linear logic. Contradictory motivations co-exist within my actions, they appear and disappear. Everything happens at the same time.

I realised that I was unable to explain my actress's way of thinking, a technique that I have incorporated through years of practice. I was simply giving a confused account of a kind of knowledge that is hard to put into words. So I concluded:

> I cannot explain; that is why I am an actress! My actions *are*; they interact with the spectators, and, if they are alive, I do not feel the need, nor am I asked, to comment on them further. To act on stage allows me to present different situations and events simultaneously, to further the conditions for an experience.

I wanted to underline that the choice of being an actress presupposes a preference for actions rather than words. Once again I insisted on the difficulty of analysing my actress's way of 'thinking with the body'.

My profession allows me to be perceived in the present. However, if I wish to link to the past and leave traces that will endure in the future, and pass on what I consider useful, I also need to find a way to explain through words. The practice of the craft finds its own transmission channels, but theatre history is also a collection of testimonies that convert practical experience into concepts that transcend both the current moment and personal motivations.

Few women have a significant role in the theatre history generally taught in schools and universities. There have been important actresses and female artists, but they have not elaborated theories, and their experiences mostly reach us through biographies, letters and news chronicles. In the century of the great theatre reformers and directors, women remain in the shadows. They are part of the multitude of people whose achievements are veiled and unrecognised.

The theme of the fourth Transit Festival, held at Odin Teatret in 2004, was Theatre – Women – Roots. I dedicated the Festival to Maria Alekseevna Valentej, Vsevolod Meyerhold's granddaughter. Maria devoted her life to redeeming the memory and legacy of her grandfather, even withstanding the Soviet government. I suppose that it is legitimate to question why I decided to dedicate a women's theatre festival to someone who had spent her life rescuing the work of a man. I had the impulse to do this when I heard of her death, after meeting her in Moscow. Everyone will remember Vsevolod Meyerhold, but who will remember Maria, or Masha as she was called?

Being an actress has taught me to believe in the power of vulnerability and to value my difference as a woman, sidestepping issues of equality or superiority. Thus, in terms of theatre history, I prefer to aim at a particular kind of visible presence, which perhaps has yet to be invented. I would like to achieve a paradoxical dream: a history in which anonymous people have a face and a voice. Instead of being concerned only with insisting on an egalitarian recognition of women in theatre history and theory, I would like to turn the usual criteria upside down and emphasise the importance of assisting, bringing up, organising, translating, inspiring, feeling, listening, looking after a family or a company, being on stage and allowing oneself to be guided by intuition. The word 'relationship', so important in theatre, comes to my mind when I remark that women theatre practitioners often find more satisfaction in participating in a common project than on insisting in seeing their names in print. I would like to discover a scholarly authority in their letters, biographies and autobiographies and to give them recognition by name without them having to abandon their generosity.

I would like something to change in the way theatre history is registered, researched, documented and written. I wish to give more presence to women, and to their way of experiencing and thinking, and to include their contributions in the theories and practices of the future. I would like actresses – myself included – to change their awareness of their craft. This would encourage us to go beyond what we know, to overcome the diffidence and insecurity that keeps us at a distance from theoretical abstractions and from disclosing our life experience. To ensure a visible presence, theatre women must accept the responsibility for writing their own history in words, forms and perspectives that, I imagine, are partly still to be discovered or reformulated.

Can I contribute to a different way of writing theatre history, and if so, how? Can I help outline a *rainbow theory* and trace words that recognise intuitively the implicit, non-evident processes of theatre practice? How can I include the diversity of my personal criterion of perceiving past and present events as a woman? If actions must be translated into a conceptual language, how can I transmit my experience and that of other actresses so they can be useful as practical and theoretical references and tools? How can I put into words the reality of actions, the texture of the motivations that generate them, and the effect they have on each spectator? How can I contribute to giving a correct place in history not only to the ideas and the men who have forged, written and achieved them, but also to actions and the women and men who have executed, perceived and interpreted them?

These questions are the result of a concern. Since working at Odin Teatret and listening to talks given by its director Eugenio Barba, I have often heard the names of Meyerhold, Stanislavski, Brecht, Artaud, Appia, Craig, Copeau, Grotowski ... and each time I have asked myself why there are no women among those masters. The names of Duncan, Duse, Littlewood, Mnouchkine... are rarely mentioned. In 1989 I gave the same questions to some women theatre historians with the intention of publishing their answers in the *Newsletter* of the Magdalena Project, a network of women in contemporary theatre. One of the historians commented that it was difficult for her to generalise about something she only recognised as concrete at a personal level. To describe an actress at work was, for her, still a creative process and she did not know what the result of doing this would be. To find other answers I turned to modern physics and quantum mechanics, disciplines that fascinated me at the time.

> The world of matter, as it really is, cannot be communicated verbally. Mathematics and English are both languages, useful tools for conveying information, but they do not work if we try to communicate experiences with them. All a language can do is talk *about* an experience. Words only re-present, with a description which is a symbol. Symbols and experience do not follow the same rules. Our symbolic thought process imposes upon us the categories of either/or. The difference between experience and symbol is the difference between *mythos* and *logos*. *Logos* imitates, but can never replace, experience. *Mythos* alludes to experience and does not try to replace it.
> (Freely quoted from *The Tao of Physics* by Fritjof Capra and *The Dancing Wu Li Masters* by Gary Zukav)

But what happens when I speak of theatre that is both experience and representation? As an actress I sit, speak, run, sweat and, simultaneously, I represent someone who sits, speaks, runs and sweats. As an actress, I am both myself and the character I am playing. I exist in the concreteness of the performance and, at the same time, I need to be alive in the minds and senses of the spectators. How can I speak of this double reality?

Physics told me: you cannot communicate experience, but by telling how quanta (the packets of energy in organic material) are produced and measured, you enable others to have the experience. So, should I speak about *how* I create, elaborate and repeat actions?

When speaking of theatre, I consider the subjectivity of my point of view important. I do not seek objective justifications. Perhaps, precisely because it follows simultaneously two different systems of rules, that of experience and that of representation, theatre allows me to sense the possibility for deep changes. I recognise theatre as a privileged gathering field for women who review their relationship to history. It seems to me that our responsibility as actresses is greater: we are in touch with embodied thinking and with the secrets of actions every day. It is our duty to share our experience, also through words.

As women, we generally choose to prioritise the emotional intensity of our lives, our affections and present occupations. We are less concerned with leaving a historical legacy, as we focus on bringing up our children or engaging with people close to us. As an actress, my intuitive perception of reality, my sense of wholeness and of subjective truth allow me to act without being halted by the logical and linear passages necessary to an analytical thought process. The need for integrity becomes an impediment to speech because the description appears to be simultaneously true and untrue.

What alternatives do I have, if I do not adapt to the usual means of transforming an event into a symbol with a version of reality that is inevitably mutilated, tracing a map that draws and remembers, but that is not the territory? Am I able to use the words to *tell* in a different way? Quantum mechanics uses the 'probability of knowledge' because it is convenient. Can I do the same, accepting the distortions and limitations of narration to say what can become useful subjectively?

While I was directing the performance *Seeds of Memory*, with the Argentinian actress Ana Woolf, I constantly remembered the Mothers of Plaza de Mayo in Buenos Aires. They taught me to challenge the absence of the *desaparecidos* by recreating their presence through detailed everyday memories of how they were when alive, smiling and full of hope for the future. The Mothers warned me that political dissertations did not give these young people their lives back, but that the description of their everyday doings kept them alive in our memories. I remember this when I am preparing the opening speech for a festival or a lecture. Formal headings do not help me speak, but daily practice and learning from mistakes does. My compass is to listen to others and concentrate on what is stimulating in the situation and avoids sterile antagonisms.

Sometimes, when I describe a creative process, I am accused of being dull, of becoming technical, as if I were renouncing passion, interior life and everything that remains invisible and mysterious to spectators, historians and even to me. The simplicity, paradoxical logic and apparent coldness of the processes I apply in creation provoke a rejection in the listener. The exposition of my professional development has even been considered pedagogically dangerous because it might mislead people into thinking that a few simple stratagems are enough to become a better craftswoman.

So it would seem preferable that actresses – just like women in their everyday lives – remain draped in an aura of secrecy and enigma, so that the craft can retain an obscure hidden sense, and the task of referring and analysing is left to others. I do not want to give up my intuitive intelligence, my way of being an actress and a woman, my intimate world that not even I know how to decipher, but I would like young women who approach theatre to be able to establish a dialogue with a woman rather than a man when looking into the past.

I find myself confronting a paradox. If I continue to defend the wholeness and singularity of experience that cannot be communicated, I will never be able to formulate a different kind of reference, theory and knowledge. However, if I cease defending them, I will write a history that is not mine. I need to pass my experience on, but I also need to discover how to do it.

The collective work of editing *The Open Page*, the annual journal of articles by women theatre practitioners, and the contact with the network of the Magdalena Project have taught me to confront the contradictory needs of being tacit and conceptual, invisible and present. When I read an issue of *The Open Page*, I realise that few articles have an autonomous historical or literary strength, but that, through the relationship established between the individual texts, each author participates in making audible a clear and remarkable voice. The presence is constructed through a shared collective commitment that amalgamates in the reader's mind.

Most of what I know is rooted in my practice as an actress. I would like to base my efforts to make women visible in theatre history on the experience of my stage presence. I feel the need to establish a relationship between being an actress and my way of writing, organising and directing.

Often students and workshop participants ask me if I have written about my work process. They would like to find the exercises and advice I have given them in print, so as to remember them more clearly. I have always resisted this proposal because the written word is cloaked in a shroud of objective truth, while in practice I inevitably contradict myself, depending on the situation and the people in front of me. In the concrete work, what is valid one day is not the next. I am afraid that the extremely personal bond and warmth that are so fundamental to teaching would be lost in the writing. The communication that passes from body to body, from sense to sense, from cell to cell, which is at the base of my actress's knowledge, would be missing. However, the request has become ever more insistent, and the work demonstrations, even though available on video, do not meet the demand.

I feel obliged to leave some written traces of my experience hoping that my words will not seem pedantic or appear to give definitive certitudes and

6   *Introduction*

truths. I would like to satisfy those who have asked me to write even though I know that I am not able to dismantle the barrier between reality and words on a page.

Usually, at the end of a workshop, I wish everyone good work. I know that one cannot teach, but only learn. I know that the road is long and that everyone must translate and betray each piece of advice through personal practice. I will try to write remembering what I have often repeated during workshops. There will always be a residue, something unsaid. I accept this responsibility with the illusion that these pages can be useful to an actress in search of *her* voice. I begin driven by the need to dialogue with the past, to forge words that may orientate and also to see women's names in theatre history books: a history that dances with a vulnerable and subjective power.

The Castle of Holstebro
Julia Varley
Photo: Jan Rüsz

1 First steps

Becoming an actress

I realised that I was an actress after writing this profession in my passport. I had already been working for a few years at Odin Teatret, the Danish theatre group founded in 1964. As a teenager I never contemplated becoming an actress, a job I associated with falseness. I was shy, it was hard for me to speak in public and I would never have imagined myself on a stage.

A film I saw when I was ten is the first memory I associate with theatre. It was projected in a theatre in Milan that usually showed English-speaking comedies. It gave me a pleasant feeling. It told the story of a group of shipwrecked children and their adventures on an island. A year later, my grandmother took me to see my first real theatre performances. In London I saw Rudolf Nureyev dance and I watched a matinee of *A Midsummer Night's Dream*. I counted the times Nureyev crossed his legs when he lifted off the floor in a leap that seemed eternal, while in *A Midsummer Night's Dream*, performed in a park, I enjoyed seeing the characters appear from behind trees. I knew of Shakespeare from a children's book in which his tragedies had been given happy endings; when a few years later I saw Franco Zeffirelli's *Romeo and Juliet*, I filled a whole scarf with tears as I did not expect the sequel of suicides.

Survivors on islands, physical activity and actors in the open air: these first images of theatre reappear today in my actress's work as reality, constriction and necessity. The floating islands of the Third Theatre, training and performances in unusual places, are nowadays recognised as part of the variegated world of theatre. However, to get in touch with them, I had first to replace the sensation of falseness I associated with the theatre profession, as presented on television and in magazines when I was a teenager, with the concreteness that becoming an actress would demand of me.

The first place I worked with theatre was a garage in Milan. Three times a week Teatro del Drago rehearsed there, after removing the cars. The floor was dirty with oil. Our costumes consisted of jeans and blue t-shirts. The group had started a year earlier with some students gathered by Massimo Schuster, an Italian who had worked with the Bread and Puppet Theater in the United States. Bored by my school and its slowness and lack of challenge, I had joined

8 *First steps*

an evening class in German to use my time in a better way. There, one of my classmates spoke about underground theatre. The word underground caught my attention: in those days, in Italy, political terms were more fashionable. It was November 1972 and I was eighteen years old.

I watched Teatro del Drago's rehearsals one evening, returned another day and was immediately included in a scene: I was a nurse in a staging of Bertolt Brecht's poem, *The Dead Soldier*. We wore masks, which helped me hide my embarrassment and the feeling of being totally ridiculous. Theatre seized me without waiting for me to choose it. I was attracted by the garage, the people and their commitment: there was rebellion in the air without time-wasting discussions. There I met Marco Donati and Clara Bianchi.

In order to take part in rehearsals on Tuesday and Thursday evenings and Sunday mornings, I had to give up athletics, volleyball, riding and skiing at the weekends. However, these same sport activities provided the first basic knowledge for my theatre craft.

The skiing competitions taught me the importance of preparation: the trainer made me study all the gates of the race by climbing up the mountain with my skis on, following the course in reverse. I needed to be familiar with all the

Rehearsal of *The Dead Soldier*, a poem by Bertolt Brecht, 1972
Clara Bianchi, Marco Donati, Mario Maffi, Julia Varley
Photo: personal archive

angles, bumps and sheets of ice in order to be able to ski down without hesitation and with complete concentration. My gymnastics teacher explained that I should never think of the race ending at the finish line, but imagine it continuing much further. This would avoid a reduction in speed caused by believing the end was in sight. I was the volleyball team captain at high school. Awareness of being part of a group and the cooperation of each single team member were essentials to winning. I had learned this when we managed to turn a game around in our favour after I had encouraged my fellow players during a break. At fourteen and fifteen, I spent my summer holidays teaching smaller children to ride. I was not an excellent rider, but the responsibility for guiding others taught me to show self-confidence.

With my friends of Teatro del Drago, I saw *1789* by Théâtre du Soleil in Paris. This performance, directed by Ariane Mnouchkine, changed my vision of what theatre could be and, still today, is an important reference. For the first time I experienced promenading spectators (who personified revolutionary masses and a market crowd) encircled by actors. We had walked to the theatre in the morning along the Bois de Boulogne, to try to get tickets for the sold-out evening performance. It was the Christmas holidays; we lived three to a room in a hotel used by prostitutes and we had no money. Ariane Mnouchkine, who was busy working on her film *Molière*, despatched us to the box office with an instruction to give us free tickets. Two years later, Teatro del Drago was invited to a festival of anti-military performances by another company from the Cartoucherie in Paris, and I could see how the Théâtre du Soleil had been transformed completely for *L'Age d'Or*.

Teatro del Drago split up after an internal argument: I was no longer part of an underground theatre, but of a political one. I had been an anarchist and then an activist of Avanguardia Operaia (workers' avant-garde), one of the groups of the revolutionary Left in Milan. In those years, 1972–6, making theatre was my way of participating in the students' and workers' struggle. In the time off from Teatro del Drago's political duties and the making of masks and puppets, we asked ourselves how we, as people who presented performances and made theatre interventions, should prepare. We wanted our theatre to be useful and inform by entertaining. The word actor was not a part of our vocabulary. There were no directors. We accepted leaders and positions of responsibility in political parties and in grass-roots organisations, but in theatre we were unruly radicals. Marco Donati, one of the founders of Teatro del Drago, was more effective on stage than others, but this did not give him the right to make decisions.

We had moved from the garage to a cellar, then to a political collective's meeting place and finally to a squat in Via Santa Marta in the centre of Milan. Here we opened a theatre, music, design and film school as part of the activities of the Circolo La Comune, an organisation originally set up to support Dario Fo's and Franca Rame's performances. Before each rehearsal we would clear away the chairs that cluttered the space after the meetings and empty the ashtrays. Hundreds of young people attended the courses. One of them was

Claudio Coloberti, who was to become a member of Teatro del Drago. I organised workshops and classes, contacted professionals, taught, wrote leaflets and press releases, prepared festivals, moulded masks, acted in performances wherever we were called, drove our old blue van, got in touch with journalists and trade unionists, entered discussions, called and presided over meetings, took part in the courses, recycled clay, painted the walls of the squat . . . I worked in the morning to earn money, in the afternoons I went to university and in the evenings and at night I did everything else. Enthusiasm, passion, political belief, deep convictions, little rest, no money, meetings and more meetings, assemblies, protest marches, community fêtes . . . were my daily bread.

Although I showed my colleagues some gymnastic sequences to use as a warm up, we were taught our first real theatre exercises by members of La Comuna Baires, an Argentinian theatre group exiled in Italy, and by Teatro del Sole, a Milanese company that made children's theatre. We exercised each part of our body separately, moved our shoulders and hips, and played with an imaginary ball throwing it with an impulse from different parts of our bodies. We did forward and backward somersaults, over and under tables, jumping over people and chairs, overcoming our fear. We called it physical expression. During an exercise, I walked with my eyes closed, smelling and touching objects in various parts of the room. In another, I ran happily in a circle, while someone on the outside gave directions to make us change the position of our arms.

The streets, universities, factories, neighbourhoods, markets and community fêtes were our real school. We would arrive in our old van with English number plates – my father had given it to us after winning it at backgammon – unload our props and present the performance. If we were lucky they would give us 50,000 lire, which, at that time, would just about pay for the petrol.

One of our performances condemned the 1973 military coup in Chile. Wearing a death mask made of wax, I represented the political party of the Christian Democrats. During a stage action called *Carillon*, which showed the links between the industrialists of various countries, I wore a bowler hat. In an anti-war performance, I was dressed as an American marine. During the campaign for the referendum on divorce, I carried bride and groom puppets with the faces of Almirante and Fanfani (two conservative Italian politicians) dressed in a rubbish bag and the bridesmaid's dress I had worn at my aunt's wedding when I was six.

We took part in protest marches using big masks that we constructed especially for each occasion. At an anti-imperialist demonstration I was inside a giant paper tiger; on the march for the right to work I walked in front of a four-metre-high red cloth elephant.

I saw Odin Teatret for the first time on television. My comrades of Teatro del Drago, Santa Marta Social Centre and Circolo La Comune were with me. The programme presented various 'barters' carried out by Odin Teatret in the villages of Salento in southern Italy. We were sure our world would interest them. Mela Tomaselli and Luciano Fernicola, collaborators from our theatre

Counter-information performance about the military coup in Chile, 1973
Marco Donati, Julia Varley
Photo: personal archive

Parade for the divorce referendum in Italy, 1974
Julia Varley carries the couple Almirante/Fanfani, conservative Italian politicians
Photo: personal archive

school, had already been in touch with this Scandinavian group. They went to Pontedera, where Odin Teatret was on tour, to invite some of the actors to give a workshop and suggest a barter with us when they came to Milan.

Torgeir Wethal, one of the founders of Odin Teatret, came to Santa Marta. Two other actors, Tage Larsen and Tom Fjordfalk, went to Isola, a social centre with which we had joined forces in order to host Odin Teatret, who had been invited to Milan officially by CRT (Centro di Ricerca per il Teatro). We discussed at length how to organise the workshops and choose the participants. We asked ourselves whether it was right to accept the availability of the mythical Nordic actors during the day, when we considered ourselves workers who made theatre only at night.

I heard of theatre training for the first time. Torgeir guided us in the development of individual exercises where the arm was the starting motor and always walking on tiptoe. We made up walks, runs, jumps and skips, backwards and forwards, with stops to maintain our balance and never resting on our heels. We all worked together in the same room, but by ourselves, isolated from each other. On one of the three days of the workshop, Torgeir asked us to make an improvisation about an important event in our lives. He explained that the improvisation should be done in silence, letting our actions be inspired by episodes from our biographies. As a point of departure I thought of my grandfather, of how, when I was twelve years old, he had forbidden me ever to cut my hair. It was the first association that came to my mind and it allowed me to use my hair as a tangible object. It was the first time that I improvised alone, without props, masks or puppets.

We also did some acrobatic exercises with Torgeir, during which I cut my chin. I had to be stitched up in hospital. The exercises resulted in my calf muscles hurting so much that I could only walk upstairs backwards. This is how I arrived to see *Come! And the Day Will Be Ours* (1976–80), the first Odin Teatret performance I experienced as a spectator. I did not understand it. Later I found out that the performance was about the meeting between European immigrants and the indigenous people of the Americas.

Meanwhile I organised the barter. I took Torgeir to Avanguardia Operaia's centre in search of audience seating to use in the deconsecrated church of San Carpoforo, where Odin Teatret would present part of their performance *The Book of Dances* (1974–9). In the church I witnessed the cornice crumbling beneath Iben Nagel Rasmussen's feet, as she got ready to descend from it. She was hanging on a long rope, dressed in her white costume and using a drum covered in colourful ribbons. I saw Tage Larsen dance with his big orange and purple flag, Tom Fjordfalk jump as he twirled a long stick while Roberta Carreri accompanied him playing drums. Else Marie Laukvik had been excused from taking part in the performance. We had arrived with our puppets and masks. The church was packed; many spectators remained outside, including my mother. I watched the performance from afar, but I recognised something familiar in the colours and dances of Odin Teatret. I felt affinity with this tribe, although I could not have explained why.

I cannot say that there was a first day in my apprenticeship as an actress, rather a long period characterised by all the experiences I have mentioned. Of the second period of apprenticeship, I remember an immense solitude. I had gone to visit Odin Teatret in Denmark with the idea of learning as much as I could in three months, in order to return to share my knowledge with my comrades in Milan. During the period in Holstebro I sought to understand stage presence by repeating handstands and back exercises against the wall whilst, day by day, my identity as a responsible, secure, socially active and politically involved person grew weaker. I could not speak the language and, anyway, they did not talk much in the North; I was not involved in any public performance or activity; I was not of use to anyone and I was confronted every day with my professional ignorance.

Three months were enough for me to feel the ground disappear from beneath my feet. I knew only one thing: I could not return to Milan and continue to be responsible for hundreds of young people with only the support of enthusiasm and words. I had chosen theatre as a way of saying 'no', of being rebellious through actions, because I couldn't stand sitting at a desk at school or in an office. At Odin Teatret I discovered that I did not really know what an action was. The only choice I had was to learn this in Denmark. My mother was happy. The 'years of lead' were starting in Italy. Many activists were to be arrested and I might have been one of them. Politics could have become my only horizon. Instead, I began to take my first steps as an actress.

Odin Teatret

I arrived at Odin Teatret, in Holstebro, Denmark, in October 1976. I did not know that before me, during the twelve years of the group's existence, hundreds of other aspiring pupils had visited the theatre. I was not aware that what was new for me was already old for the group I had met only a month earlier. I had spoken with Torgeir Wethal and Iben Nagel Rasmussen in Milan, and then accompanied them on tour in Lombardy. I wanted to enquire whether I might follow their work for a period with the intention of returning to Italy to transmit my new knowledge to my colleagues there. A misunderstanding between Torgeir and Iben led me to think that I had been invited to Denmark. Iben had asked me if I was interested in learning as a director or an actress. I didn't understand the question: directors didn't exist at Santa Marta Social Centre or Teatro del Drago. I reached Denmark at night, loaded with bags and suitcases, after a long journey in Odin Teatret's van, which I had offered to drive to make myself useful. The theatre gave me the impression of being incredibly tidy, clean and rich.

During a meeting, which I did not attend, Eugenio Barba asked who was going to be responsible for me. It was customary that all guests should be looked after by a member of the group. No one offered. I imagine it was an awkward situation. After the meeting, the 'old' actors organised a series of classes for me, while Eugenio behaved as if I did not exist. He thought this way of introducing me to the theatre was unjust. Eugenio and I tried to ignore each other, even when we met in corridors.

During this second period of apprenticeship as an actress, my day was divided between composition (different ways of walking that I invented, watched by Silvia Ricciardelli, a pupil at Odin Teatret), acrobatics (led by Toni Cots, another implacable pupil), work with props (using flags and small stilts together with Francis Pardeilhan, supervised by Tage Larsen) and voice (with Iben Nagel Rasmussen, until she became ill on tour). It was during the first session of voice training with Iben that I realised that I did not know any songs, so that I had to resort to endlessly repeating a nursery rhyme.

I still remember a funny walk, among the five I fixed under Silvia's guidance: I walked with my legs straight, lifting the points of my toes, with my arms straight and my hands held flat and perpendicular, pointing in opposite directions. I repeated the five different walks for hours, changing speed, order and direction in space.

When Odin Teatret went on tour to the outskirts of Copenhagen, there was much less time to take care of guests and pupils. I got up at five o'clock in the morning to work before the group began its own training at seven. I continued alone while the 'elders' rested before the performance. In the evenings I sold books and programmes and helped to show the audience to their seats.

My whole day was dedicated to trying to create a personal training, using my previous experiences in Milan, the first workshop with Torgeir, and the composition, acrobatics and work with props that I was learning in Denmark. When I was not in the room, I spent my time writing pages and pages in my diary.

I did the exercises created by Iben and Jens Christensen. They were called 'Swiss exercises' because Eugenio had seen them for the first time during an Odin Teatret tour in Switzerland. I had learned them from Mela Tomaselli at Santa Marta Social Centre and then seen them again in a film on Odin Teatret's physical training that Torgeir had shown as part of his workshop in Milan. What I remembered mostly from the film was not the exercises, but the final scene: Iben, after having improvised for a long time with the exercises, had gone to kneel at Eugenio's feet as he spoke and explained. Iben's submissive silence had embarrassed me as much as her mysterious power in doing the exercises had fascinated me. In the film Iben showed different ways of kneeling, sitting and lying on the floor, getting up and changing direction. I tried to assimilate and master these exercises by repeating them endlessly. I never felt as clumsy as the day when Eugenio came into Odin Teatret's white room, showing a new secretary around the theatre. I was trying to get up without using my hands from a sitting position with my legs folded sideways.

After spending three months in Denmark, my dream of returning to Milan replete with knowledge that could be transmitted was crushed. The only certainty that remained was that I knew nothing. I could not go back to my old colleagues and sustain their work only with the illusory strength of ideology and the anger provoked by injustice. I was beginning to understand the difference between words and actions, between ideals and the capacity to actually realise them.

I decided to stay and I was 'adopted' by Tage. Adoption was the solution devised by Eugenio to satisfy the desire of the 'elders' to have new young people in the group. Eugenio felt no such need and demanded that anyone who did should assume the financial and didactic responsibility for those they invited to stay. Tage took on the burden of making me grow, together with his other pupil, the North-American Francis Pardeilhan. During the same period Iben was responsible for the Italian Silvia Ricciardelli and the Spaniard Toni Cots. Tage was my first teacher, and later also my husband. I went back to Milan for three months to earn enough money to be economically independent for as long as possible. Then I returned to Odin Teatret with the intention of staying, with Tage's backing and against Eugenio's will.

Teachers

From my very first days at Odin Teatret, even before I was officially accepted as a pupil, I followed the clown performance, presented in Danish schools by Silvia Ricciardelli, Toni Cots and Francis Pardeilhan, as an assistant. I learned to pass the props in the right order, to clean them and pack them neatly after being used, and to make litres of shaving foam for the final comic scene.

Whenever possible I watched the performance *Come! And the Day Will Be Ours*. I sat among the spectators and watched the evident transformation that took place in the bodies of Roberta Carreri, Tom Fjordfalk, Tage Larsen, Else Marie Laukvik, Iben Nagel Rasmussen and Torgeir Wethal. I stored images of tensions, impulses, jumps, walks, falls, voices and songs in which the story being told merged with technical tasks, and the emotions with sweat.

I began making theatre in Italy at a time when the body was the centre of attention. Many young people wanted to be on stage and few wished to be spectators. Doing was the priority. There would always be time to watch and learn later. Theatre was the answer to collective needs and rebellious urges in the pursuit of total involvement and fun. It was not a profession because, as such, it was considered distant and false. Physical training and finding teachers was not the consequence of wanting an apprenticeship that would give the right to a job, but a way of widening the horizons for social commitment through theatre. Seriousness was not determined by professionalism, but by the value given to theatre. Groups learned by themselves. Young people gathered to exchange what they knew and what they pretended to know. The older generations were looked upon with suspicion: they represented conservative forces and practices that could no longer be considered interesting.

When I arrived at Odin Teatret in 1976 I learned to recognise the authority of the actresses and actors of the group: they were teachers and masters. They had skills acquired through years of experience, made apparent by the effect of their actions both in and out of the theatre spaces. I had to build from my foundations to be able to exist again, taking inspiration from the examples I had before me. I sank deeper and deeper into the certainty of knowing nothing.

Among the Odin Teatret actors, Tage Larsen took the responsibility for being my teacher. He created the conditions that allowed me to learn and guaranteed the continuity, patience, daily presence and trust for me to make the necessary mistakes as a pupil. For several years, while I learned to take my first real steps alone, he was the crucial silent company at my side.

I made two scenes for a performance, overseen by Tage; one with Francis using flags as props, and another with a Danish pupil, Torben Bjelke, playing bass drums. I created different ways of walking inspired by Indian dances. Introducing this work, Tage had spoken of classical Indian dances, but I had misunderstood. Thinking that he was talking about American Indians, I called my notebook 'Geronimo'. I made vocal improvisations during which I nervously hid my hands in my skirt pockets, squeezing my fists so tightly that I cut myself with my nails. Tage sometimes executed exercises or particular ways of walking so that I could imitate him, but mostly he behaved as if we were carrying out research together, where my contributions, solutions, capacity to invent and my persistence were as important as his.

For the first two years I followed Odin Teatret on tour and helped out where I could. In France, Spain, Norway and Germany my only preoccupation was to find a free room where I could work alone or under Tage's supervision in the time spare from the group's other activities. On the stage of Théâtre Paul Éluard in the suburbs of Paris, I had a revelation: after having endlessly repeated exercises I had been taught, I thought I had finally understood what composition was. In another space, in Lecco, in Italy, I discovered that it was possible to tell a story with the intonation of the voice independently from the meaning of the words in the text, whilst some months earlier, in Bergen, in Norway, I had cried desperately because of my total incapacity to improvise and develop a given theme with my voice. On all these occasions nothing special happened, it was just the fleeting feeling that my body had understood. For a moment experience revealed its intrinsic meaning and suggested the way forward. Results arrived suddenly and unexpectedly after months and months of insistence along apparently sterile paths. I felt as though I had made a leap forwards, only to return to my daily climb from the same point. The memory of the leap, however, gave me confidence.

In December 1977, in Rennes, in France, the 'families' of Odin Teatret's adopted pupils made a 'barter' to show their training to each other in public. For the first time, Francis and I, led by Tage, and Toni and Silvia, led by Iben, met to expose the daily secret work in front of the eyes of spectators and other members of the group. The time normally dedicated to each exercise passed quickly and we sweated more than usual. The different 'families' showed their dances, music and songs with the ambition of being recognised as part of the same tribe.

I was officially accepted as a pupil at Odin Teatret in 1978, after a period of three months during which the group separated to pursue individual interests and I worked with Tage. Some travelled alone, in couples or in small groups to far away countries like India, Bali and Brazil, others stayed in Denmark. Just before starting to work together again Eugenio announced that the 'children' 'adopted' by Tage and Iben were no longer distant satellites, but part of the group. Eighteen months had passed since I first arrived. From that moment on we would receive a quarter of a monthly salary and we would share both the privileges and the burdens given to each member of Odin Teatret. At that point Iben decided to take on the pedagogical responsibility for the younger members of the group in return for dispensation from having to give workshops outside.

Iben introduced us to the 'samurai' (different grounded steps with very bent legs, using the strong energy of a Japanese warrior) and made us fix a sequence of actions, falls and jumps that, with newly invented elements, grew longer day by day. I trained every day, even on tour, in a variety of spaces, with Francis, Torben and Ulrik Skeel (an actor from an earlier production, *My Father's House*, who had returned to Odin Teatret after an absence of three years). I tried to make my actions firm and precise, but there was always something in excess or something lacking; I did not manage to contain the impulses and my body bounced as though made of rubber.

In 1981 Eugenio went away for three months to direct the second session of ISTA (International School of Theatre Anthropology). He asked Ingemar Lindh, an ex-assistant of Etienne Decroux, to take responsibility for the younger generation at Odin Teatret during that period. We studied the basic figures of corporeal mime for an hour a day and then concentrated on improvisation using fixed elements that we had learned or created during the training. Ingemar insisted on teaching us the explosion of energy of an impulse. During the training Francis was Vaslav Nijinsky, Ulrik passed from being Salvador Dali to Sergei Diaghilev, and I was Isadora Duncan. Ingemar wished our exercises to be *sublime*. We had to be aware and ready so as not to miss the opportunities offered by chance and by circumstances, as though the training were a kind of practical prayer. The training ought to develop like a day of sunshine, from sunrise to sunset, always ending with a performance. He urged us to move like horses and not seals, to be aristocratic, to show nonchalance when in difficulty and to be at ease like a worker opening a bottle of beer. We walked on all fours, pushing our heels into the floor like athletes, maintaining the tension in our legs like horses, floating in the air while compensating with our hips, or pushed forward by an impulse of the pelvis.

Ingemar encouraged me to work with the character of Lady Macbeth. I learned a monologue from Shakespeare's *Macbeth* and an aria from Verdi's opera. Ingemar was the first person to make me dance in space as I sang, forcing me to forget that I thought I could not sing. During my spare time I trained with a long wooden stick and a bowler hat to make a scene for a street performance.

In 1983 Eugenio took a sabbatical year from Odin Teatret. He announced his decision just before the summer holidays and left us soon afterwards, obliging us to find a different way of functioning internally in order to deal with the planned tours. At that time I worked with Silvia Ricciardelli and Ulrik Skeel on the performance *The Night of the Vagabonds*, directed by Else Marie Laukvik. Else Marie would make us improvise entire scenes, texts, music and dances together, only repeating occasionally to cement certain elements that interested her. Else Marie taught me the possibilities of creative disorder and encouraged me not to respect the literal meaning of a situation.

I learned a lot from Iben and Else Marie, even though I was aware that they did not consider me their pupil. Marco Donati at Teatro del Drago, and Tage and Eugenio at Odin Teatret are, on the other hand, my most persistent teachers: all men. I had to strive to find an autonomous image of an actress who could be feminine, yet strong. I could not even see the examples close to me.

Some years later the Magdalena Project, a network of women active in contemporary theatre, became the space in which I could exchange professional experiences with other women. This environment gave me confidence in my questions and my curiosity. It helped me discover a personal language and encouraged me to reflect and write about my work. Ever since the first festival in Cardiff in 1986 every meeting with these women has represented a new challenge for me.

From the beginning of my apprenticeship, training has been important, but the performances constitute the biggest factor in my progress. This is why I say that characters are my real teachers. Mr Peanut, born for the street performance *Anabasis*, taught me to dance and improvise freely. Mrs Peachum and Ilse Koch from *Brecht's Ashes* forced me to smile even when I did not feel like it. With the Woman-in-Black of *The Million* I discovered how to transform my inability to sing into a way of interpreting a text. Joan of Arc helped me conceive a scenario that followed two autonomous, parallel stories during the rehearsals for *The Gospel According to Oxyrhincus*. I faced a whole performance alone with the Woman-in-White of *The Castle of Holstebro*. Kirsten Hastrup, the anthropologist in *Talabot*, taught me not to seek results but to let them happen, Doña Musica from *Kaosmos* to be and not to be, Daedalus in *Mythos* to enter the labyrinth with confidence, and Scheherazade of *Andersen's Dream* not to fear being veiled. The characters introduced me to the rigorous territory of the performances, where to be skilled as an artisan is an obligation and learning its inevitable consequence.

Practice teaches. In one of my work demonstrations I define an actress as a person who makes actions. I reached this simple definition after years of work with Odin Teatret, in an attempt to explain and share my process with others. It seems obvious, but I know it is not, as I rediscover every time I ask participants in workshops what an action is. It is difficult to find a common definition. I ask them to count the actions in a physical sequence or in a scene and identify the personal logic each of them uses to recognise an action. When we still do not agree, I try to point out even the minimal transformations, the changes of muscle tone in the torso that signal to me the transition between

The Million
Tage Larsen, Julia Varley
Photo: Jan Rüsz

one action and the next. The action exists when something alters and reality is no longer the same.

It is not easy to understand that an action is the smallest fragment of a complex movement, nevertheless my experience as an actress lies precisely in this detail. Actions create changes. The smallest change originates in the torso of the person doing the action and can be noticed in the tensions that involve the feet. Turning the world and the usual patterns of opinion on their head, I would like the intelligence of the feet to be acknowledged for its effectiveness in dynamic reflection. The actress who thinks with her feet recognises intuitively the will of her well-rooted body. Also, in order to explain my experience, I start off from a thought that has roots in my feet. With Odin Teatret I have learned to listen to what my feet tell me, with the Magdalena Project to make my feet walk in search of the female image of a master.[1]

Note

1   The female of master is mistress. It is shocking for me to note the different meaning generally given to these two words, to the point that I dare not choose the second one. I have to admit that my battle with language still has a long way to go.

2 The dramaturgy of the actress

Personal terminology

I aspire to have wholeness as an actress, without artificial divisions among body, mind, imagination, senses, emotions and deliberation. My physical and vocal actions aim at affecting the spectator. For my work as an actress, dramaturgy is the instrument that helps me organise my behaviour on stage, it is the logic that links my actions and it is the technique that allows me to act truthfully in fiction.

In my creative process as an actress I pass through different stages that change in importance and priority depending on the phase and development of my work. These stages are the building of presence, the creation of stage behaviour through improvisation or composition, the memorisation of results and their repetition, the interpretation of a text and character, the elaboration of fixed materials, and the repeating of performances. To each of these stages I apply a specific personal dramaturgy.

A theatre performance is composed of a weaving of representation with a complex dramaturgy. Dramaturgy is usually considered in relation to the story and the text, however at Odin Teatret dramaturgy is defined as a simultaneous and coherent succession of events at different levels: organic (or dynamic), narrative and evocative. Allowing myself to be guided by these divisions I could say that for an actress the dynamic or organic dramaturgy corresponds to stage presence, the narrative dramaturgy corresponds to the interpretation of a theme, text or character, and the evocative dramaturgy corresponds to a personal universe made of necessities and rigour, imagination and impulsiveness.

But words that divide life into closed compartments confuse me. Interpretation depends on intonation and movement, which is to say on the faculty of the physical and vocal actions to convince, which is to say on presence. The underlying principles of presence determine the actions of an improvisation that conveys a meaning. Sometimes a character is alive because of the way in which it walks, other times because of what it says, still others because of its context. Rigour is also the consequence of doing exercises to acquire stage presence.

What is so clear when actually doing is difficult to explain in words that follow each other one by one. A part of my experience is left out as soon as I write about one aspect of my craft, whereas my stage narration jumps continuously from one domain to another. For me as an actress, there are explicit and implicit narrative threads: explicit when declared and understood by the spectators, implicit when hidden and contained in the action. The implicit narrative, that I also call hidden illustration or motivation, enriches my work as an actress with details that do not necessarily need to be decipherable from the exterior.

The potential of an action fascinates me. I seek what in my work terminology I call the essence and 'heart' of the action and, at the same time, I explore all the possible, even opposite, meanings it can convey. The stage action is an infinite field of adventure and discovery. Through repetition I come across the vast amount of information that an action contains, which does not reveal itself immediately in its first execution. To do this I repeat a sequence of memorised actions, focusing my attention on a different aspect each time, without interrupting the process.

Sometimes I concentrate on my feet and on how my weight shifts, other times on my hands and the different tensions in my fingers. Then I go to my eyes: I dilate or half close them, I push and pull with them, I change the distance of focus. Subsequently I work with rhythm, diminishing and increasing the speed of the actions from slow motion to fast forward. I amplify the size of my actions to invade space like a giant. I reduce the external form until the actions become barely perceptible, or I 'think' of them just preserving the succession of impulses. I repeat the sequence separating each action with a stop, to underline the beginning, progress and end of each fragment, almost like the mechanical segmentation of gymnastics. I eliminate all evidence of a link between one action and the next to move in a continuous flow. I dance the sequence of actions as a waltz, a samba or rock and roll. I repeat the actions as heavily as a steam-roller or as lightly as a butterfly. I move as though the air were made of stone that opposes my movement, water that caresses me or wind that lifts and transports me with its gusts.

I continue to explore the sequence of actions as though I were Medea advancing towards her children, then Ophelia gathering flowers at the river, a barbarian preparing for war, an astronaut walking on the moon, Hamlet questioning the meaning of life, a humming bird flying from flower to flower or the sun melting the snow. Then I let Hamlet dialogue with Ophelia: one foot is Ophelia the other Hamlet, one action is Hamlet and the next Ophelia.

The sequence of actions is the same, yet everything changes. Changing the circumstances and concentrating each time on a different task, I assess whether the actions vary enough in rhythm, volume, energy and direction in space. I check that the movements are not symmetrical and that my weight does not rest in a static posture. Above all, by altering the thoughts that accompany the action, I experience how the action includes many more possible interpretations than a concept. By repeating the same action I discover each time a meaning of which I was previously unaware.

I enhance my actress's dramaturgy as instrument, logic and technique with a personal terminology that I use to explain my experience to myself and to try to make it accessible to others. For example, I speak of cells that breathe. My frequent use of the word 'cell' comes from a healing massage I received many years ago. As the masseur's hands gently rocked my neck, I answered her questions. Suddenly I remembered an accident that had happened to me and that was the probable cause of the pain I felt in my chest. I had the sensation that these small parts of my body retained memories better than I did and that the cells, that completely renew themselves every seven years, passed this information on without me knowing about it. The discovery of this independent life fascinated me.

One day, during training, while I was experimenting with ways of emanating and retaining energy without moving in space, I thought of breathing with the cells of my body. Without shifting from where I was, I felt every minuscule unit of my muscle fibre participating in an outward and inward movement of retained power that alternatively offered and stored energy. I did not change position in space, yet I had the sensation of reaching the most distant walls with my vibrations. It was like a total breath. I called it 'cell breathing' and this became my definition of a technique for making my presence felt even when keeping completely still.

I also speak of the 'heart' of the action to indicate that nexus without which the action does not exist. It is an inner knot, made of tensions in motion, which cannot be seen, but is clearly perceptible. It is located in the torso, but, instead of beating like a heart, it travels like blood, flows like water, bringing vital sap, nourishment and motivation to the action. It runs beneath the bombed bridge like the river that carries the memory of war to the sea.

I witnessed this 'heart' when Tage Larsen took me to see Auguste Rodin's museum in Paris. He enthusiastically showed me the secret contained in the dynamism of those armless and legless figures. The expressive power of Auguste Rodin's sculptures is still inspiring to me when I have to indicate the essence of an action.

To give examples, I use words that can seem absurd. For instance, I often use the adjective 'abstract' for an action. In my personal terminology, when speaking of an action, abstract is not the opposite of concrete, but of realistic or figurative, as in painting. The comparison with painting is useful to me because an abstract painter must also go through a long apprenticeship of copying from real life, of imitating reality. In the same way, during my first years of learning as an actress, I had to respect all the details of the realistic situations I imagined, in order to understand the necessity for precision. Abstract painting, distancing itself from the principles of the figurative reproduction of reality, concentrates on rhythms, colours and directions in space. I proceed in a similar manner when I allow my body to think and decide for itself. Abstract is the name I give to my actions that think and decide by themselves, because I no longer have a guiding reference that can be described in images, active verbs or stories. The abstract action is concrete in the thought of my feet and in my cells' breath. It is the result of a reaction to something I feel and know, but that I am unable to paraphrase.

Associations and equivalences are other recurrent technical procedures of mine. An association is the intuitive consequence of a reaction to a stimulus, the free equivalent to an event, the next step in a rapid alternation of changing images. I find it useful to think associatively when creating. It allows me to jump from motivation to motivation following a personal logic that has no rules. I can associate a tree with a shelter, a shelter with a cave, a cave with an octopus and thus move my arms like the branches of a tree in the wind with the softness of an octopus in the water. I can associate Lady Macbeth with the witch in Snow White, the witch with an image of the mirror, the mirror with a dialogue with Narcissus, and thus improvise on the beauty and vanity of Lady Macbeth who sees her reflection and vanishes in the bottom of a well.

Equivalence is the ability to find an action, form, image, dynamic structure, scene or thought that corresponds to the point of departure without being the same. Equivalence uses similar but not identical forces, it transports the same rules from one world to another; it is analogous to translation. I find it useful when I have to elaborate my actress's material, or pass from one reference context to another. After I have created a sequence of actions sitting down, I can find an equivalent of the actions while standing, with my voice, or moving the chair instead of my body. Looking at the whirling movement of a dance, I can create an equivalent sensation with my costume, in a hand gesture, while putting a book on the table. I can take some steps using an equivalent rhythm to the lines of a poem, give a character the equivalent vivacity of a folk tune, and say a text with a touch equivalent to the colours in a Van Gogh painting.

It is difficult to judge my own quality of stage life as an actress. It is clearer to me when I look at other actresses. I can perceive that some of my actions are more interesting than others, but, at the same time, I need to be open to the observations of the director who reacts and judges from outside. I don't say very much when I work with young people who want to learn from me. I insist on the same principles, in different countries and theatre environments, even though I am faced with very dissimilar individuals. But the terms and phrases I reiterate are not general rules. Every body, memory, person and actress is different from each other; what is a problem for one can be the solution for another. I indicate principles as advice useful to acquire stage presence, but these need to be translated into a personal language, in which often what actually happens is the opposite of what one thinks or is useful to think.

The echo of silence

We were at the Teatro Argentina in Rome for a seminar. Odin Teatret's entire ensemble was sitting in front of hundreds of students who were asking questions. One of them said: 'Aren't you afraid for your voice?' 'I am afraid *with* my voice,' I replied and burst into tears. The previous morning, during a rehearsal for the Italian version of *Mythos*, one of the performances we were to show in Rome, I had been asked to make the interpretation of a song more spoken. To speak the song I had to change its tonality and rhythm and my voice began to croak as it does sometimes without me being able to do anything to control it. My voice reveals the sense of insecurity that always accompanies me even though I have learned that this vulnerability – and the capacity to offer it as it is – is part of my strength as an actress.

It is said that singing is merely breathing. Merely?!? In 1976 I wrote in my diary of the terrible sense of anguish I felt during a course at Santa Marta Social Centre when I was asked to breathe with my abdomen while lying on the floor. I felt a pressure on my heart as though my body were too small for all it contained. During the early years at Odin Teatret, Tage Larsen made me run, improvise a description of places and people, and sing to his violin. Iben Nagel Rasmussen asked me to direct my voice backwards, to speak with my head, chest and belly, and to find work songs. Eugenio Barba first assessed that I did not sing with my guts, that the lower half of my body did not participate. Then he tried tying belts round my waist, making me lie down, or push him while he opposed my movement in order to let go and make me speak normally. Else Marie Laukvik asked me to make up stories as I went along, to keep my mind busy.

A phonetician I went to when I had serious voice problems advised me to produce relaxed sounds with a breathed 'H' before each word, and to increase the volume as though I were blowing. Ingemar Lindh made me guide my voice with impulses from my body and use an operatic voice. Kozana Lucca of the Roy Hart Theatre (a theatre company that specialises in voice) asked me to growl with a broken voice, and Sacco (an Italian musician and singer) made me hold one note for a long time. John Hardy, an English musician, suggested that I relax. Michael Vetter, the German musician with whom I have worked longest, made me begin by improvising gently following the tones of an Indian tambura.

I have been asked why we don't pay more attention to vocal technique when presenting our work at Odin Teatret. Physical presence has a material consistency: the physical limits of the body can be seen clearly, it is possible to describe in which direction a knee is moving. Voice, on the other hand, is completely individual; it is only definable by metaphor, through medical terms or the laws of physics. Consequently it is more difficult to speak about. The voice is mysterious; its boundaries cannot be touched or easily described: voice travels near and far, it laughs and cries, it sits and flies. It belongs to a space that is found in between the speaker and other people, in between us and the stars that show us the way. The variations of voice are infinite. It is possible to imagine the form of a warrior's stride, but a warrior's voice has such a wide range of possibilities that it is problematic to circumscribe it. The voice has tonalities, colours, timbres, resonators, harmonics, directions, pauses, tremolos, trills, glissando, musicality, air, body, volume, amplitude; the voice vibrates; it fills, extends or limits the space . . . the resonators and the dimensions of the body, the hollows of the mouth and nose, the shape of the head, the position of the teeth and the size of the tongue – all of this

The Echo of Silence
Julia Varley
Photo: Rossella Viti

influences the quality of the voice. Endless and tiny details constitute the particularities of voice.

The translation of the principles of stage presence into a personal language, for which what I think or is useful for me to think is often the reverse of reality, is even more necessary for voice. Voice recognition, like the eyes and fingertips, can be used to guarantee that only one person can open and lock a door. No voice is exactly the same as another; knowing this has helped me understand that what is useful for one voice is not necessarily useful for another. In the same way as I work in empathy with my body, without wishing it were different, I have to acknowledge and accept the sound of my voice, with its specificity and natural inflexions, without flattening it out by forcing it to reach hasty results for the stage.

I think the voice reveals personality more than the body does. It is said that the voice is the mirror of the soul. For me the voice *is* body, in the most complete sense, because its muscles and blood, its cells and vital essence are disseminated in my whole being. Like my body, my voice is supported by my feet being well placed on the ground and it addresses itself to a world that is all around me. I don't find it useful to think of the voice as vocal chords located in the throat or of the breath sustained by the diaphragm, even though this is true physiologically.

With the body it is easy to learn by imitation, even to copy a teacher. With voice, searching for one's own vocal characteristics, I think that direct imitation can even be harmful. I prefer to think of imitation as inspiration rather than an exact copy, in order to avoid trying to reach the same identical results through willpower. The vocal skill that others have obtained serves as orientation for me to figure out my own way forward.

For one of my first vocal improvisations during training, Tage asked me to reproduce the sounds, voices and noises of a film studio. I could not. Even today I feel embarrassed if I imitate, while it helps me to imagine correspondences or equivalents of my own images or the theme I have received. Then it is no longer a question of imitation, but rather a personal process that exploits figurative representation as a point of departure and that cannot be judged on the basis of similarity.

I have had to accept that people with great vocal abilities are not always the best teachers. While teaching, they would like to transmit their technique by presenting it as objective and universal. Especially in singing technique there is a tendency to want to impose a single way of singing or breathing, affirming its 'correctness'. A technique that has given results is not a guarantee of success in general. I believe that different needs co-exist and that we all have to find the most suitable technique for ourselves. I believe that a thousand ways of breathing and singing exist and that each person has to recognise her own. Finding mine is still a continuing process, full of mirages and misunderstandings, discoveries and concerns.

Open, closed, relaxed, sustained voice, using resonators, head voice, bel canto, thinking, not thinking . . . the theories and suggestions I received at the beginning of my apprenticeship made me more and more confused. My private voice is timid; for theatre I had to give it volume. I wanted to get results, to be proficient like the Odin Teatret actresses who were my examples; I wanted to 'function' on stage. I only achieved an imbalance between my breathing and my vocal production. After four years of work, forcing provoked problems. My voice had cramps, I couldn't release it continuously, it was broken and I didn't feel like entrusting it to anyone. Half my face was numb and one of my neck muscles swelled more than the other. My mother was convinced that my trombone playing was the cause, since the breathing power I had developed fought with my voice instead of supporting it. I could produce all the artificial voices (falsetto, nasal, growls . . .) without difficulty, but I could not speak in a normal voice, not even in private. I was incapable of talking on the telephone or with someone sitting beside me in a car. I couldn't find volume at close distance. My voice trembled; it was introverted and false. It was full of ruptures and boundaries: between theatrical and personal, nasal and guttural, sung and spoken.

I visited doctors, dentists, phoneticians, neurologists, throat experts, psychologists, and each of them suggested a different solution to my problem: submit to a dental operation, enter therapy, take penicillin for a whole year . . . all I could do was ignore these suggestions and follow my intuition instead.

Vocal warm-up at the XI ISTA session in Montemor-o-novo, 1998
Photo: Fiora Bemporad

I had to learn to recognise my personal voice again without worrying about the techniques necessary for theatre. Repeating ordinary sentences in simple and normal tones, breathing in a relaxed way, putting an aspiration before every word, doing warm-up exercises, gradually I regained my confidence.

I alternated vibrations and the placement of support with M, N, Ñ, V, B, Z, then with R, BL and BR. I pronounced whole words slowly passing from air to sound to speech, I varied tonalities and colours as much as possible, I spoke everyday sentences with the intention of recognising my own personal voice without consideration for the voice I had developed through training. I yawned, breathed without hurrying, sighed, purred like a cat and puffed like a horse. I encouraged myself to smile, to open my eyes and nostrils, to understand that my voice is forced when I decide to scream, not when I call to someone. I found images and tasks that stimulated me to react and open up vocal possibilities, fighting against the temptation to *want* to achieve a certain effect, to *want* to make particular kinds of voices, to *want* to reach a specific tone or volume.

A full rounded vocal quality and the desire to explore unknown tonalities, timbres and colours materialised when I started to accept my voice as it was, without requiring it to be loud, strong and deep. During a journey to India, away from all those who knew me as an actress, I was taught a song. While I repeated it, my voice vibrated differently: it was mine. It still trembled, but it didn't matter. It was soft, but it didn't need to be strong. From that moment my voice started to grow.

My difficulties and the solutions I have found to overcome them have generated characteristics that have been appreciated. I am perplexed and surprised: my weak point seems to be admired. Many people ask me to work with them. Then I insist on thinking of the voice as something to offer, send like a message or donate as a gift, without holding on to it as though it were a possession. For this reason I prefer not to speak of *my* voice, which underlines a sense of self-direction. I would rather refer to the echo of my voice and recognise it when it comes back modified and amplified, thus focusing my attention outside myself. The voice is a letter that, once written, no longer belongs to me, but to the person to whom it is addressed. For me a voice that vibrates in space is generous.

Even today, hesitations, breaks and flutters, the consequences of my first years of apprenticeship, can be noticed in my voice. The difficulties have been an incentive to invent exercises and find expedients that helped me. More than other practices, vocal work has taught me that resistance is the motor of freedom, that obstacles are signs that show us the way forward, that the river's current needs banks to contain its flow.

Stage presence

What follows does not have anything to do with an aesthetically perfect body. An incredibly fit and agile body could be theatrically insipid and inert. The theme I wish to deal with refers to a physicality that might have plump legs, short sight and convulsive movements. A young, athletic body bursting with energy can deceive, but I think that the 'organicity' of an actress is observed best in stillness, when all the superfluous movements have been eliminated.

It is not my natural features that make me attractive or not on stage, but the behaviour of the character and how this contrasts and collaborates with my own features. For me, as an actress, being 'alive' and organic on stage is different to what the spectator may perceive as such. For the spectator an actress's 'organicity' in a performance depends on a series of factors: the theme, text, space, other actresses and actors, the director, story, genre, culture, political vision, time of the performance, the willingness and mood of the spectators . . . all these elements participate in creating a sensation of 'life'. On the other hand it is not sufficient for an actress to have stage presence in order to appear luminous, vulnerable or seductive. As an actress I can dance my actions and yet cause indifference, vibrate with intensity and yet be boring. An actress's magic on stage and her ability to capture attention also depend on discipline and experience, on personal need and trust in practice, on conviction and luck.

Stage presence is the premise for transforming ideas and wishful thinking into persuasive actions, for the internal creative forces to be revealed and to take on a communicative form. If I have presence independently from the context in which I am placed, it is more possible that I will be able to contribute to the life of the performance. It is no coincidence that I had to develop my theatrical identity by doing endless handstands against a wall: having left the world of ideology and naïve enthusiasm, first of all I had to learn to think with my body in order to exist as an actress.

The first exercises I did at Odin Teatret served to strengthen the muscles of my back and legs, to increase my balance and stamina, to develop the readiness of my reflexes and stretch my tendons so that I could move freely.

I bent one knee at a time, in various directions, with the soles of my feet on the ground or on tiptoe. Standing facing a wall, I flexed my arms at head height and stretched my calf muscles. Vertebra by vertebra I bent my back forwards and backwards. With my back to a wall, I walked my hands down the wall until reaching a bridge position and then came up again. I walked on all fours, then crouched as low as possible before kicking with one leg. I did headstands in different positions. I sat and got up from the floor in various ways. I jumped forwards, backwards, sideways, with my feet together, apart, bringing my knees up to my chest or stretching my arms as if swimming through the air. I did acrobatic exercises and danced with and without music. The continuity, the passage from one exercise to the next and the rhythm were important, as if I was always dancing to an internal and external tune.

I exercised what I call the breathing of the body while keeping still and I pushed my energy in various directions without moving. I stored the sensation of huge power, as though I could jump like a panther, fight like a samurai, run like an antelope. The memory of this sensation, which finally arrived after four years of exercises and immediately vanished, motivated me to persevere in finding it again. Sometimes I imagined expanding the space around me so that the halo emanating from the actions pushed beyond the walls; at other times I started every movement from the centre of my torso or concentrated on a force in opposition to the direction I wanted to follow.

My own definition of stage presence is that of a body that breathes and in which energy is in motion. For me an actress is organic when energy, or the breathing of cells, flows through her whole body. Only necessary tensions are exploited, carried by continuous waves of new impulses. Every part of the body participates in the action, paying attention to concurrent or differing details. Presence is based on some principles: balance is moved away from the centre, weight transforms into energy, actions have a beginning and end and the trajectory between these two points is not linear, actions contain oppositions and have a coherence of intention. In this breathing body certain characteristics are apparent: the body is whole, precise, decided and the tensions in the torso change constantly.

Pursuing oppositions

Opposition, for me as an actress, is a complementary form of thought, action, sensibility, will, intention and result. Opposition is characterised by antagonist tensions. Oppositions keep me upright: the will to look up contrasts with the inert weight of my body; muscular energy holds the structure of the skeleton erect although it is attracted to the ground by the force of gravity. Oppositions are related to technical principles and to the capacity for combining discipline and freedom, vigour and vulnerability, speed and immobility, the euphoric desire to move on and the appreciation of the final result.

On stage my body generates oppositions if it is rooted, which is to say if it is in good contact with the ground and, at the same time, reaches upwards, stretching my spine as if to touch the sky with the nape of my neck. I try to keep a solid secure base, even on tiptoe, and simultaneously to continue elongating; to fight against 'the tired man' with the rounded back and hanging head so well described by Etienne Decroux. Reaching up with my arms like the branches of a tree, I must not forget to have roots that sink into the ground. Moving or still, gravity pulls me towards the earth and an angel holds me up.

Jolanta Krukowska, an actress with the Polish theatre group Akademia Ruchu, taught me an exercise for making good contact with the floor. Jolanta showed me how I could open and close my toes rapidly, as though trying to dig a hole in the sand. To extend the spine and give people I am working with the sensation of hanging, I often pull their hair from the back of their heads. Opposition, which allows me to reach upwards while keeping my body well rooted, lets me walk silently like a panther and prevents me hurting my back as I would if I stamped my heels down at every step.

Opposition also means that my body is not symmetrical and that my successive actions are never identical. For every action I distribute my weight differently. My hands take on different shapes from each other and avoid the symmetry that can be seen in gymnastic exercises that do not give an organic impression. When executing actions like pushing a wheelbarrow, pulling a rope, embracing a child, filling a plate or opening a door, the hands and fingers always take on different positions and tensions, and the weight is rarely equally distributed between both legs.

Opposition, for me, is also the equivalent of executing actions simultaneously and of playing with balance. I move my balance in one direction, risk losing it and then secure it again. I play with balance with large movements in space, but also with the individual steps of a particular walk. While walking I delay or anticipate the instant of falling when I pass the weight from one foot to the other. I maintain or let my balance go by using pressure in the opposite direction to my feet.

I achieve opposition when I build resistance. I kneel as if pushing my pelvis upwards: I resist the downwards trajectory of my bending knees by striving to keep my pelvis up. In the end my knees touch the floor noiselessly and without hurting myself. When I walk I can place a resistance to my advancing steps, as though something hinders and pushes my feet backwards. The double intention – going forwards and being held back – and the resulting contrast in tension, clarifies the pattern of my movement. I often hold on to workshop participants so that they can experience the resistance of a contrasting force. I restrain them by their shoulders, arms, legs or feet in order to oppose the direction of their movement and make them aware of the effort in a specific part of their bodies.

To create a resistance I move as though passing through mud, a brick wall, water, a wheat field, a stretch of soft snow, solid air, or as though buffeted by sea waves, gusts of wind, a tennis racket or a landslide. The element of resistance can also surround me completely and oblige me to involve my whole body. I play with an invisible hand, which holds me back unexpectedly, to shift the accent of resistance in my body from my knee to my torso, from my foot to my elbow. Or I work with a colleague who blocks each of my movements by mirroring them and pushing in the opposite direction.

I use opposition to achieve a change in rhythm and prevent the condensed milk effect, characteristic of monotonous uninterrupted movements. Opposition is also useful to stop the puppet effect, whereby movements succeed each other disconnectedly. The condensed milk effect is often the result of swollen, unnecessary movements (with the torso, for example) or of the exaggerated trajectory of a pleasing gesture. The puppet effect is often caused by accentuating the beginning and end of an action while forgetting to give equal importance to the multiple phases that occur between them.

Opposition is revealed through divergent tensions: I lift an arm to point up while I kneel down to pick up an object from the ground; I look in the opposite direction to the movement of my head; I begin an action with a counter-impulse in the reverse direction to that which I intend to follow.

The Dead Brother
Julia Varley
Photo: Fiora Bemporad

Whispering Winds
Julia Varley
Photo: Fiora Bemporad

I discover opposition mostly in what at Odin Teatret is called *sats* (a Scandinavian word): the impulse to do, the moment in which all energy is retained and calibrated, ready to execute an action. It is easy to understand what *sats* is by thinking of sport: in order to throw a ball, the arm begins by going backwards; to jump, the knees bend to find the impulse; to kick, the leg withdraws before making impact. The *sats* is muscular and nervous engagement, precise withheld action, moulded energy that is ready for action.

Opposition – resistance – permits expression, to 'ex-press', to press out. Resistance, understood as limitation of movement, an obstacle to overcome, constriction in space and a force that opposes the obvious directions and tendencies, helps me perceive the body's form and precision clearly. Constriction is obvious in physical actions: for example, weight inhibits me from flying. In vocal actions this constriction is less obvious because the vocal borders are not so apparent: the voice flies and creates space. Nevertheless, it is always opposition that gives my voice a base. Technically speaking it is given by my diaphragm, but I prefer to think of the earth. I gather the power of my voice from the ground by pushing my feet downwards, feeling my roots sink into the floor, as though this tension were the origin of speech and song.

Thinking in oppositions helps my voice: if I have difficulty in producing a high tone I concentrate on letting my voice slither along the floor; if I cannot reach a deep tone then I surprise myself by addressing my intentions upwards;

if I have difficulty in breathing in quickly I pause between every intake of air. Often when I focus my attention in the opposite direction I realise that the problem has solved itself.

With breathing exercises, contrary to what is usually practised, I begin with a complete exhalation in order to connect the out breath to an active tension and the in breath to a moment of relaxation. During vocal warm-ups I extend my spine during the exhalation, increasing the tension and activity while I relax my belly and torso as I inhale, allowing the air to enter by itself to occupy the empty space. The sensation of opposition that comes from relaxing while breathing in instead of while breathing out helps me control my breath.

In an exercise I let my voice follow spiral hand movements. I choose to start with a low note as my hand leaves the ground and I lift the tone gradually following the movement of my rising hand. Or, in contrast, I again begin with a low note and gradually raise it as my hand descends from high to low; then I decide which choice supports me best.

On stage, the smaller an action is, the more I must permeate it with a precise, controlled energy. The more I contain the volume of my voice, the more I try to keep it round and full, concentrating also on making the diction precise. It takes twice the effort for me to execute a fully dynamic action, which was originally done standing up, sitting on a chair or lying on the floor. Restraining an action so that only a minimal part is shown, while maintaining the nature of the original intentions and the precision of the impulses, tires me much more than executing an action freely in space.

Developing oppositions in my actions has helped me gain stage presence. Thinking in oppositions has taught me to find acting principles that are equivalent to the logic of everyday life. My body, alive on stage thanks to these oppositions, has prepared me to think in a paradoxical way. I take pleasure in confronting problems that give me the opportunity to find surprising solutions.

Rodin's torsos

In a theatrically alive body the tensions in the torso change continuously. I return to my definition of the actress as a person who executes actions, and of the action as something that changes, differently to a movement. Change for me means to influence reality in such a way that it is no longer the same: once a chair has been moved, the situation is different. The same thing happens in my actress's body: the action determines a change in tensions in my torso and consequently affects the perception of the spectator.

By tensions, I do not mean superfluous or static muscular contractions like cramps. Changes in tensions have a purpose: they flow, transform and transport, and can be perceived as muscle tone variations in the torso. If I pick up a child, I can detect the impulses in my back that allow me to bend down, hold, lift and then carry. The four phases each have a purpose and therefore a different impulse (*sats*). The passage from one phase to the next changes the tensions in the torso and, even though minuscule, these variations can be perceived by the spectators.

The changes of tensions allow me to control the difference between a 'real' action and one that is only executed as an external form. To look and see are actions that create almost imperceptible changes in tension. If, as an actress, I look and *really* see something or someone – and do not just pretend to look and see – the tension in my spine is altered by the action. It is a process that is discernible by the spectators even if they cannot see my eyes directly.

In everyday life we are not aware of the changes in tension that take place during the trajectory of an action. Thus, as a young actress, I concentrated on the descriptive aspect, forgetting what lay behind it, what nowadays I call the essence or 'heart' of the action. Seeing a person stroking a pillow, my superficial observation perceived the hand moving gently. But if I carefully watch the back of the person stroking, I notice minute modifications in tonus. It is this mutation, of which I have become aware, that I reinforce when I want to execute this action on stage and that determines the quality and rhythm of the hand's movement. The awareness of the 'heart' of the action is especially helpful when I stroke an imaginary pillow. Real objects and situations force the body to react and adapt, whereas imagination is more easily content with description and approximation. The alternation of tension allows me to re-find the meaning of an action, its true quality, even in a gesture that mimics.

On stage the distribution of weight and the way in which the tensions operate in the body can be opposite to the model that inspires them. If I wish to give the impression of carrying a bucket full of water without the bucket, I accentuate the weight on the opposite foot to the one which would support the real bucket. In order to produce the image of pushing a pram, I recreate the weight with resistance in my arms and backward pressure in my feet.

Pointless, superfluous tensions often manifest themselves in rigid hands, tense fingers, a frowning forehead, open mouth and protruding chest and chin. These are provoked by the desire to express, beautify or emphasise actions, or by the determination to guide those actions conceptually rather than trusting the body's intelligence. It takes humility, skill and patience to limit myself to doing only that which is necessary.

The most significant change in tensions is perceived when an actress seems to levitate in space while remaining still: weight has become energy. An exercise I learned from Isso Miura, a Japanese Butoh dancer, gives tangible proof of this transformation. I begin crouched with bent knees, ready to spring upwards; then I jump as high and far as possible, opening my arms and dilating my chest with a shout. I land in exactly the same position I started from and repeat the jump fluidly. Isso did this along kilometres of beach.

In the course of an action, the weight shifts from one foot to the other, or it is distributed differently on the sole of each foot. As an exercise in recognising variations in muscle tone, I change the point I am leaning on, which then requires a redistribution of my weight, thus having an immediate repercussion on the rest of my body. The shift of weight from one foot to the other is characteristic of dance.

It is not the form, but the sense, rhythm and intention – the information – contained within the form that determines the nature of my actions and the corresponding change of tensions in my spine. If I push my hands against the sky, it is not important that my arms are stretched above my head, but that they contain the necessary pressure. I can repeat the same pushing action with my arms more or less bent; showing or hiding what I am doing. The information contained in an action – a certain way of pushing – is maintained when the external form changes; the consequent tonal variations take place even in the reduced form. I try to pay attention to these small details without limiting myself only to big forms. It is in knowing and using these processes – processes that provoke minute changes of tension – that my body reveals its particular kind of intelligence.

Reaching the limit of a movement, or extending my limbs to the maximum, means that I am unable to continue the action in stillness or maintain a tension that goes towards a target without ever reaching it. If I point at something, in order to clarify where I am pointing, I will not extend my arm fully, but rather keep my elbow slightly bent in order to continue the action. The energy flows without interruption so that my torso is linked, through my arm and finger, to what I am pointing at. An extended arm, that is taut and inert, risks being only an unmotivated external form.

The voice also makes actions. It acts, transforms itself and transforms the space by rejecting, stroking, squashing, attracting, hitting, carrying, encircling ... My voice adapts to the active verb and finds its own variations as soon as it is given precise tasks: the voice that strokes like smoke is different from the voice that falls like rain or that cuts a ripe peach.

The continuous variations of timbre, volume, direction, intensity and tonality, all features of a living voice, are also the result of the connection between vocal and physical actions. My voice dialogues with, and adapts and reacts to what I am doing. A fast run, a jump, a light touch, a fight, a fall, an embrace – these all influence my voice, so that the tensions of the physical actions manifest through continuous changes. Instead of controlling my vocal production, as though my body were not involved in a physical activity, I try to use the actions so that my voice and body collaborate. I allow the tension changes to be reflected in my voice and avoid thinking that this may give the appearance of fatigue or lack of control.

A predetermined idea of what is right or wrong risks flattening my voice into a forced pitch, and rendering it monotonous or exaggerated. The desire to pre-establish a certain kind of expressivity or the involuntary habit of repeating the same intonations as in a nursery rhyme remove the organic effect from the vocal action and therefore its credibility.

The voice should be free of superfluous tensions in order to fly and float in space like a soap bubble or a flying carpet. Supported by the floor, avoiding useless contractions in my chest and throat, and using my body to expand my presence, I try not to push my voice, but to have the sensation of letting it go.

In search of vocal variations I imagine that my words follow a fly around the room. I take inspiration from the speech patterns of different languages, and imitate the calls and sounds of animals and birds. I have improvised conversations between: an imaginary Finn who offers vodka to an Italian; a Chinese man shopping in a New York supermarket; a Japanese tourist who chases a boat along the Mekong; an English aristocrat who drinks tea; a German spitting out judgements and an American chewing gum. Imitating animals has allowed me to discover vocal tones that I did not know I possessed: a cock waking the town at dawn; a flock of sheep passing through the centre of Madrid; an Alsatian and a Pekinese dog barking; the insistent mewing of my father's hungry cats; a cow disturbed by someone walking through its field; a snake approaching water; a dove bringing a message to a prisoner.

To emphasise a word in a sentence, it is enough for me to insert a negative. To underline the word 'spaghetti' in the sentence 'today I would like spaghetti with tomato sauce' I say 'today I would like *spaghetti* – and not rice – with tomato sauce'. The change of tension in my voice when saying the emphasised word corresponds to the change that occurs in the passage between the beginning and end of a physical action. The change in vocal tension is used to accentuate one or more words in a sentence, in a musical phrase or in part of a text.

To control the variations in my voice I repeat the sentence, deciding which word to underline each time. The emphasised word is said slower and with lower volume, like a secret. The logic is the same as what makes us hold on to what we consider important, without throwing it away. This vocal exercise has its equivalent in the physical action when the tonal accent is moved: in an embrace I can change the moment in which I squeeze; picking up an imaginary object the impulse to grasp it can come a moment earlier or later; jumping from stone to stone to cross a river I can vary the moment when I lift my foot. This change in accent helps me find variations in rhythm.

I repeat: for me the secret and 'heart' of the action, be it physical or vocal, lies in the changes of tension in the torso so well depicted in Auguste Rodin's sculptures. I can eliminate the external form and what is anecdotal from an action, even choose not to show it at all, but the pulses of tension, even if they are only impulses, remain essential in giving life to my stage presence.

Precision and decision: the whole body

The execution of actions helps my body be whole. I believe that in theatre an action need not necessarily be realistic, but it must be 'real': it must recreate on stage an equivalent of the forces present in everyday life. Making 'real' actions presupposes precision and decision. The precision of a 'real' action on stage is achieved by its beginning and end, and by the passage between these two points, which is not linear, but contains a change of tension. Faithfulness to the intention and the particular concreteness of the 'real' action forces me to be present here and now, to concentrate on what is necessary. In this way I enrich the action with details, without anticipating the next action or bringing with me qualities and characteristics from the previous one.

The body of an actress making an action on stage seems whole to me – which is to say precise and decided – when there are no blocks (especially in the knees, chest and neck) that inhibit the dynamic flow and the passage of energy from one part of the organism to another. The movement of the feet, fingers and eyes are linked by an invisible yet perceptible current that passes incessantly through the torso like vital blood. The spine assumes an elastic position that does not obstruct the breath or the muscles' suppleness.

Mikkel Futtrup, a friend's son, has played violin since childhood. He taught me that, in order to keep the torso in an elastic position, I should leave room for a sparrow under my armpits. The elbows do not wave in the air as if to accommodate an eagle, but detach themselves just enough not to squash the little bird. The knees are always slightly bent, though ready to spring up, so avoiding a locked position and allowing the energy that comes from the earth and feet to pass through the body. Getting up from the floor and lying down again, I try to follow a line of movement that neither hampers my breathing nor provokes tensions, for example, making me jut my chin out or bend my head to my chest in the effort of lifting my torso.

The actions of the extremities are connected to the trunk and the pelvis. The movements of the arms, legs and head begin from a centre that is situated in the torso, or provoke a consequence there. If the position of one part of my body is exaggerated to an extreme, I find a counterpoint that helps me maintain stability and the readiness to act. As an actress, even sitting down, if I act with my whole body, my action does not end in my pelvis as it rests on the chair leaving my legs inert. I always maintain a connection that flows from my toes to my eyes.

I remember that the world is round: I try not to establish a frontal point of view for each of my actions, nor do I finish my actions always in the same place. The choice of counterpoints, of variation in rhythm, of segmenting one or more actions, of isolating an articulation, engages my whole organism and relates each of my actions to the next.

The precision of the extremities – my hands, fingers, feet and eyes – reveals faithfulness to my intention and to the 'real' action, helping me to be believable as an actress. My way of walking, using my hands, looking, changes according to the situation I am in. It is different to imagine walking on sand or on ice, to feel wet grass or earthenware tiles under my feet, to touch a rabbit or a hedgehog, to point at a sign or a galloping horse, to pick up a book or a cushion, to throw a javelin or a ball, to look far away or at my own nose, to observe the sun or a glass of wine. The details that are an essential part of the imagined reality generate the precision characteristic of a true reaction.

Precision is often associated with the ability to repeat a scene in the same way. For me, to act with precision does not mean to repeat exactly, but to

The Flying Carpet
Julia Varley
Photo: Francesco Galli

execute the action necessary in that moment. I realised this during rehearsals for *Brecht's Ashes*. Else Marie Laukvik repeated a scene, always adding new details to it while Eugenio Barba commented: 'It is amazing how precise Else Marie is!' I tried to understand what the director saw that I still could not detect. Precision makes the drawing of the body in space incisive and clear. As the letters in a book are not written down haphazardly, but are organised into words, sentences and chapters, so in a precise body the actions follow an order and are linked by clear beginnings and ends. The actions are put into focus, as in a photograph or film frame, and do not seem confused or faded like a fuzzy television screen.

Precision is the premise of decision. To be decided I must be convinced. Even if my action is apparently ridiculous or absurd, to believe firmly in what I am doing helps me persuade those who watch. It is important that I am able to throw myself completely into what I do, like someone who learns to swim by jumping into the water, without first testing the depth or having a lifebelt handy. With time and experience, conviction comes from inner necessity, from a personal logic that selects exactly this action and not that. A decided body is the opposite of an awkward and embarrassed body that makes the spectator ill at ease. It is not afraid of making mistakes, it is not subjugated to the need to be beautiful and perfect, it also knows how to lose control and take risks, it accepts moments of inconsistency, unexpected explosions and storms of contradictory impulses. If my body is whole, which is to say precise and decided, I fall and find myself on my feet, I jump over an obstacle and find myself on the other side, I run and have a reason to do so.

A body that is whole is believable. Credibility, for me, does not mean intelligibility: it is not necessary that what I do as an actress is understood for my actions to be believable. Precision and decision allow an existing logic to be perceived, even if the nature of this logic eludes the spectator. When something does not convince me in a young actress's actions, I ask her to verbalise her actions. Often I receive a vague answer, with adjectives and nouns that describe a state of mind instead of verbs that pinpoint the skeleton of the action. Or I receive answers in which the verbs do not correspond to what I was shown because the actions do not include the details that are the necessary consequence of the chosen verbs. Often the absence of credibility, linked to a lack of decision and precision, is caused by a preoccupation with being original and by the fear that the action is too simple and concrete.

It is not the volume of actions that makes me alive on stage, but the 'reality' or precision of those actions. Working with Viajeros de la Velocidad, an Argentinian theatre group used to strenuous physical exercises, I invited the actress and actors to sit on the floor with a pencil in front of them. I asked them to make the movement of picking up the pencil, but without actually taking it; to behave *as if* they picked it up. Immediately afterwards they were to actually pick the pencil up, paying attention to what was happening in their backs. The imitative movement caused no change of tension in their backs, whereas the real action, even though small and easy, contained a tension, a miniscule passage of energy, in the exact moment that their fingers closed on the pencil. Repeating the movement without the pencil, while being aware of the change needed for the action and the precision required to lift a pencil (and not a carrot or a book), the added miniscule tension gave a precise and believable quality to the action. I often use this experiment in my workshops to explain the difference between movement and action. The action that engages the whole body can be discovered in a miniature tension, by using a pen or a piece of paper.

Consistency helps my body be precise and decided. Consistency does not depend on my everyday way of behaving, but on respecting both a chosen way of thinking and theatrical convention. I construct an equivalent, but different logic to that used in daily life, which allows me to focus my intentions, model my actions and vary my energy and thus act with precision and decision. The coherence can be given by a principle established for an exercise, by an attribute chosen for a character or by the style of a particular performative genre. For example, in training, I can walk at length only on my toes or without lifting my heels from the floor; I can move with an impulse from the hips or in the opposite direction to that of my arms; I can use movements that are always either round or straight.

I would like my body to be whole, decided without having to decide, expressive without wanting to express, precise or ready to react and intervene in any situation, powerful but not heavy. For me, an actress's body possesses these characteristics when she is centred and at the same time aware of what happens all around her, when there is no discrepancy between being and wanting to be, when thought does not interfere and slow down the ability to react. Neurobiologists state that we act before we think the action. I would like to be so whole in my stage behaviour that my actions always precede my mind.

Precision and decision: the whole voice

Just like my body, my voice also seeks precision, decision, wholeness. Science tells us that one hemisphere of our brain determines our ability to sing and the other our ability to speak. In my work I behave as though this were not true. I strive not to create artificial separations, to speak texts as though I were singing and to sing as if I were speaking; and to act on stage with the same kind of voice that I use in everyday life. Despite the different variations, colours, resonators and tones, I think of my voice as whole, with a unity whose various features only belong to me.

For me the characteristic of a whole voice is that its centre is situated in the trunk, that its support is found in firmly grounded feet and that a link is maintained throughout its entire range, which is to say that a sense of being rooted is not lost when I speak in a high pitch, nor do I lose the ability to lift a cavernous voice to the sky. The high tones start low and the low tones vault upwards. A body that is whole with its voice dances, thinks and sings while it walks, acts and speaks.

My voice is whole, or secure, precise and decided, when it has a reason for invading the space: it is not important to sing 'well', but to put the child to sleep with a lullaby, to maintain the collective rhythm of work while laying the rail tracks, or to declare passionate devotion in a serenade. My voice is decided when I call the driver to stop the bus, when I sell fish at market, when I defend my pups like a hyena confronted by a leopard. The fear of high or low tones, of making mistakes, of hurting myself, causes a hesitancy that can be really harmful. I would like my voice to be free to react, forgetting any obligation to be interesting or expressive. My voice automatically acquires weight if I actually lift a load, or if I am able to recreate the reality of an imaginary weight without showing it through futile effort or exaggerating the body's movements. If I pull, push or throw something, using my whole body and not just my arms, head and chin, my voice automatically participates in the action and supports it.

The precision of my voice is given by the concreteness of the intention and the kind of actions it executes, by knowing to whom or to what it is directed and where my interlocutors are. I should know whom or what I am addressing: only one spectator, a whole group, myself, an actress beside me, the tree in the garden outside the theatre, a friend on the other side of the world, the sun ... my voice reacts and adapts. Every spectator has the right to hear and my amplified voice needs to direct itself to fill the whole space. I am aware that an audience of one, three or thirty rows of spectators demands a modification of my vocal actions.

The precision of the voice can be remarked by its capacity to react quickly. The voice adapts to changing circumstances and to the location of the person it addresses without losing elasticity, suppleness and flexibility. To verify the voice's ability to free itself from technical habits and to adjust to a situation, I use an exercise in two stages. First, I ask person A to listen to B saying a text. A moves about, approaching and distancing herself from B, making sure that B does not shout when A is close and that she can be heard when A is distant. An increase in volume should not provoke tensions in the chin or forehead, but comes from the body's commitment and the firm support of the feet. Then the exercise is repeated, but instead of reciting a text, the speaker makes ordinary conversation on an interesting topic. The difference in vitality of the voices and bodies in the two versions of the exercise depends on the engagement of the listener. The awareness of being captivating contributes to giving the voice precision and decision. The speaker no longer thinks about the volume of the voice, or of distance and interpretation, but simply about maintaining contact with the listener who is moving around. The voice adapts automatically without superfluous tensions.

To help achieve precision, I invent imaginary listeners for whom my words or songs are important. I can call to someone on the roof or tell a story to a child sitting on my lap. It is not necessarily a human being who listens, but perhaps walls, ghosts in the cellar, or caterpillars in the kitchen garden that can capture my words with their particular ears.

In a whole body the voice is synchronised with the physical actions. This does not mean that each word has to have a corresponding action, but that my voice is in harmony with my body as when I dance to a rhythm, in dialogue with it or making counterpoints. It is as if my voice dances to the music of my body's actions, so that they become one. The physical and vocal actions interact like two simultaneous musical scores in the same composition. In everyday life, gestures always follow the rhythm of speech. On stage I must know how to reconstruct this synchronicity in the montage of my physical and vocal actions. As an actress, through repetition, I reunite the individual transformed and deconstructed elements until the divisions belonging to the building process can no longer be perceived. Then my way of speaking should appear spontaneous, although it is artificially constructed. If, however, my body and voice follow two autonomous rhythms, with no inter-relationship, the spectator feels a sense of estrangement.

The unity of my voice and body helps my voice expand in all directions. To give substance to my voice, in order to obtain volume without shouting, I do not only direct my voice in front of me, but also behind, above and below me: I work with the sensation that my voice widens and invades the air around me like a ball. I use the image of the Michelin Man, whose body is made of tyres: big, fat, squashy and elastic. The voice becomes round and broad because it includes all the surrounding space. Other images that have helped me are: the feeling of the sun radiating heat; the consistency of kneading bread; the deliciousness of ice cream as it melts in my mouth; the roundness of an orange or a yawn.

My own voice tends to tremble. At times it is fragile and shy and gives the impression of being broken as if I were crying, but nevertheless I continue to seek decision. I am still perplexed by the mysterious ability of the voice to follow its own logic, which I cannot control. It is up to my creativity as an actress to devise situations in which I can feel safe and that I can trust, in order to protect my vulnerability.

I try to bring together speaking and singing techniques by thinking, for example, that speech always has changes in tone that are musical variations. In song, the tones are held at the pitch determined by the musical note, whereas in speech the variations are faster and use fractions of tone. But both in song and in speech I recognise sounds that I understand as music.

While singing, precision prompts exact tuning. When the tuning is supported by an action or an image and one can forget the technical problem, the voice tends to regulate itself and to match naturally what it hears. I have heard choirs sing more in tune together when they sang as if their voices were snow falling on the Monte Bianco in January, or fog embracing São Paolo, or a cat in love with a stray dog, than when they were worried about being correctly in tune.

In intonation, precision is given by maintaining the tone in movement. Brigitte Cirla and Helen Chadwick, two singers I have met through the Magdalena Project, taught me to think of a tone as a continuous flight upwards, which never stays still. Precision and decision are not fixed: being whole follows an essential course.

3 Training

Aspects of training

'Do you still train?' I am often asked this question. After thirty years of working at Odin Teatret it is difficult to answer: yes, no, it depends! What is 'training'? What does this word – never translated and so common among theatre groups all over the world – actually mean? How can training be defined in the aftermath of Stanislavski's Studies and Meyerhold's Biomechanics, the experience of Jerzy Grotowski's Teatr Laboratorium and the Living Theatre, and the vast long-term exploration of Odin Teatret? It is apprenticeship, learning, workout, coaching, work on oneself, preparation, active meditation, gymnastics, physical and mental discipline, a process of integration with an environment, a refuge, a competition with oneself and others. All of this? Something different?

Thanks to training I have discovered my own language as an actress and the principles of stage presence. I have learned to direct this presence in space, to react, to combine the dynamism of physical actions with the sonority of vocal flow, and to distance myself from all that I had learned before in order to seek out new paths. Nowadays training is my microlaboratory where I search for outcomes that perhaps eventually will be addressed to a spectator. It is a non-public zone within the professional domain where I discover a terminology of my own. It is a fertile and personal resource from which ideas and characters, initial montages of texts, songs and sequences of actions can sprout. It is privileged terrain where I allow myself, as an actress, to fail while I search for new material and proposals. It is the interstice of independence from the director and from the current dominant interests and aims at Odin Teatret.

Training offers me the possibility of confronting difficulties, giving myself tasks that will help break entrenched habits from the previous performance, discovering new points of departure; it is a space in which I can reawaken and satisfy my curiosity, contrive challenges, find relief from the wear and tear of rehearsals and the obligation to present performances. I start from something simple that I then develop: a piece of music, a theme, a poem, a photograph, a painting.

Training is my independent time. I like to be alone in the rehearsal space. It is a luxury that I can no longer give myself every day, as I did when I was first beginning. To spare time for these occasions is difficult now, with touring, performances, teaching, directing, editing *The Open Page*, the computer, emails, planning festivals and organising numerous associated activities. I am happy when there is a period when I can remain for four or five hours in the working space without knowing where I will end up, but conscious that I am planting the first seeds for a new performance about which as yet I know nothing.

After thirty years of training, during which I have confronted different aspects of the complexity of the actress's work, I feel the desire to turn back and have a simpler and more rudimentary relationship with my body, to encourage and treat it well. For me now training is also a kind of gymnastics to rediscover, reawaken and re-experience a primary energy: exercises to strengthen my back, align my bones, maintain the muscle tone and prevent pains and contractions. Since regular daily training is no longer easy to realise, the work demonstrations, workshops and performances, with their variety and quantity, are opportunities to keep alive the curiosity of research. Nowadays I also do voice training in the car, to the accompaniment of recorded music, or during the holidays when I have the whole theatre to myself and know that no one can see or hear me.

'Training' for me is a term that maintains its English origins in several languages. I trained for ski competitions, and in general one trains to learn something. Training allowed me to acquire stage presence: I would never have been accepted by Odin Teatret or any other theatre group if I had not trained. Training has been my rite of passage to becoming an actress.

Training is characterised by various phases that depend on the stage of development and experience of each actress and on that of the theatre group to which she belongs. At the beginning of Odin Teatret the first phase included the rudiments of mime and ballet techniques, acrobatic elements, some exercises that came from Stanislavski's books and others learned from Jerzy Grotowski's Teatr Laboratorium.

In a second phase the training was personalised. Odin Teatret's actresses and actors started to invent their own exercises and execute them while adding variations and following individual rhythms. In the morning, everyone trained together, but each person worked independently despite being in the same space. The training was a completely separate world from that of rehearsals and performance. There was no direct connection between these different aspects of the work, although the form of the exercises might colour an actress's movements when improvising or creating a composition.

The third phase began in 1973, shortly after making the didactic physical and vocal training films. The exercises started to lose priority as they gave way to the personal curiosities and questions of each actress and actor, at times in relation to research or tasks for a new performance. During this phase the pre-established forms of the exercises were replaced by a tendency to follow various principles and the capacity for directing energy in space was enhanced by working with props. The customary dark training clothes were replaced by colourful costumes. Then, in 1974, a revolutionary development: during a residency in southern Italy, Odin Teatret presented a performance composed of training elements to the local population. It was *The Book of Dances*. Spectacular sequences and exercises with sticks, flags, coloured ribbons and musical instruments were exposed and performed outdoors. The material was assembled in a basic rhythmical structure that did not tell a story (hence the title). From then on the worlds of training and performance started to influence each other more directly. Nowadays it is common for a character to begin to emerge or for the first sketch of a scene to take shape during training.

Training has always functioned as a test for young people who wish to join the group. It is an initiation that serves as an introduction to Odin Teatret's culture. In all its phases, training remains the place in which to confront one's own limitations and resources. Each actress faces the solitude and everyday necessity of this humble and anonymous activity, and will continue to do so even when, after many years, the training has developed into something different from the usual format of exercises executed in a rehearsal space.

At Odin Teatret it is mostly the women who have persevered with patience and curiosity and have continued to develop a personal training that renews its sense. I imagine that, for us, training is not an instrument that helps master a technique or confirm a skill, but a subjective space in which to discover ourselves and others.

My own training

I hated running. At seven o'clock in the morning, rain or snow, in the dark of winter mornings or the light of Nordic summers, during the early years at Odin Teatret the day always began with a thirty to forty minute run. I did it because it was obligatory, distracting myself by looking at the landscape or learning texts. When the training passed on to the personal phase and I could devise my own programme, I substituted some physical stamina exercises that I had learned on a martial arts course for the run. The hours dedicated to acrobatics also belong to my first training phase. I was not terrified of the chair that I had to somersault over, but of the hard mattress on the other side on which my flat back would bounce.

From the very beginning I worked with props: two flags and small stilts. Others were added a few years later: a bass drum, a black stick, a bowler hat, a monocycle and higher stilts. Throwing, catching and manoeuvring the flags or the long stick, I learned to react with my whole body, combining these sequences with acrobatic exercises that required impulse explosion and control. Later still I found other kinds of props, less spectacular in appearance and size; they kept me company when I worked alone, without a colleague with whom to have a dialogue or a teacher to observe me. Music was another support in overcoming solitude and giving me a partner with which to interact.

I started by learning exercises from others, but I was immediately encouraged to invent my own. I could organise my training freely, applying

Training in Odin Teatret's red room, 1983
Photo: Christoph Falke

principles or seeking to resolve difficulties, building stage material and putting sequences together. An exercise that first gave me a sense of feeling rooted was the samurai walk as developed in the training by Iben Nagel Rasmussen. Keeping the weight downwards, the solidity and width of the steps, the sensation of vigour and the need to re-establish immobility after each move, required a good foundation and a concentration of energy in the pelvis, with the back well aligned on top. On the other hand, the walks developed by Tage Larsen, inspired by Marilyn Monroe's undulating hips, and those invented by Etienne Decroux that I learned from Ingemar Lindh, taught me to float through the air without lowering or raising my head, keeping an even distance between my shoulders and the floor. Practising these walks I discovered how to compensate with one part of my body for the activity of another.

At the beginning, to find the precision of an action, I let myself be guided by detailed images: walking through clover, being pinched by a crab, gathering daisies and making a chain of them, packing a suitcase, chasing the waves of the sea . . . the images steered me towards the making of 'real' actions. Over the years my body has learned to think by itself and to chisel out the precision of an action without thinking about it beforehand.

The composition exercises were followed by ballroom dancing and a variety of walks accompanied by an assortment of march music. Then I worked on the different phases of a step, sitting on a chair or on the floor, improvising with the character of Shakespeare's and Verdi's Lady Macbeth, dancing to Irish rhythms. As the years passed, the presence of Tage, Iben or other occasional teachers dwindled. The training became more and more personal and solitary. The exercises I had learned or invented were replaced by different principles I applied; composition was overlaid with montage technique to amalgamate texts and physical actions, songs, costumes and props. More recently I have concentrated mostly on vocal training, accompanying songs with postures, dances and actions.

In fact, I have always experienced training at Odin Teatret as predominantly individual. There might be many of us in the same room – and obviously each person's process in some way influences that of the others – but the choice of approach, exercises and rhythm is taken alone. Even if we were all immersed in the same music (as happened in 1976 with a repetitive samba record, or when the Odin actor-musicians played), each of us followed specific personal motivations, objectives and principles.

In certain periods we trained in pairs or groups in order to establish the source of a scene, rehearse music or songs, or discern common starting points that we could develop for a new production. We called one of these periods of communal training *Fiskedam* (fish breeding pool). It was in 1978. We took turns to play in the orchestra that accompanied the work; we improvised characters, some of which were later introduced in *Brecht's Ashes*; we went wild doing all kinds of things, until the director intervened and got rid of roller-skates, exotic costumes and monocycles.

For a month, in 1979, Torgeir Wethal guided the younger members of the group, teaching us exercises that we had only seen on film. I had a taste of what it meant to stand on my head in every possible position, to fight with white plastic sticks aiming at a colleague's head or feet, to follow the impulses

Training at a theatre group meeting in Huampani, Peru, 1988
Photo: Tony D'Urso

of every part of my body in the 'plastic' exercises and to work for hours on acrobatics and sequences called bridges, half bridges, handstands, jumps, worms, cats and dolphins.

Over the years other elements have enriched my training. An awareness of the general principles verified in Odin Teatret's training and in other codified performance forms is the consequence of meetings with masters from Asian, European and Afro-Brazilian theatre, especially during the first sessions of ISTA (International School of Theatre Anthropology) founded in 1979. From then on the terminology used for explanation in workshops and work demonstrations became more explicit. The training was no longer carried out and transmitted only in silence, but was also theorised through words and concepts like 'real actions', the 'pre-expressive level', the 'organicity effect', 'form and information', 'segmentation', 'energy shaping'. Despite all of this, when I am in the room training, I don't need these words: training continues to be a privileged universe of action.

The purpose of training

There are actresses who are naturally alive on stage, who do not need to work to acquire this quality. I am not one of them. I have had to sweat to obtain stage presence and learn to realise 'real' actions, incorporating the principles that make my behaviour visible to the spectator. Does one become a better actress by doing exercises and training? I know that, if I had not done them, I would never have been able to become an actress. Probably I would not even have been attracted to theatre.

For me training and exercises are a way of keeping in contact with concrete tasks, the proof that an apprenticeship for the actress's craft exists and that the commitment is serious: we need to practise, just as a musician or dancer does. Inspiration, the need to express myself and be creative would not have helped me. Hard work and physical effort are better suited to my need for wholeness. I train in all possible ways. I need training: it prevents me from disappearing or dying little by little as an actress. Training continues to teach me to think with my feet.

I learned to make 'real' actions and discovered my stage presence by obstinately continuing to execute exercises that induced my body to think by itself. I repeat: a well-composed and well-executed exercise contains the principles of a 'real' action. It has a precise beginning and end; it includes oppositions and changes of tension in my torso; it displaces my balance from the centre, changes weight into energy, demands coherence, decision, continuity, rhythm and resistance, precise intentions and impulses.

At first the exercises created a distance from my everyday behaviour and built a formalised way of being and acting that used an exaggerated amount of energy. Then, when this acquired stage behaviour became mechanical, the invention of new exercises wiped away the form that had taken me so much time and effort to assimilate.

Training during the X ISTA session in Copenhagen, 1996
Photo: Fiora Bemporad

I join the single exercises together in an uninterrupted sequence. The transition from one exercise to the next creates knots, impulses and counter-impulses, further changes. If the exercise teaches me the principles of an action as though it were a single word, the continuous flow of the training directs me towards composing dynamic sentences. I link the actions one after the other in such a way that the end of one becomes the beginning of the next. Then I introduce punctuation into the phrase, moulding the flow with stops, suspensions, staccatos, legatos and crescendos.

In the training I have learned to act and react, to model my energy through the wholeness of my physical and vocal presence. I observe what happens around me so that I can turn it into a stimulus. I project other people, fantasy beings, animals or objects into the space and interact with them even though I am alone. Participants in a dialogue can be other people in the rehearsal room, but also noises coming from outside, like helicopters flying overhead or children playing in the courtyard; or the squeaking floor, the shape of a prop, the size of a room, the texture of a costume. My imagination keeps me company and populates the work space, while I place and direct my actions outwards, and develop my readiness to react. I listen to my colleagues practising, to the crickets singing, to music that is playing, I pay attention to marks on the walls, to a ray of sun coming in through the window . . . I try to avoid the training closing me in on myself; instead I let it provoke a dance of actions and reactions to all that surrounds me. The imperative is that energy should continuously flow from me to the outside, and from the outside back towards me.

Training gives me the sensation of having learned something and of having a skill, but this sensation only lasts a second. If I look back on the years of training I can recall moments in which I thought I had understood something and taken a step forwards, and then long periods of disheartened frustration that followed these flashes of revelation. There is the danger of becoming a prisoner of habits induced by a training that has lost its purpose: legs that are bent too much just to walk from one place to another; a voice that loses elasticity because I want it to be stronger; counter-impulses that become automatic because they are on display; a torso in continuous movement in order to have the illusion of being active.

Despite experience and embodied knowledge, new problems continue to present themselves in different ways each day. In confronting them I must start from zero, repeat the first steps, and not give into laziness: even this is a form of training for me these days.

When I am asked how to build a personal training, I advise searching for oppositions: choosing some actions that are easy and others that are difficult, some slow and some fast, some big and some small, working with a strong and then with a soft energy. It is best to be simple in the choice of exercises, slowly adding new tasks until reaching complexity. It is essential that the exercises are executed with fluidity, with variations in rhythm, suspensions and small pauses, but always as part of an ongoing flow. I find it useful to single out something that I like in the training, something that suits and satisfies

Roberta Carreri and Julia Varley executing the 'three-three exercise'
Photo: Fiora Bemporad

me. It becomes a point of support and a stimulus with which to confront the difficulties and periods of stagnation characteristic of creative work.

Training helps overcome limits, but it should not be harmful. Generally this is obvious in the physical work: blows become bruises, stiff muscles prevent me from walking upstairs, and falls provoke cuts that need stitches. With care it is possible to avoid these accidents, but without surrendering to easiness. When I lead young people I suggest that they should not fall too heavily on their knees and should walk using the absorption facility of their feet, knees and hips so as to protect the spine. Training should not be torture. The daily repetition goes through monotonous phases, but should also include moments of pleasure and fun.

The point of balance between tension and relaxation, courage and caution, pursuing new results and preserving stability, motivation and blinding ambition, is mobile. I try to find this point every day in my training. Sometimes, during vocal training, it is useful for me to shout, other times to relax and sigh while imagining the pleasure of sunbathing or taking a cool shower. Sometimes I try to distil and purify my voice as much as possible, eliminating the air almost completely; other times I add breath to the sound so as to soften the onset of speech.

Many people ask me how to understand whether they are harming the voice while trying to go beyond their limits in vocal training. Here are some tricks that have helped me: directing my voice to something outside myself; not requiring immediate results; not listening to myself; avoiding touching my body to check the points of resonance; giving myself concrete tasks that allow my voice to react independently. In order to achieve volume I have learned to be patient and not to push. I wait for the voice to grow bit by bit as I learn to use my body to amplify its size.

In training, time is one of the great masters. Working for oneself and on oneself, without interruption and for the long term, teaches us to overcome our conditioning and discover hidden sources of energy and unknown resistances. Beyond the threshold of tiredness, other forces begin to guide us and one day, suddenly, a fall is transformed into the impulse to get up again.

Training the 'three-three exercise' with ISTA participants in Montemor-o-novo, 1998

Photo: Fiora Bemporad

I do not force the process to obtain results, just as I do not pull up a small plant to make it grow. I till the earth, water and manure it, and after some years, with a bit of luck, the tree blossoms and gives fruit. It has been the hardest lesson to learn: as an actress I have to give myself concrete tasks without conserving energy or limiting the number of times I try and I must be prepared to begin all over again without the satisfaction of easy success. I have to trust that time will bestow results exactly when I no longer expect them.

During a particularly difficult period for me, while rehearsing my first production at Odin Teatret, I decided in a gesture of dismay and revolt that training was my own free territory. I would do as I wanted there without worrying about 'functioning' for an outside eye. On exactly that day, after four years of daily work, Eugenio Barba commented that there was nothing that disturbed him in my training.

Reduction

At the beginning of my apprenticeship I found it useful to do exercises that had large dimensions so as to use my energy to the full while learning to shape and give form to stage actions. The dilation of the movements and their trajectories prepared me to expand my physical presence to fill the surrounding space. Acrobatics demanded alertness in reflexes, precision and decision, to avoid hurting myself. Work with large, heavy and difficult props made my body react while grasping, throwing, manipulating and manoeuvring these work companions that possess their own independent temperaments. Dances and jumps forced me to renounce the security of the floor, while falls and walks re-established a trusting contact with the ground. Imitating a cat, snake or leopard infused life into my spine. The reproduction of manual chores – to dig or saw, carry loads or ring church-bells – taught me the necessity of counter-impulse.

Once this knowledge was incorporated, the next stage was to execute actions while withholding and compressing my energy. I did the exercises while remaining in one place, or sitting down, using smaller props, adapting to different spaces, positions and situations without losing the essence or 'heart' of the action, which is to say the impulses and intentions and their resulting changes in my torso's muscle tone. I replaced the flags I had worked with during the early years with handbags, strings and ribbons, butterflies and handkerchiefs; the somersaults and jumps with almost normal steps and dialogues of pure impulse; the stilt dances with fluid movements accompanied by music from various cultures and small child-like skips. The songs used in street performances were exchanged with vocal improvisations accompanied by a violin; the texts with a sustained level of sound with grandmothers' tales.

Even today, in training, the exercises interact with other elements: music, texts, props such as a pair of shoes or a fan, and, of course, my colleagues. When I think I have exhausted all the possibilities and start to feel bored,

I discover unexplored potential by simply modifying a detail. To launch into a dance wearing a pair of boots instead of barefoot, to decide to move without using my arms or legs, to accentuate or diminish the intensity of my eyes, to peel an orange or read a book, to replace my usual training clothes with an elegant dress, are some examples of how the introduction of new tasks reawakens the readiness to react. I introduce these new circumstances into a sequence that is already fixed, finding a justification for the new situation each time.

The process that at Odin Teatret we call the reduction or absorption of an action is one of the most useful procedures I have learned. It is primarily an extremely effective means of 'cleaning' stage behaviour of exterior anecdotes or formalistic habits. The easiest way of describing this process is to think of an inflated balloon: if you reduce its volume, the compressed balloon takes up less space, but contains the same amount of air. Instead of executing the stage action in its original dimensions, I 'reduce' and 'absorb' the outer form. I show it shrunken, smaller, miniaturised, taking care however to maintain the initial energy and changes of tension in my torso. A sensation of implosion replaces that of explosion. First I move like a giant filling more space than my own body does, reaching the extreme of my possibilities, then I absorb the volume to show progressively less and less of the external form. The difficulty consists in respecting the information contained in the 'heart' of the action, which is to say the changes in muscle tone that safeguard the purpose and sense of the action.

The dimensions of an action can be reduced by half, or almost entirely, as long as the original intentions and impulses are preserved. A jump becomes the mere impulse to jump; a complete twirl is executed by turning only a little, but with the same amount of energy; and instead of lying on the floor, I only lower myself slightly. If previously I lifted my arm above my head, when I reduce the action, my arm remains by my body keeping the original tensions and intentions but showing them only through the hand that veers upwards.

In absorbing the form completely, only the immobile body that 'thinks' the action is left. This 'thought' is a dynamic preparation, an inclination to act, a *sats* that I perceive from my body's centre to its extremities, from my torso to the intensity of my eyes and to the tips of my fingers and toes. The variation of dynamism and the succession of 'reduced' actions can be identified in the change of pressure in my feet.

When experimenting with the reduction technique for the first time I tended to make mistakes that prevented the energy from flowing within the reduced form. I didn't pay attention to details; the action was no longer 'thought/acted' by my whole body with all its minimal reactions because I concentrated only on how to reproduce the most obvious changes. I tried to shrink the space, lifting my shoulders and inhibiting the breath so much that the action became cramped. Instead of allowing the impulses to live, I tried to contain them in a closed box. I didn't allow the energy and flow of impulses to be directed outwards, as though the reduction of the outer form arrested the action instead of increasing its compression and therefore its dynamism. If the reduction was done sitting down, I often forgot the pressure of my feet on the floor, so that only the upper part of my body was active and it lacked roots and oppositions.

I have applied the principle of reduction to my voice, to see how far I can maintain the energy while decreasing the volume. In doing this I discovered a silence saturated with sounds, songs and words, a silence alive with tensions, equivalent to a quietness that is not inert, but ready to jump, lie on the floor and move in any direction. Immobility is not a dead state of suspension, but an expectation pregnant with surprise.

My vocal work demonstration, *The Echo of Silence*, was born from the process of reduction as I absorbed my vocal actions until they became implicit. Just as there is a white that contains all the colours of the rainbow, there is a silence that, for me, contains all possible sounds, from whispers to screams. The voice vibrates with a withheld power, ready to glow. The 'heart' of the action is protected.

4 Improvisation and composition

The creation of material

With the term 'material' I allude to autonomous work done by the actress before the director's intervention or the definitive montage made during rehearsals. For me the actress's material consists of sequences of actions, scenes, walks, dance steps, ways of sitting down, of looking and using the arms, with the intention of building a particular kind of stage behaviour that is usually considered as the creation of a character. At Odin Teatret besides the word 'material', we use 'score', a term originally employed by Stanislavski: instead of musical notes, the score is composed of the actress's physical and vocal actions.

The material, or score, is the point of departure from which I confront a text, theme, situation, scene or character. The material, or score, is like a block of marble quarried from a mountain ready to be sculpted and receive its final form. It is like the cultivated earth in which seeds are planted, or the vegetables that have been prepared to be cooked and seasoned, or the written page that needs to be corrected again for inclusion in a novel. It is my presence as an actress, a personal way of being that begins to take shape and be elaborated in relation to a theme.

At Odin Teatret material can be created by composing one action at a time and adding them together, or by improvising. Composition and improvisation are two more terms that have several meanings according to the tradition and the specific framework in which they are used. Improvisation – for me as well – does not imply one single activity, but at least three, each different from the other: to invent from a given theme; to make variations on given elements; to change imperceptibly some details within a fixed score. I use the word composition, instead, to designate a process where I construct one action after the other. I compose the single elements separately, with parts of my body or with my whole body. I start from associations or exercises, from the weaving of a story or text, from the application of the principles of stage presence or by giving free rein to my imagination.

I create sequences of actions composing or improvising and memorise the results physically so as to be able to repeat them without resorting to conceptual memory. Memorisation of the material can happen through personal repetition or progressively during rehearsals. In both instances, the assiduous repetition of actions and behaviour invented however accidentally is the premise for safeguarding the thousand reactions, colours and details that originally characterised the score. The actions are created with an underlying logic. This logic is the fundamental reference during rehearsals, which also allows me to improvise without losing the initial quality even after the performance is finished.

The sources from which the material springs are various: a theme, text, image, music, association, character, costume, situation or technical task (for example, to move a chair from one side of the stage to the other). I make a preliminary montage of my material myself and then present the result to the director so that we can elaborate it further together.

With composition and improvisation, even when they are inspired by everyday situations, I almost always create non-realistic actions. These are 'real' because my torso contains the changes of muscular tone equivalent to those which would be done off stage, without being their exact copy. The space, objects or people involved in the situation I imagine provoke concrete reactions.

Improvising on the theme 'The secrets of the past', I might bend down to enter the low attic where my grandparents' trunks are kept. A particular way of bending will be apparent in my material: the 'real' action necessary to go through the small door of the imaginary attic. I have to bend exactly in that way, even though I am not describing the door realistically. The spectators and the director will not see the door, nor will they understand that I am entering an attic. They will only perceive that there is a logic that dictates my behaviour and, if this is precise, it will probably be believable to their senses as well.

Making a composition on the same theme, I might walk with careful steps like a person moving in darkness, rowing with my arms as if I wanted to go back in time, puffing out my chest to imitate my grandfather in his portrait, with old age's lost empty eyes and the inquisitive face of a detective. Putting all these attitudes together builds a synthetic behaviour that doesn't illustrate a realistic or reasoned succession, but is anchored to a different logic based on associations, simultaneity and a movement that goes forwards and backwards in time.

When I improvise or compose, I respect the principles of stage presence and exploit the faculty for making variations that I have incorporated with training. My technical foundation – or particular way of thinking with the body – allows me to confront a theme and unravel it from beginning to end. I enter the theme; I find an opposite point of reference in order to avoid illustration; I create connections and divergences between the starting point and what I invent. For example, if I imagine I am caressing a cat, I will automatically increase the energy and tension in my hand, arm and back, to carry out the action with my whole body as I have learned in training. Then, in order not to remain fixed in one single position, I might glance back at the

Improvisation, Copenhagen, 1996
Julia Varley, Sanjukta Panigrahi
Photo: Torben Huss

armchair the cat has scratched and, to change my height, I could sit there to read a book. I could choose not to hold the book with my hands, but with my feet, and to read in it stories about panthers that make me withdraw the hand that strokes the cat with a counter-impulse, as if frightened by a growl.

When I receive a starting point for an improvisation or composition – a text, word, poem, image, piece of music, character's name, technical task – from the director or when I choose one myself, my first undertaking is to translate the theme into a personal language, condensing the information and focusing on what attracts me and triggers my curiosity. To explore the character, text or theme, I set off in search of clues that resonate with my experience and appeal to my imagination, and so encourage me to be creative. I can be inspired by the title or a single word, a sentence or the general meaning of the text, a whole image or a detail, the complexity of the person or the shape of her or his legs, a song or a note. Then I let my associations run wild or, following a more literal interpretation, I seek the tangible stimuli that provoke actions.

For example, starting from the theme 'My wife lost her health', the course of my associations could lead me to make an improvisation over a weak flame that I try to keep alight. The associations start from imagining the wife looking at the black circles under her eyes in a mirror, then move on to a valley darkened by clouds, to a storm that fuses the lights and to a frightened child looking for a candle and matches. Or instead I could compose in a literal way how the wife lies down, then an action of losing something – racing behind the tram and missing it, trying to catch a ball and dropping it, or failing to grasp the hand of a child who has tripped – and then tremble with a feverish quivering.

I find it useful to start from the opposite of my target, for example to build on silence for a demonstration of vocal technique. I can also use a corresponding but dissimilar element as a point of departure, such as birds singing as a way for my *Mythos* character Daedalus to speak. The choice is not accidental, although it seems so at times. I follow the clues or hints that my intuition or actress's intelligence can recognise, but is not able to explain in advance.

I improvise from the stimuli set in motion by the theme. The improvisation plays out through successive images and actions imposed by the rhythm of my body that thinks and decides without any conscious or rational deliberation. The improvisation requires me to have simultaneous reactions and translate immediately from image to action and from action to image, with a whole body-mind that acts and reacts.

The improvisation is generally characterised by an uninterrupted flow of reactions. The difficulty resides in reconstructing it in its smallest details. The composition is a process that adds one detail at a time, concentrating step by step on different parts of the body or on different images, deciding the succession of forms that my body assumes in relationship to the starting point. The created elements are put together and added one after the other and become 'material'.

Composition is a method for constructing material that allows me to reach repeatable results quite quickly. An improvisation can have a more surprising quantity and quality of reactions, but I need more time to fix it. Improvisation is a special process that requires protection, while I can work on a composition more coldly. The improvisation seems more alive at the beginning, but feels as though it loses its value when I repeat it for the first few times. Composition, by contrast, builds gradually and immediately becomes stronger as I go through the actions again. The results of both procedures acquire incisiveness with time: assiduous repetition and elaboration deepen and allow the material that emerges from such different methods to mature.

When I create material I find it useful to think of the verbs. In the text 'Last night I dreamt of saving other lives than my own', 'dream' and 'save' help me more than 'last night' or 'my own' to make actions. A transitive active verb implies an action (to dream or to save what?) that engages the torso, while names, adverbs and adjectives incline me to describe and be satisfied with the anecdote narrated by the arms, hands and face.

To create material, improvising or composing, I find it useful to make actions in a different rhythm from the everyday, slower or faster; to vary the size of the space that I occupy, making it bigger or smaller; to bring closer

Improvisation, Montemor-o-novo, 1998
Julia Varley, I Nyoman Budi Artha
Photo: Fiora Bemporad

or distance the people or the imaginary objects to which I address myself. In the improvisation or composition I can jump from a close-up to a landscape view, as in film editing. I can show the house and then the wrinkles on the face of the person at its window.

To avoid linearity, I respect neither the watch nor the calendar, but jump back and forth in time. My actress's material can be based on the story of an old man who plays football as he did when he was child, who teaches philosophy to a student and is simultaneously remembered by his friends after his death. Or I present a comet star that loses its tail, the Magi who look for the star in the sky, then Jesus on the cross and last year's Christmas.

My stage actions take place in a world that is not flat, but spherical and multi-sided. I address myself to different directions at the same time and avoid always facing front. I can grasp an object in front of me, or beside, behind, above, under me; to move forwards I walk in a circle, backwards, sideways, on top of a chair, sinking in quicksand, zigzag.

My facial expression and the movements of my arms and hands reveal the stories of my inner images. At times I choose to show the material without moving my arms and hands, and with an expressionless face. To conceal the banality of a facile obvious anecdote I resort to reduction, preserving all the tensions of the actions without showing them in their external form.

When I improvise or compose, I find it useful to change subject. I am myself, the actress, the artisan doing her work, the person who narrates, what I am talking about, the person who comments and observes, and all the circumstances that intervene in the story. I can simultaneously be more subjects with different parts of my body or with the different details of a single action: for example, wind, rain, bird, tree, cellar, person, character, river, mountain, food, Julia ... or, more simply, I can pass from one subject to the next as in a dialogue. This helps me find variations in space and change the muscular tone of my stage behaviour.

I don't confine myself to describing only the theme with my material, but try to orchestrate a context, a fresco, a whole landscape. I can be the different characters, animals and objects of the environment I am presenting, as well as myself and a storyteller. I can be the only character in the text and whatever is contiguous to it. I can follow the words of a poem and remember the author's biography; present historical figures and the era in which they lived. In an improvisation or composition on sunrise, I can include an owl looking at the sun, the sun on the horizon, an old person who tells or remembers the episode, the sunrays, the light covering the ground, the colours of the sky, the baker intent on baking bread at dawn, the alarm clock ringing beside my bed, the rooster that sings three times and Pontius Pilate washing his hands.

I strive to treat the improvisation and composition as if they were poems and not prose. In a poem every word is necessary, the connections between them tend to create oxymora; the sentences are condensed, there is musicality, the information is given with the fewest elements and it is synthetic and complex. If there is an action in my material that I want to repeat, because the information is contained exactly in the reiteration, I will do it in a slightly different way each time. I am concerned with changing rhythm, size, strength or direction. I repeat, but like the flames in a fire. I am conscious that the repetition of three analogous elements already establishes a sense of continuity. Above all I avoid symmetry.

Improvisation, Holstebro, 1993
Julia Varley, Sanjukta Panigrahi, Augusto Omolú
Photo: Jan Rüsz

I create material, through composition and improvisation, alone or with other people, with objects or without, in silence, accompanied by live or recorded music, using the voice or not, in costume or wearing training clothes. I choose the condition that stimulates me most so as not to formulate stage behaviours I have already experimented with previously. An improvisation that I make alone, without partners, usually reaches a depth of motivation that withstands time. A group improvisation tends to allow behavioural clichés to emerge: fights, submission, seduction and games. However, it can be useful to provide a framework that can be filled subsequently with individual material.

The actress's material is my opportunity to contribute to the creative process in a personal way and therefore to influence it. The concrete behaviour that I propose introduces my perspective into the development of the performance. To obviate the danger of illustration, of remaining too tied to the text or the theme, and therefore producing obvious material, at an early stage I move away from them. I encounter them again in a subsequent phase with the understanding that springs from the material I have accumulated. If I aim straight in the direction designated by the text or theme, my actress's material risks only emphasising an existing story and therefore being redundant.

The necessity to distance myself from the theme is similar to the need to hide narratives that are too explicit in my actions. I believe that if my material is structured in an open way it is a better resource and gives more opportunities for elaboration to the director. For me, as an actress, it is the most favourable approach to maintain a creative tension with the director and with the potential meanings of the performance.

Stimuli, strategies and procedures

I don't have incredibly original or brilliant ideas; my images are simple. Often, to avoid images being recognised, I transform them slightly or I put two or three of them together simultaneously, while safeguarding above all the precision and dynamism that gives them life. To hide the obviousness, in addition to repositioning the action in space, I can transpose it to another part of the body or deconstruct the movement into different segments that follow divergent directions. I continue to elaborate the material and conceal the descriptive nature of the actions. I have this freedom because my actions don't need to explain anything, but rather to suggest and transmit manifold allusions according to the context in which they are included. The additional meanings that arise after the elaboration and the director's montage merge with my intentions, stimulating and enriching them.

If the stone already possesses the statue's shape, what is left for me to carve? If the tree already bears fruit, what can I sow? The quantity of contradictory information contained in one moment of stage behaviour is one of the factors that makes it interesting for me. It is not necessary for the director or the spectator to be aware of the motivations that allowed me to create that particular moment.

If I follow a cubist logic, the composition of material becomes deconstruction. I could deconstruct the image of riding a horse like this: I hold the reins with one hand above my head and the other at knee height; I perform the pelvic movement on the saddle with the nape of my neck and walk tightening my elbows as if they were knees pressing against the horse's flanks. Even though I displace the single parts, I preserve a coherent precision equivalent to the situation I am composing; I recreate the 'real' action without it being realistic. Starting from simple elements, I keep the image to myself and offer the director a more complex synthesis that can be used according to her or his personal interpretation or to what is necessary for the development of the scene.

Why not directly use the action of riding for a scene that shows someone on a horse? If the horse really existed, I would not need to invent any stage behaviour because the literal action would also be real and sufficiently theatrical to speak for itself. If the horse is not there, the literal description seems to me too simplistic, resulting in a performed mimicry that, for me, gives an impression of artificiality and untruthfulness. It does not represent the hidden tensions and contradictory and contiguous characteristics of reality. The literal image appears one-dimensional to me, like a colourless drawing. I aspire instead to give my actions a strength equivalent to that of reality, a density of active tensions that escape the control of an over-linear cartoon.

'And what about feelings?' I am often asked. In my work as an actress, emotions are not a point of departure, but rather reactions that arise unintentionally, as a consequence of something that happens. The characteristics of a physical or vocal action – looking with my eyes while keeping my head lowered or an irregular interrupted way of breathing – provoke an affective reaction in me that is different from that of the spectator. I imagine that emotion can be an important creative reference for other actresses. If I happen to start a process from a feeling I am careful not to generalise. Love? Yes, but what kind of love? The tenderness for my dog that runs around my legs when I come home and scratches me with its rough fur until I feed it? Or the predilection for the red silk shirt that I wore to dance salsa at the Teja Corrida in Bogotá? Or a father's possessive and suffocating feeling for his teenage son? Or the sensation of sensuality provoked by hot sunshine while lying on the beach looking at seagulls in the company of a lover?

Early on I found it helpful to follow clear images. I asked myself concretely what I was doing, how I could respect the imagined reality and return it in the precision of my action, while also eliminating superfluous movements. The sharp, exact image to which I reacted, perceived with all my senses (touching, hearing, seeing, tasting and smelling), materialised through a variation of rhythms, impulses, directions and forms, demanding gestures, silences, expectations and pauses, and engaging my torso. A generic image would have made me lose coherence and describe only an idea. To be the wind, I need to know if it is a storm or an evening breeze, if the wind is sweeping autumn leaves or making a feather dance, if it whistles, blows or

64 *Improvisation and composition*

Improvisation, Londrina, 1994
Julia Varley, Tjokorda Istri Putra Padmini
Photo: Emidio Luisi

hisses, if it passes through a mountain creek, glides over a plain or enters a crack in the window of a city apartment, if it brings news from the sea or reminds someone of an appointment . . . The details of the image, of the inner actions, impart a particular colour to my perceptible actions and to the tensions of my stage presence.

With years and experience, my body has learned to think by itself without the need to project an imaginary film in order to create material. Other eyes see, a different imagination acts; my cells think and their memory and intelligence offer me simultaneous and opposite information. The action already contains its reason for being in the moment it is realised and I am free from having to explain, even to myself. When I create material nowadays I am immersed in a continuous alternation between actions that determine images, stimuli that determine actions, and actions without images that speak for themselves. At present, thinking with my body, the images of an improvisation or a composition sometimes come with the actions and, at other times, as a result of the actions.

The images and memories I resort to when creating material tend to show up again and again. They are no longer an effective incentive for discovering endless variations. My imagination repeats itself: the same events reappear, and these produce similar behaviour and mannerisms. The fundamental life experiences that evoke childhood and adolescence, nature and love, replicated in my mind, no longer serve as an inexhaustible source of differing actions. The depth and value of episodes lived in the past risk becoming banal if, when repeated, they are not slightly or radically transformed. So I have searched for unusual starting points that might have the same suggestive capacity and importance as key personal events.

I invent reactions to a colleague's actions and I even adapt training exercises. I create material starting from photographs or drawings; I translate in space the movement and the dynamism of a painting, depicting with my actions the shape of the subject, the sense of perspective, the different directions that the eye pursues while looking at the image. I can realise a score by copying the positions of the characters in a painting by Botticelli and reproducing the lines of energy of the same painting with physical attitudes. After I have reproduced the figures, I link them together, finding a dynamism that reveals a story and enriches my understanding of the painting. Looking at 'Lara's Death' by Delacroix – a woman lying in the arms of a man who is bent over her – I walk backwards sideways, as if an invisible hand tugged my head (in order to follow the direction of the main movement I have detected in the painting), I look upward as if I were lying down, then I turn my arm with the roundness of the man's embrace and finally I resume the head's impulse to underline the main focus.

I often take inspiration from music. I let the music determine my actions, allowing the rhythm, and onset of instruments and song, to lead me. The slow beat of a melody becomes slow-motion steps on the spot, the half tonalities turn into an uncertain waving of the hand, the low notes a way of bending over, and the high pitches an anxious smile that is fixed on the horizon. A fast rhythm can provoke small running footsteps. The addition of another musical instrument to the same rhythm can induce me to combine my arms with the way of running. The insistence of the rapid tempo transforms the arms' movement into a gesture that protects my face. I slowly lift my arm when the fast rhythm is interrupted by a note on the piano. The music builds expectantly and I point far away. Suddenly the voice enters and I lift both my arms with a feeling of abandonment. The text of the song speaks of wings and I close myself up like a cocoon. The music continues with nail-biting high notes and I lengthen my backbone as much as possible with my hands open. Some bass drums intervene and I advance with my face contracted and my fists at chest height.

Props and objects also help me create material. I reproduce the aspect, outline, structure, consistency or function of an object: an apple, book, door, flag, ring. I can be a stone that rolls, a shutter that is pulled up, a piece of cake eaten by a mouse, a tree that bends in the north wind. I become thin and long like a stick, I open like an umbrella, I cover myself like a hat, I bounce like a ball.

To create material, I have learned to let my thoughts proceed by association, quickly, without hesitating. What I don't know about a theme, I invent.

66 Improvisation and composition

Improvisation, Wroclaw, 2005
Akira Matsui, Julia Varley, Augusto Omolú
Photo: Francesco Galli

What I don't remember, I evoke imaginatively. The material becomes, for me, a field of exploration: a search for enigmas, surprises, contradictory meanings that will be refined in the elaboration subsequently by being put into relationship with the improvisations and compositions of other actresses and actors. I know that my material will be distorted by the context in which it will be included and by the intervention of wishes and sensibilities external to my own – namely the director and the spectator. The material is the thesis or antithesis in the dialectical process between actress and director. It is the proof that I exist as an actress; it is the form in which my identity reveals itself.

Repetition, memory, fixing

In theatre, spontaneity and improvisation are generally associated with the freshness of immediate execution. To be spontaneous means to act naturally without hesitation, premeditation or studied reactions. One of my aims is to behave *as if* it is always the first time. I imagine that there are actresses who are able to appear spontaneous every evening on stage without having to work for this result. I am not one of them. I achieve freshness in a character or stage action only after assiduous repetition. This allows me to recover a kind of spontaneity based on incorporated and 'forgotten' memory.

In performance, the effect of spontaneity for me comes from repetition, from memorising and assimilating my score during rehearsals. With time, this

Improvisation and composition   67

triple process becomes incorporated awareness, a way of making actions and of being. It is a kind of spontaneity similar to that of the pianist who interprets a symphony by Beethoven for the *n*th time. Also, when I have to improvise in front of spectators, for example during street performances, or when I respond to sudden technical problems and mistakes, or when I present a new scene during a demonstration, the point of support comes from the long practice of repetition, from the security given by previous memorising and rehearsal. In this case repetition doesn't consist of going over scenes that are already fixed, but comes from the experience of having had to face difficulties many times without any sort of hesitation. Combining a succession of acrobatic exercises in training, resolving a person's particular problems during a workshop, having a sense of geographical control over unfamiliar spaces so as to get into the appropriate position in a street performance, are some examples of situations that have taught me to react instantaneously and to improvise.

I have danced countless times in alleys and squares with Mr Peanut, my character with a skull head. Performances of *Anabasis*, Odin Teatret's most elaborate street production, forced me to learn to orientate myself quickly. The length of time dedicated to rehearsals for a performance provides me with the freedom and security that enable me to face unexpected incidents. Years and years of interaction with Odin Teatret's actresses and actors have made me attentive to their signals and impulses so that I can transform them into immediate reactions. It is as if they give me the ideas, the spontaneity and the sense of what I do.

During Ingemar Lindh's training, I would improvise every day with elements that I knew very well. The improvisation consisted of making continuous variations in a combination of previously fixed actions. The vocal improvisations that I also present in public, alone or accompanied by a musical instrument, are different each time and exploit my ability to manage counterpoint, rhythm, flow, diversification, surprise, harmonic and atonal sequences. I have developed this skill by constantly repeating exercises with the purpose of assimilating principles with which I can create stage material and performances.

Observing the scores that Odin Teatret's actresses and actors have repeated for years, Eugenio Barba declares that he is fascinated by the quality they radiate. This 'radiation', fruit of repetition, has a life independent of the score even if the latter is extracted from the context to which it belonged originally. Performances such as *Inside the Skeleton of the Whale*, *Ode to Progress*, *Itsi Bitsi*, *The Castle of Holstebro* and *Doña Musica's Butterflies* use scores that partly originate from previous performances. In the new setting and grid of relationships, the scores assume entirely different meanings, primarily because of the organic charge they convey.

It is important to be aware that this organic quality doesn't depend only on repetition, but above all from the need – while repeating – to convince the director or the spectators, and hence to be decided. There is a difference for me between repeating for myself, to memorise or practise, and repeating in front of others who watch me. The external eye demands maximum engagement and the highest quality of energy from me every time. Under these conditions the score, seen and heard, is not repeated and incorporated mechanically, but is pervaded by the necessity for precision, a tension towards excellence that sharpens the sense and desire to *say* something.

I try to make the freshness of the score, inherent in an exercise, scene, improvisation or composition, or in a complete performance, re-emerge while respecting two conditions: the accurate repetition of its dynamisms, rhythms and actions; and mobilising each time the motivation that the specific relationship with the spectator requires. This deep-felt tie between actress and spectator – or actress and director – gives an intensity of experience that I wish could shine through my whole organism without separation between thought and body, logic and feelings. I deduce therefore that the evolution of an actress depends above all on performing – even if for one lone spectator – and on the response of the rigorous director who works with her.

When I begin to repeat an improvisation or composition, I have the feeling that it loses its vitality and detail. During an improvisation the motivations – concrete stimuli, internal actions, images and physical impulses – dictate their rhythm, and I react without hesitation. The action/reaction seems to be the only possible one: no judgement impedes it. I proceed without interrupting to remember and without worrying about how I will re-discover what I have done already. When I repeat in order to fix, I am aware of losing the freshness and verve of the improvisation at first: everything seems mechanical. The intensity I remember doesn't correspond to my physical recall and what appeared fascinating to me previously now seems banal and meaningless. Only after I have memorised the score with my body to the point where I am able to forget it, can I re-find the suppleness that allows surprises, sensations, images, rhythms and meanings to re-emerge from my actions. I discover that the original result contains much more potential than I had imagined. Like the pianist whose fingers move autonomously, I am free to interpret and 'improvise' when I am no longer subject to technique, when I have incorporated and 'forgotten' the score that has become an integral part of me by now.

Before, during and after improvisation

There are various ways of improvising and composing and there are many useful procedures for repeating and remembering. Normally at Odin Teatret an improvisation is fixed in its smallest details. All the steps, ways of looking, body angles, weight distribution, tensions and expressions must be recreated identically. When I repeat an improvisation for the first time, I try to remember as many details as possible without interrupting myself. I activate my body memory and let the flow of actions help me proceed. I don't interrupt myself by using conscious memory or correcting myself. For the subsequent

Theatrum Mundi rehearsal, Bologna, 1990
Tjokorda Istri Putra Padmini, Haruchiko Azuma, Julia Varley, Sanjukta Panigrahi, Tjokorda Raka Tisnu

Photo: Tony D'Urso

repetitions, though, I read the notes that I took immediately after the improvisation, look at the video recordings or listen to the observations of my colleagues who have written down my improvisation.

Immediately after the improvisation or the work of composition I take notes. My annotations evoke images, movements or even things that I have noticed around me. They are key words or drawings that don't describe the action, but help me fix it as a physical memory. The position of a foot, a direction, a rhythm, the number of steps, an association: the writing doesn't follow a narrative or psychological logic, but it gives synthetic and independent data that helps me find the action again with my body.

I can make an improvisation applying what I call a 'hiccup' technique. It is a simple procedure that I often use when working alone without external assistance. I make a certain number of actions that I am sure I can remember, I stop and repeat them, and then continue from the point where I broke off. This 'hiccup' progression is similar to composition as a way of creating material and it doesn't usually reach the depth or intensity of a free improvisation.

Sometimes during an improvisation I make mistakes or elements appear that I don't like. However, the first time I repeat a sequence of actions it is useful for me to keep everything, without censoring myself, or adding or subtracting anything. I don't eliminate mistakes or 'black spots', huffs or puffs, embarrassed giggles or cries of impatience. They may become elements of surprise and participate in changing the rhythm and colour of my material. They are usually actions that have escaped my control and it is a challenge to justify them. At first it seems impossible to include them in the logic of what I am doing. They seem insubstantial and absurd, but finding a solution that will make these foreign cells congruent with the rest of the organism that is developing allows me to distance myself from my habits and clichés. At Odin Teatret it is almost a given that the director selects our mistakes during rehearsals.

When creating a scene or a character, the usual tendency is to throw away anything that is disappointing. Dissatisfaction persuades us to change every time and abandon working patiently in depth. I try to keep to what I have created, even if I haven't reached the result for which I was aiming. If I alter things immediately, I will not be able to accumulate, to distinguish what is valuable from what is superfluous, and fathom the potential of the first result. I try to emulate the fisherman who, after pulling his net out of the sea, carefully examines the seaweed before throwing anything away.

During rehearsals for *Brecht's Ashes* – when I was still a beginner and didn't know how to defend my pride with concrete proposals – I imagined that the director, Eugenio Barba, contrived a thousand ways for me to be noticed as little as possible. I found it relatively easy to explore, but difficult to choose and fix. Nothing seemed good enough to me. I didn't dare believe that my actions might be interesting. One week of work with Eugenio was enough to change my attitude. From the ten walks and ten ways of holding a handbag that he had asked me to prepare, he chose the ones that I considered most boring and banal. Then he combined a walk with an arm position and a way of holding a handbag and suddenly everything was transformed and acquired a meaning and coherence that I would never have imagined.

I achieve *density* by weaving together simple elements and creating connections between them. I am aware that my material has to pass through various phases of elaboration before it is satisfactory. At Odin Teatret I have noticed that the experienced actresses and actors tend to compose or improvise with simplicity. They know that the *elaboration* will make their presence and their actions interesting eventually. They know that repeating something simple will allow them to appropriate the material more quickly and so be able to focus on the long phase of elaboration. In contrast, the younger generations use improvisation as a special occasion for expression; they strive to present something that they consider to be worthy of note already.

Repetition creates roots; it gives stability and autonomy to my material before it is introduced into a complex process of relationships: with other scores, space, lights, images, objects, music and text. The confidence I acquire from repetition prepares me to safeguard my material but also trains me to be open to the changes and drastic interventions of the elaboration. The

Theatrum Mundi, Bologna, 1990
Kanho Azuma, Haruchiko Azuma, Sanjukta Panigrahi, Julia Varley, I Wayan Berata, I Made Pasek Tempo, Tjokorda Raka Tisnu, Kanichi Hanayagi, Roberta Carreri
Photo: Fiora Bemporad

material gives me an identity and with this I am ready to meet the other and others. At the point when the physical and vocal scores are so incorporated that they can no longer be separated from my way of being on stage, repetition gives me both conviction and persuasive power.

Elaboration: from the actress's point of view

At Odin Teatret elaboration is the most important phase of the creative process. It consists of retouching the scores derived from improvisations and compositions, cautiously refining the smallest details by repeating, chiselling, distilling and modifying them. During this phase the symbiosis between text and action, actress and character, score and space is achieved. Slowly, despite all the artificiality of the montage, life reasserts itself. It is the moment in which the performance begins to decide for itself. During the elaboration, the texts, the material I have contributed, the ideas or images proposed by the director, meet and clash and transform into something that surprises both me as an actress and the director – a reality with a life of its own. The context and the individual biography determine finally the meaning that each spectator gives to the performance. An identical performance, in different countries or

72 Improvisation and composition

different milieux in the same city, acquires distinct meanings and values. The last word is with the spectator.

The capacity to convert a subjective reality into stage behaviour has an important function when I improvise and compose. During the creation of my material, thoughts and feelings manifest themselves through actions, which I fix and memorise, so that they become precise physical forms and expressions. During the elaboration, however, it is my capacity to react, modifying and adapting my material to the relationships and circumstances that arise from the new assignments, that is important. For example, I have to be aware how my position influences the perception of the stage space as a whole and be able to recognise the impulses in the actions of another actress. It is interesting to note how the actions of one of my scores, which the director perceived as organic when I performed them alone, might lose their 'life' momentarily as soon as the material is introduced into another context.

At the beginning of rehearsals, the shape, volume, rhythm and strength of my actions depend on the motivation that has produced them. When an action is placed in relationship with the text, the space, other scores, music, etc., its characteristics have to be adapted in order to calibrate the effect it needs to generate in the scene that is being created. In adapting a score, I try not to lose the original attributes yet simultaneously take into account everything around me in order to justify my stage behaviour in the new situation. It is

The Island of Labyrinths, Copenhagen, 1996
Julia Varley, Ni Made Sariani
Photo: Fiora Bemporad

not a rational process that explains or connects an effect with a cause, nor does it develop according to narrative criteria. It is a way of proceeding that acknowledges the primary organic signs and elaborates and cements them, almost casually creating black holes from which meanings surface for me as an actress, for the director and for the spectator. It is an intuitive process of physical sensibility that knows how and how much to reduce or change my actions so as to make them acceptable and believable.

During rehearsals, the elaboration of a dialogue with another actress, based on impulses and counter-impulses, on actions and reactions, adjusts the rhythms, direction and intensity of the single scores. From this comes an unplanned source of further creation. Reacting to the space, to changes of light, to lines spoken by others, to a new costume, is also a way for me to detect the potential of a character or of material I have previously prepared. During the daily rehearsal of the fixed scenes, I do my best to create connections – synapses – between my own material and that of my colleagues on stage. This is a way in which I can fill empty moments and technical passages, and be 'present' so that the director doesn't forget that I exist. The character and/or my scores ripen day by day as I react to what is happening, remembering the sequences and refining the deliberate or accidental combinations that generate associations. It is a repetition that involves a continuous adjustment to new circumstances, in which even the slightest alteration happens with maximum engagement because of the presence of the director.

The score is enriched by meeting with other people, with space and lights, text and stories: it modifies and adapts, maintaining the original motivations and finding new ones at the same time. If, in the score, the action is the imaginary impulse to throw a ball, and in the scene this behaviour and the ensuing physical tensions are used to take a hat from someone else, the action has to be adapted to the distance, height and size of the hat. I keep the impulse and the original motivation – which I have by now incorporated – without remaining stubbornly faithful to a form that has become strange in the new situation. The dynamic quality of the original action allows me to elaborate and justify its form in the new context, thus opening up a denser reading for the spectator who perceives distinct dynamic information in addition to the anecdote of the removed hat.

Without the tension between fidelity to the dynamic core of the original action and the ability to adapt to a new context, my material would show little possibility for development. To protect its essence, when I elaborate, I must recognise the 'heart' of an action. I need to know how to maintain the centre of impulses in the torso, the weight distribution and energy flow, particularly when I reduce the outer manifestation of the action as much as possible. The dialogue between respect for the subjective and objective characteristics of the original material and the necessary changes creates a tension. From this tension images and suggestions emerge that suggest a new and surprising understanding of my action.

The point of balance between loyalty and variation is not absolute. I find the boundaries within which to move every single time, so that variation does not make me lose the original points of reference nor fidelity prevent me from integrating into the new situation.

At Odin Teatret the moment when we choose the texts and stories to be presented, like the moment when names are given to the characters, varies from performance to performance. Sometimes characters or texts are a starting point, at other times a result. Usually the decisions are taken during rehearsals. When the general narrative thematic frame is established, my actress's material is once again confronted by a situation that changes its effect and meaning, and so demands further elaboration.

Elaboration: from the director's point of view

At Odin Teatret, Eugenio Barba, as director, has developed an acute practice of observation that allows him to understand when an action can be adapted to a task without losing its 'heart' or particular tensions. His comments, when correcting the material of an improvisation or a composition, treasure the somatic characteristics of the action, its entrenched dynamic information, without intruding on my motives.

In our many years of work together, I don't remember a single occasion on which Eugenio has not respected what, for me, is the deep-rooted information of the action. If the material that I present does not interest him, Eugenio cuts or eliminates it. If, on the contrary, it provokes associations, he starts following them, elaborating my actions and connecting them with other scores, texts, objects or melodies.

For example, during rehearsals for *The Castle of Holstebro*, part of the material I presented to the director was a way of running with a slight limp and my hands turned up towards the sky. This score originated from *The Gospel According to Oxyrhincus*, where it was Jeanne d'Arc who ran after the angels and conversed with them. Eugenio adjusted the actions, asking me to keep the palms of my hands facing the ground to work with the poem *The Bitch* by Essenin. In this text a bitch slips on the snow as she runs after her master who intends to drown her litter. Eugenio did not suggest that I should run like a desperate dog, nor did he offer propositions that would influence the 'heart' of my actions. He asked only that I change the position of my hands, without allowing this to upset the deep-rooted connotations of my score and physical impulses. The energy that previously was addressed upwards, with the new position of the hands, is directed towards the ground. The image of Jeanne d'Arc is overlapped by that of the dog. Jeanne d'Arc doesn't disappear to give way to the bitch, but remains as stored experience giving more density to the score. These meanings are implicit: usually, when I present that score during performance, I don't think of either the dog or Jeanne d'Arc.

Nowadays, the first thing Eugenio does at the beginning of a process of elaboration is to eliminate those actions that seem static to his eyes and alter my material to strengthen the organic effect of the individual actions. In the next phase, long before we have a clear idea of the result for which we are aiming, Eugenio improvises using my scores; he changes the sequences of actions, their volume and rhythm, he cuts and sews up again, deconstructs and recomposes following the red thread of his own associations. My stage behaviour – which may be recognisable as a character already – leads him into the unknown landscape of the forthcoming performance.

I make an effort to accommodate the director who accelerates or slows down some of my actions. He transforms their energetic quality from strong to soft, or the other way round, or he alternates these qualities; he submits the actions to a process of reduction; he distorts the rhythm of a whole scene. He subdivides an action, thus underlining the different phases of its composition; he asks me to colour them with introverted or extroverted characteristics or to transpose an action that involves the whole body to a single part of the body. He makes me find an equivalent to the score with my voice, or to manoeuvre and use an object. A scene can be deconstructed and some details, peripeteia, vicissitudes or ideas may even be passed on to another actress or to the whole group.

In order to improvise and discover what he still doesn't know, the director often feels the need to remove anecdotal elements from my stage behaviour so that only a mass of energy, tensions and dynamisms remains with a potentiality of conflicting meanings. The director 'washes' my facial expression and the futile tensions of my fingers, arms and legs. He works with the associations aroused in him by the 'heart' of my actions. It is my dance of impulses and tensions that prompts his imagination and incites him to react and be creative, encouraging him to move towards disconcerting solutions, unexpected combinations, *quid pro quo* and contradictory points of view. At the same time he continues to offer technical suggestions that, detail by detail, coalesce into a dense ball of autonomous narrative threads that – sometimes amalgamating, sometimes clashing or remaining parallel – subsist in the finished performance.

The understanding of the numerous meanings and associations that the score can assume and arouse belongs to a kind of tacit knowledge that cannot be easily explained. In order to allow this embodied intelligence to work, during the elaboration of the material at Odin Teatret we don't speak of our deep-rooted motivations, but rather choose to communicate in technical and neutral language. The score is where the actress and director meet.

It is during rehearsals that the performance grows. The daily repetition of the accumulated material, with all the actresses and actors in the working room, is a fertile situation for distillation. Small scenes are added, an infinity of details are changed or eliminated, the performance gradually emerges from the fog and, mysteriously, reveals itself as a *kasba* with one thousand alleys in which both the spectator and I can get lost at first, only subsequently to find a single and personal way out.

When I create actress's material, to avoid pretence, I find it useful to invent equivalents to the reality I am depicting. The same is true for the elaboration, when we face circumstances that cannot be reproduced directly in theatre without being trapped in falseness or bad taste. Torture, madness, death and the act of love are experiences that need to be recreated through a complex montage of equivalent situations. Speaking of Ophelia's mad scene in the *Theatrum Mundi*, Eugenio explains that to represent insanity – which means to offer the experience of this particular state of the mind to the spectator – the whole scene has to be crazy, overturning the usual rules of the interaction of space and time.

Usually, as a starting point, the director presents a text, a collection of texts or a theme as inspiration for the work process. Eugenio makes an oral improvisation. He introduces his 'material', his bricks for the building of the house: a collection of images, visions, evocative oxymora, familiar words to be cracked like nuts, contradictory questions to be confronted and knots to be unravelled. The themes of Odin Teatret's performances include: biographies and the works of authors (Dostoyevsky, Brecht, Hans Christian Andersen); the clash between European emigrants and the native tribes of the Americas; the funeral of an anthem (*The International*); the biography of a living anthropologist; the story of Kaspar Hauser . . . For *The Gospel According to Oxyrhincus* we started from a single image: mad lions in the desert. For *Kaosmos* the first step was the theme for an improvisation: the three births of a wolf. We have begun to prepare performances in the most disparate ways: without text but with many scores; with many volumes of poems but without actress's material; with a written play from which some characters have been eliminated; with fixed improvisations but without a common theme; with a set design or piece of music; with dances or costumes; without knowing which story we would narrate or port we would sail into at the end of our exploratory journey.

The title of the performance – which may change during the elaboration – is a stable point of reference. It is the compass that directs rehearsals. With the title, the questions we ask ourselves as actress and director become more concrete and guide the work. With the title, a new tension is established between the elaboration of the material and the theme and this contributes to the complexity of the dramaturgy.

Time is a fundamental factor in the elaboration. The hours, days and months, with their difficulties, uncertainties and the meticulous chiselling away at details, seem to always be the same. The periods of monotony are endless. It feels as if there is a complete lack of wind in the sail and only rare puffs of breeze indicate that the boat is gently gliding forward. In this attenuated, intense atmosphere, fraught with tension, the performance laboriously takes form and becomes a being with seven lives. I cannot describe the complexity and simultaneity of this phase, because it would take the same amount of time as it does to live it.

To get valid results, we must confront obstacles and challenges, pass through moments of crisis and discouragement, and have the patience to wait for results to appear when the time is right. In this phase the relationship between actress, director and all those people who collaborate in the birth of the performance, intensifies in highs and lows, passions and conflicts, fatigue and recuperation, mutual admiration and mistrust. The daily rehearsal schedule, new proposals, dedication to shared work, the surprises that each of us manages to bring are supportive and essential aspects of the professional relationships within our group. We engage in trying to give each other confidence, without any certainty that finally the performance will rise from the ground and fly.

At Odin Teatret the last phase of the elaboration usually involves open rehearsals for students of all ages from Holstebro. In return they each write a response. Reading them, we discover whether our work carries energies that move the spectator. The finished performance has a life of its own that follows its own tortuous path, independent from the motivations contained in the actress's material or the stories that the director believes he is telling. The intentions of the actress and director disappear to make room for a living fresco in which the individual brushstrokes are indistinguishable.

5 Score and subscore

A useful but wrong word

An aura of mystery and respect, which irritates me at times, is fashioned around an actress's way of thinking. This *terra incognita* becomes a mirage that blinds those who observe it. I sense that occasionally my presence in a performance fills with magic and that this happens quite independently of the constant level of professionalism I demand of myself. It is a magic that I cannot control. It is this kind of magic that causes the mirages.

In Theatre Anthropology the word 'subtext' has been replaced by 'subscore', a more appropriate term for the not necessarily text-based forms of theatre in which an actress builds her stage presence with a kind of vocal and physical behaviour called a 'score'. The term 'subscore' includes all the mental and psychic processes on which an actress bases her work. Mixed in this concept are personal techniques, elements of support that keep the score alive, starting points for creating material, the actress's thoughts before and during the performance, a character's motives, the inner world, emotions, energy, memories, sensations, and everything that cannot be conceptualised.

In my work as an actress there are places where I do not care to venture with too conscious an eye. I want to preserve the possibility of letting myself be guided by forces that I do not control, as I know that they collaborate with my creative process. Only in this way do I feel that the magic – that illuminates the unique moment when my necessity as an actress meets with my experience – can be released. But there are also ways of working with the subscore that are deliberate, looked for and led by the practice of the craft. If, as an actress, I manage to absorb the methods and rules, exercises and training, and turn them into a personal technique, I also locate a pragmatic strategy that helps me achieve results.

Eugenio Barba uses the image of a 'blind horse' when he describes the part of himself that conducts his creative work on a performance. To try to understand the way that the 'blind horse' thinks is not useful, but it is important to know *how* to let the horse work. This presupposes a personal technique that does not need to be analysed, but that can allow space for a gallop. The subscore is, for me, this personal technique, this disposition to follow or determine the mental processes that will support my actions.

The subscore is not restricted to a conscious mental process based on images. The course that a subscore follows can be linked to physical sensations, abstractions, information processed in different ways by the brain and remembered/forgotten by a memory, which I place in my cells rather than in my thoughts. As an actress I choose the way that best suits my professional and personal curiosity and the needs of the role at that moment. The subscore is, for me, an invisible physical/mental process, which accompanies, both in a fixed and fluctuating way, the actions that the spectator sees.

The paper song

At Brecon, in Wales, during the seventh session of ISTA, my 'paper song' prompted a discussion. When I was asked to create a sequence of actions on the basis of the title 'the book', my first concern was not to repeat myself.

On that occasion, in the big sports hall where we worked in Brecon, I did not have anything with me except my notebook. So I translated 'book' into 'paper'. I ripped a piece of paper out of my notebook and reacted to whatever I could make it do, using the sounds it produced, the shapes it took, the resistance I felt while tearing it, the direction in which I threw it or made it fly. The torn, folded, crumpled, flapped, gnawed paper, and the way I used it to blow through, dry, cut, became the points of reference for creating a sequence of physical actions. I simply responded to the stimuli I received from the paper/book.

It was difficult for some observers to accept and hear my 'paper song'. That I worked in such a way, with a process that did not resort to the deep emotions of a first love or a dying father, caused animated discussion. Once again I had to listen to the assertion that, as an actress, in order to provoke emotions I should experience them and that communication with the spectator depends on the depth of my feelings. It is true that to create dynamic material, the information I start from should be important and dense, but this for me means rich in details.

It was interesting to note how the critical observers saw *results*, which did not function for them, instead of material in the first phase of a *process*, which still needs to be elaborated by me as actress and later by the director. The noise of a piece of paper tearing could reawaken the deep echoes of a lived experience: a letter arriving too late, the possession order demanding the furniture belonging to my home when my father could not pay his taxes, my first drawing, a poem by Montale ... Why should I have to be able to consciously recognise and describe these deep echoes of experience that had been transformed into actions through my technique as an actress? Why is it so difficult to understand that the body remembers and that an action contains so much more information than consciousness can master?

I was reading an article on the 1992 war in former Yugoslavia. In the text I found the word 'omission', which had recently been used in a letter I had received from a person who is not fond of me. Two unpleasant experiences were linked. I can recognise this association now, but I would not be able to point out the numerous connections that are part of my fund of knowledge. Yet it is precisely these short-circuits of experience that are essential in imparting a certain quality of colour, rhythm and intensity to my actions. It is not necessary for my mind to be aware of these passages separately, but for my actress's integral body/mind to use its particular intelligence in actions that already contain them. During the work process, as an actress, I am not interested in an introspective journey of self-knowledge. I prefer to protect the incomprehensible way of thinking of the cells and to concentrate on how to open up spaces for that thinking to flow. I would rather deflect the attention away from my person, without explaining what I feel to myself, so that I can dedicate myself to the steps that are necessary for the work and in order that what I produce is able to speak to me.

Thought

The idea that an actress has to be totally present in the action, at one with what she is doing, gives a picture of a body/mind in which thought is indissolubly bound to action; as if I ought not to think of anything else. Nevertheless, during a performance, while present in my action and totally concentrated, I discover the simultaneous presence of other thoughts: technical observations, practical considerations, new interpretations of the performance. I can think: 'Why hasn't the light come on?', 'T's zip is broken, I'll let him know in the next scene', 'I've forgotten to put the shawl in its place', 'We are slowing down the rhythm', 'The tone is too high'. I can think: 'I've got a stomach ache', 'What a nice old man in the third row', 'The restaurant is closed tonight', 'We have to strike the set afterwards'. I can think: 'Those are the coins which paid Judas' (while looking at Tage Larsen, who as the Great Inquisitor in *The Gospel According to Oxyrhincus*, throws away the bracelet of coin charms and rubs his hands), 'This is the sound of a rocking chair on which an old person in a home waits for a relative to visit' (while, as Doña Musica, sitting on the stool during *Kaosmos* I grumble and wait for the Man from the Country after having just said 'And there he stayed for days and years'), 'Ah! But I am addressing Death, not a person . . .' (while, as the girl dressed in white in *The Castle of Holstebro*, I recite a poem by Sappho with my arms stretched out towards Mr Peanut, the character with a skull head).

Do all these thoughts have any influence on the spectators? I think that I can be *occupied* by different thoughts without these detracting from my presence on stage, but I cannot be *preoccupied* by them. The thoughts must not be at the centre of my attention, nor should they determine the accent of the whole picture. Most importantly, I should not think about the score and thus create a separation within me as an actress, so that I remember, decide and perform the action, instead of being action. When my mind flows with the action, concentrated and free to venture in different directions, ready to discover, to comment and take decisions, I know that I have managed to build a situation in which I fight against the danger of becoming a robot that only follows its established course. My thoughts are free even if deeply rooted and present in the action.

I am ready to react to anything that happens; I am present through the precision of the score that I have incorporated, not absent in a schematic structure that hides the surroundings from me. The body is intelligent, ready, not mechanical, after it has liberated itself from the difficulty of remembering.

So those exciting moments of enlightenment, when two elements suddenly meet and I think I have grasped something, can occur as flashes during the performance. To achieve this state of being for me it is necessary that the score has been memorised so completely that it can be forgotten, that continuous repetition has turned upside down the freshness of the first time and now returns it, and that the restriction of the fixed components has been transformed into a well of as yet unknown visions. To achieve this state of being I work obsessively on details during rehearsals and until I have played the performance at least thirty times.

As an actress I pass through various phases, and each phase has particularities that keep the work alive and interesting for me. At first it is the difficulty of remembering, the emotion and fear of encountering the spectators. Then it is the difficulty of adapting to new venues on tour. Next, when the certitude of repetition is achieved, I confront new tasks in performance or choose a parallel activity during the day that might act as a stimulus. In every performance I discover unexpected perspectives, new stories, relationships and meanings, details hidden in the actions that have been repeated in the same way for years.

The subscore of creation

I should take a step back to focus on the subscore at the stage when the first material is created and then elaborated. This is the only way to understand how the subscore in performance embraces all the information from the distinct phases of the process in an indissoluble and coherent texture that forgets and remembers, and goes forwards and backwards in time.

During my first year of work at Odin Teatret, training, improvisations and performance belonged to separate worlds for me. Only after Eugenio Barba's long and patient work on one of my improvisations, during which he adjusted each movement a few centimetres, did I realise that the 'I' who was learning to be present on stage, to mould her energy and make her actions 'real' through the training exercises, was the same 'I' who needed to shape my inner images in an improvisation and adapt them to the conditions imposed by the performance.

During the early years, I wanted to be expressive and I created material with conceptual images and linear stories. The resulting material, even though it made sense to me, often failed to surprise me or function in the process of building a performance. Today I know that the pragmatic rules and pre-expressive principles – the work on presence, on how to be credible for the spectator independently from what is represented – determine both what I say in an improvisation and the meanings that the spectator will take from the performance.

In rehearsal, elaborating a sequence of actions, the strong or soft quality of energy, fast or slow rhythm, extrovert or introvert characteristics, different directions in space, kinds of balance, the chosen framework, will all weave into variations and oppositions, which make the stage behaviour organic. Following these principles, in an improvisation or a composition, a character's way of being, the meanings or feelings, are not preconceived, but something that can surprise me. I discover that *I am told*, when I abandon the perspective of the person who *wants* to tell.

As an actress I lean on the subscore first to create material, then to keep it alive, and later still to feel alive. To create a character, embody a text or a choreography, resolve a technical demand, the issue is always *how* to translate the task, theme, imaginary person, word or concept into a tangible form of behaviour that will give a sensation of fullness and life.

The subscore becomes the personal strategy I choose to create references to which I can react. I can decide to analyse a character's traits to influence the way it walks or to walk in a certain way to build a character's traits, but the creation of rooted material always entails a process that branches out into details. To generalise does not help me. At the end of the process there will no longer be a 'psychological', 'physical' or 'distanced' actress, but a character which, if believable to the spectator, contains all the contiguous and contradictory aspects of a human being.

I have followed many different procedures and the logic of the subscore used at the moment of creation has changed a lot over the years. With *The Million*, the material was built from a dance in which a couple never let go of each other's hands, the discipline of European ballroom dancing, marching rhythms, from the real fear I felt, and from wanting to show off a beautiful Mexican dress. *The Castle of Holstebro* was born by letting Mr Peanut – the stilt character that already existed in the street performances – speak in a work demonstration.

I have made improvisations in which, after being given a theme, I begin by letting my mind become immersed in a flow of associations. I then start to move following clear images and sensations, with a commitment to continue without stopping until I have finished. I have built sequences of actions from verbs in a text, from ways of sitting on a chair, from the opposition between head and eyes, from walking across stepping stones in a river, from the impudence of youth, from ten ways of holding a handbag or infinite ways of using a handkerchief. I have created characters starting from the opposite of their known characteristics and I have let divergent material create nameless roles. To improvise without a theme I have substituted the flow of music or the dynamism of certain paintings, the intonation of a song or the rhythm of a text for sequences of images and associations. The pleasure of dancing, the sensuality of energy that vibrates and breathes, or the beauty of a movement that finds its strongest expression can become references that help me find and fix the score during the phase of creation.

Chaotic order

But still the question remains: listening to that music, thinking of that theme, looking at that painting, why is the consequence this particular action and not that? Different factors decide: received information, the principles that vitalise my stage presence, and chance. In the same way that the colour red is troubling and blue gives a sense of tranquillity, a musical phrase determines a certain kind of movement, the dynamism of a painting makes me follow certain lines in space, the implicit knowledge of a theme provokes certain associations that I manifest through actions that for me are linked to the point of departure.

The actions are induced by a logic that can only be personal, which transforms and translates at the same time as reacting to the information received. But even when the starting point is detailed and precise, and even when the principles of stage presence are respected, there are still thousands of actions that could result. At this point it is chance that decides, I say to myself, following the same chaotic order that rules the universe, the order that makes a hurricane depend on a butterfly's wing beat.

I do not dispute chance. After the action is chosen and I have done it for the first time, I try to be faithful to it. I find it again, look after and repeat it until the time comes to change it during the process of elaborating a character or performance. This moment only arrives when I have incorporated both the original material and its motivation – the score and its subscore. During rehearsals the material can be cut, reduced, transformed, manipulated until it is almost unrecognisable. But the final result will contain all the previous information and every phase, enriching the texture of impulses and intentions. The original motives, the new meanings that emerge, the actions that no longer exist, the contradictory information and the logic that belongs to different stories: all this experience is part of the final result and is remembered/forgotten by the action.

The subscore of repetition

Once the score is created and fixed, my problem is to keep it alive and appealing. As an actress I am and, at the same time, I represent. Improvising around details that don't change the score but enrich the references I lean on, I find it useful to jump between these two levels: to be possessed by the action and to comment upon it. Identifying and creating distance are points of view and ways of proceeding that converge in the action and are necessary to one another. I work with the consciousness of having and of being a character.

In *Talabot*, for example, in the divorce scene during which I had to destroy a nest, the interrupted rhythm with which I spoke the text, the tiredness caused by the previous scene, the tickle in my throat provoked by inhaling the thyme that covered my face, resulted in feeling like someone who first tries to control tears and then lets herself go, giving in to depression. When repeating this scene I tried to keep it alive by controlling the breath that had been broken by the rhythm of the text, the itching thyme and by interpreting the destruction of the nest with a greater or lesser hand pressure. To underline the desolation I could let out all my breath in the pause in which the text changed from information to comment or reproduce in one word the moaning tone with which some Norwegian children speak. I could cry, let myself cry and sing the crying.

I find it difficult to believe these motivations as I write them down. The written words, like rational thought, are too slow for the time available to me as an actress when I am on stage. In that situation, which I don't know quite how to reproduce on paper, these inner references travel at a higher speed than that of the scene, they co-exist and come into being by themselves. The subscore that keeps the fixed score alive is a jungle of motives, sensations and opinions, which precede thought.

Talabot
Julia Varley as Kirsten Hastrup
Photo: Jan Rüsz

Repetition can have a negative influence on the ability to keep the score alive when the performance is presented regularly for two, three, four or even ten years. To help prevent this deterioration I have either given myself new tasks or created processes that are independent from the performance. For example, the change of language when we play in different countries gives me an obstacle to overcome. I can oppose the established features of a character with tiny, new aspects, render the obvious expressions slightly ambiguous, give value to each syllable rather than only to the words of the text, look for any remaining dead moments in the performance and introduce some postures or miniscule movements. I can let the presence of the spectators and of other characters influence my perception of the scenes more or I can enrich the general symphony of the performance by introducing small sounds.

Independently of the performance, at other times during the day, I can dedicate myself to other activities, which have a complementary kind of energy. This revives my motivation and resolution to continue playing.

The subscore of performance

It is my precision as an actress that allows the spectators to endow an action with meaning and awakens reactions, sensations and emotions in them. When it is the body/mind that thinks, this same precision fills the score with meaning and affectivity for me as well. Precision provokes different reactions in the spectator and in me. While I am on stage, precision also triggers reactions in me that are not always the same.

Precision – giving life to a gesture that can only be so, an action that contains all its intentions – is the only real foundation on which I can always lean, even though I know that sometimes the aura that reverberates from it will be full of magic and at other times only of professionalism. Precision is my actress's 'intelligence', which doesn't know if the intention or the action comes first: it is the score that has become subscore and vice versa. I attain precision when the question of whether it is determined by an inner motivation or by an exterior physical movement is redundant, when these terms are no longer relevant and the technique has become stage life.

After the years in which I had to learn to be visible on stage came the years in which I worked on veiling technique. Then I only wanted to be a dance of energy and my ideal was a butterfly. I had thought of entitling this chapter 'Subscore: under the skin of the action'. Then, reading a book on biology, I remembered that in modern science one no longer thinks in terms of inside or outside, over or under, but that everything is matter in borderless communication, a continuous flow and interchange. So all I can say is: subscore, another useful but 'wrong' word.

Note

1 This chapter is taken from an article written in response to questions put to me by Patrice Pavis during a lecture we gave together in 1992 on the occasion of the seventh session of ISTA in Brecon and Cardiff.

6 Text and subtext

Textual interpretation

Words are difficult for me; I don't catch their meaning immediately and I need time to learn them by heart. I am not a person who generally speaks with ease. The vocal problems that I have had to face have encouraged me to sift through the usual textual interpretation techniques to adapt them atypically to my needs. The supporting elements I have found are not necessarily valid for others. The paths I have followed are only a demonstration of the relevance of a personal technique and of the need to trust one's own voice.

I sense that I have to 'forget' the text in order to let the words pour out by themselves, setting meaning free to reach the spectator, while I concentrate on something else. If I think directly about the text, my memory sometimes gets blocked: I have to improvise to continue. To remember and 'forget', I turn my attention to the music of the text, the vocal action, pauses for breath, the people and objects I address, the authors and circumstances in which the text was written, my mood, the details that determine the colour of the timbre of my voice.

Aside from the technical choices I make in articulating the words of a text, it always helps me to think in terms of vocal actions. Each inflexion, accent, intonation, pause and vibration is the consequence of an action performed by my voice. The voice is concrete, material, physical for me because it is able to act in space just as my body does. Detecting the vocal action and knowing that it can accompany, underline or oppose the meaning of the words, be indifferent to or independent from them, affects my capacity for vocal rendition and stimulates my desire to explore.

To tackle a text first means for me to decide *how* to say the words. To contribute with musicality, inflexion, characters and visions of my own to the development and direction of a scene or performance based on a text, I need to find a basis for transforming the written words into vocal and physical actions: into monologues or dialogues, songs or declamations, sonority or silences, mimed or danced verbs, rhythms, vibrations or dynamisms. To facilitate the distinction between the two processes in this chapter, I will call the basis 'subscore' when it refers to the creation of physical action scores and 'subtext' when it refers to vocal action scores.

The elements I rely on to determine *how* to say the words (subtext) are the motivations and references that I use to speak the text in a particular manner, in the same way as I use the subscore to act with a specific body behaviour. My motivations and references can be historical, sensorial, psychological, emotional, intuitive, abstract or physical. The elements I lean on to determine *how* to say the words (subtext) can be provided by text analysis, a physical score, a rhythmic or musical structure, a melody, a vocal score, a sequence of associations or reactions to situations in which a character participates.

The subtext can be implicit in the way of saying the text, like the subscore is the disguised motivation for the physical score. But the subtext – for example, when it is a sequence of physical actions – can also be visible and audible in the scene in which I say the words. In this case the base becomes the actress's material in itself and the procedure of finding *how* to say the text becomes part of the scene to be presented to the spectators. The subtext, then, besides fulfilling its original function, also participates directly.

I use the base I consider most effective or interesting according to the text, scene, character and performance. The way of speaking the text depends on the performing situation I am in or on the kind of production we are rehearsing. In a dialogue I take into consideration the voice of the interlocutor; in a monologue I respect the vocal quality of the character I am interpreting. In a small room I don't shout too loudly. Saying the text in French I am careful of harshness with the pronunciation, in Spanish of the specific musicality of the different countries in which this language is spoken. The more tragic the text is, the more I maintain coldness and distance; the more it is poetic, the less I add vocal variations.

Textual analysis

Text analysis allows me to extract information from the written words, to turn concepts and abstract symbols that explicitly belong to the text into vocal actions and ways of speaking.

I focus on the verbs extrapolating them from the text. I find physical actions that correspond to the verbs and, subsequently, a vocal equivalent for the physical actions: I take inspiration from the verbs to fix physical actions that I later translate into speech, song or sound. The quality of the voice that results from the physical expression of the verbs colours the way of speaking the text.

For example, if the text has the verbs 'to be', 'to express' and 'to live', I make different physical actions for each verb. To render the verb 'to be' I maintain my body erect and well grounded, I lift my arm sideways, I close my fist and then rest it on my bent leg; for the verb 'to express' I push my arms away from my chest, then I suddenly let go and lift my hands to the sky; for the verb 'to live', while my torso bends back slightly, my fingers vibrate like a blossoming bud. I fix these actions that have been invented with reference to the verbs and repeat them as vocal actions: my voice closes and rests like a fist, it pushes and lets go and makes the movement of the petals opening.

I don't attempt to describe the concept outlined by the physical action with my voice, but instead to rediscover the same tensions and intentions that I have expressed with my body and manifest them through sound vibrations. Then I adapt the vocal score I have found to the text and fix it. *How* I say the text, in this instance, results from the analysis of the verbs belonging to it, as a result of a process of equivalence.

I emphasise the important words in a sentence, even articles or conjunctions, by slowing down their rhythm and lowering their volume. In this way I achieve an increase of intensity on the underlined word. Another way of changing the inflection and accent of the words is by a fictitious change in the sentence's structure, implying small affirmations. For example, I can say the sentence 'Tonight I have dreamt of saving other lives than my own' adding interpolations for myself: tonight (and not yesterday) I have dreamt (and not slept) of saving (and not of killing) other lives (and not deaths) than my own (and not your own). The result of this procedure is similar to that of underlining; the accentuation of the words that are contradicted by others that are only thought, gives a vocal logic to the text.

I extract different inflections by inserting new punctuation in the sentences and turning them into questions, half questions, exclamations or suspensions. I can say 'That man, is so good?' 'That man is so good!' 'That man! Is so good . . .' 'That man . . . is! So . . . good!' Or I can say the sentence with a meaning that is opposite to the text while overstressing its sense, for example 'That man is so wicked' instead of 'That man is so good', exaggerating the interpretation of the meaning. Then I repeat 'That man is so good' with the inflection found in the sentence that expresses the opposite. This allows me to avoid settling for the first and obvious understanding.

I can also identify characters in the text and extract them to speak with their own voices, or colour the text with sounds from the surroundings or from natural elements present in the passage. With a process similar to that of the extrapolation of the verbs, I mark out some words or concepts and I personalise them with voices, then use the corresponding vocal quality for some parts of the text.

The inflections of my voice are often suggested by associations that come from the text. I don't need to remain faithful to the meanings with which I am dealing. There are no rules for how I follow the flow of my associations and translate them into vocal qualities or intonations. I decide on the course to follow. If the text doesn't give the information, I choose whether the moon shines with a warm or cold light, whether the old man talks with a sweet or hoarse voice, whether ten or a hundred children are playing together in the school courtyard. Even when the information is provided by the text, I still have to evoke the cold or warm light of the moon with my voice: sharp or soft, sighing or plump, blue, white or silver, crystalline or full of wonder. I follow an entirely subjective logic to make the associations that the text provokes in me become sound. The text analysis thus becomes a process for tracking down more and more elements, both objective and subjective, which I can elaborate and weave together subsequently.

Physical actions as subtext

I can base a text on a physical score. In order to do this, however, I must first know how to follow and respect the rhythm, intensity, energy, direction and size of each physical action vocally, without trying to interpret the meaning of the words. I have to know the text by heart in a neutral way so that my voice can be infused with the tensions of the physical actions. I let these colour the intonation of the words I say and therefore determine the sense of the text. I must have a blank white page before applying the colours. I have to free myself from the automatic inflection that comes from the first reading and from the desire to respect the pauses and rhythm of written punctuation. I have to ignore my rational inclination to interpret the text immediately in the belief that conscious thought is more knowledgeable than the body. The consequence of a preoccupation with understanding and following the decisions of the mind is a voice that is disconnected from the physical impulses and not synchronised with the actions. To be able to translate a physical score into vocal actions, or to transplant the dynamic qualities of the physical actions to the voice, my body and mind must be one.

I translate the size of the physical action, its direction, change of tension and intention into a vocal action as if I was translating from one language to another using my own personal dictionary. In a purely subjective way, I choose a vocal equivalent, transposing and adapting the voice to the physical action. If I run, my voice runs while saying the words, accelerating the rhythm and increasing the volume and intensity as if I wanted to catch someone who is running away. If I jump, my voice leaps like someone screaming 'goal!' at a football game. If I walk normally, my voice directs itself where I look, in a calm and uniform rhythm with the cadence of a peaceful prayer. If I skip, my voice hops with a succession of light upward impulses; if I march like a soldier, my vocal pulse presses down with every step. If I advance in slow motion, the vowels lengthen; I speak as slowly as possible without breaks between the words or dividing the syllables as if I moved like a puppet. If I lie down on the ground, my voice tries to soak into the floor; if I lift myself up on my toes, my voice ascends to the sky.

These actions are simple and it is relatively easy to translate their physical impulses into vocal inflections. I have to be patient when searching for the vocal equivalent of more complex sequences that contain simultaneous and divergent information, composed of actions created through improvisation or composition. To recognise the smallest details of the physical impulses and trust my body's intelligence is a reflex that has been strengthened by time and experience. I decipher the physical score as if it contained a series of dynamic suggestions that must be transmitted to the text.

There are no rules that allow me to check if the translation from physical to vocal impulses is correct. I must trust the intuition that I have developed with years of training. For example, if I make an action that goes down low and shakes, I could sink the pitch of my voice and let it vibrate, or I could lower the volume and moan. Two steps taken as if I was pulling a thin thread might result in a slender, drawn-out and suspended voice. I reproduce the perception of my physical action with my voice by deciding on the spot whether the two hands that grab a fly can be translated into a growl or a restrained whisper, in the anticipation of surprising the prey. The intention is already action.

If I delay the moment at which I start to say the text in relation to the individual actions of a physical score or I combine different words with the same actions, I can discover a variety of inflections and rhythms for the same sentence. For example, if I begin to speak the text on a first slow action the result will be different from what I would obtain by beginning on the second action where I get up quickly, or on the third when I walk with heavy footsteps. I choose the action that affects the voice in the most appropriate way for the text and then modify it again eventually during the course of the subsequent elaboration.

If I use the physical score to find a way of saying the text without the physical actions being visible in the scene, at the end of the process the physical score is perceptible only as a succession of vocal actions. At first, it is easier for me to perform the physical actions and their vocal equivalent simultaneously. The physical action realised in space helps me verify more accurately how the impulses and physical dynamics have been translated into vocal characteristics. When the impulses and dynamics are memorised by my body, I gradually absorb the physical actions allowing only the voice to act in space. Gradually the subtext – the physical actions that support the way of saying the text – is 'forgotten' because it becomes an integral part of the vocal action. At this point a new phase of elaboration takes over: I combine my way of saying the text with other physical scores and adapt the results to the relationships I am establishing with other people on stage, with the surrounding space or the props.

When putting the text, already fixed in vocal actions, together with a new physical score, both the text and the actions must find a common dance. The impulses of the body and the voice are synchronised following an inner music whose rhythm is based on variations and counterpoints adapted to the logic of the text. I adapt the actions to underline, comment, enrich or deny the meaning of the words. The synchronisation of the physical impulses with the vocal impulses is the premise for obtaining an organic effect.

When the physical score that is employed to find the way to say the text is also the sequence of physical actions that accompanies the text – or when the subtext is the same as the physical score performed in the scene – the synchronisation between the impulses of the words and those of the physical actions is already established. In that case, I search for new variations, knowing that, for example, a strong physical action can have its correspondence in a vigorous and contained vocal action, or in a low tone or cry.

The physical and vocal actions don't necessarily have to have the same characteristics as the literal meaning of the words. A humorous sentence can be accompanied by a strong, abrupt action and a seductive intonation. The same humorous sentence can be accompanied by a strong, abrupt action and an intonation that is equally strong and abrupt. Again the same sentence can be accompanied by a soft action and a strong intonation. Despite the divergences between meaning, action and intonation, and the different formal vocal characteristics, to synchronise the text with the actions, the textual inflections should respect the beginning, change of tension and end of each physical action. The synchronisation is particularly important in that phase of the action in which the direction of the impulse, rhythm and intensity alter, which is to say in the succession of tonic passages on the journey between beginning and end. These changes of tension provide the emphasis and are a source of detailed facets and colours that interpret the literal meaning of the words, with the effect of underlining certain parts of the sentence.

The distribution of the text onto the actions of the physical score establishes the rhythm of the words. I can say only one word for the duration of a single action, exploring at length the sonority of the vowels. Or I can accelerate: I say many words during only one action, which accentuates the consonants. Or I can choose to interrupt the text with a pause: I can sustain the silence with the energy of the action. By distributing the quantity of words differently for every successive action, I can achieve the effect of variation of rhythm in the text. I play with the rhythm to interpose surprise: it is a process that needs me to have a firm sense of the unity between the physical and vocal actions so as not to lose their synchronisation.

To develop this sense of unity I find it useful to accompany physical activities with the voice. Hearing workers' and peasants' songs has inspired me to create an exercise I call 'labour'. I imagine digging the earth, pulling a bucket up from the well, polishing the floor, wringing clothes, sewing tobacco leaves, throwing a parcel . . . and I accompany the work with a sound, song, call, exclamation that helps me in my task. It is not a question of describing the activity with a noise, but of supporting the physical action with the voice. Once I have found the appropriate vocal accompaniment, I memorise and repeat it with the action, and then place a text over it. I strive to respect the colour and particularity of the voice as much as possible, but without jeopardising the comprehensibility of the words.

The different effect on the voice and therefore on the text is clearly noticeable with the actions of pulling and pushing. If I alternate the qualities of pulling and pushing in my voice, I can establish a dynamic of attraction and refusal. This dynamic is especially useful in the performances in which there are no other people on stage to whom I can direct my voice in order to create variety. Pushing, I have the impression of being antagonistic to the spectators and keeping them at a distance. Pulling, it is as if I bring the spectators onto the stage, seducing them and making them curious about the words.

Physical movement attracts more attention than words do. Interweaving the text with physical actions, and wanting to give prominence to the words, I often have to reduce the actions. In addition, the vocal action derived from a physical score can be excessive and sway the attention from the text; then I have to reduce the vocal effects. I absorb the inflections and tonal variations of the vocal actions calibrating them with the understanding of the text and the dynamic of my body. The bond between the subtext and physical actions subsists, but not overtly. The amplitude of pitch, the volume and particular sounds are reduced to an almost everyday way of speaking, yet the roots of the vocal action still enliven my voice and the words.

Vocal actions as subtext

In *Talabot* I decided to use vocal actions as subtext instead of physical actions. I journeyed with the voice in different directions prompted by ways of singing and speaking, by noises and music, which I fixed in a pattern of sounds that I then transferred to the text. Imitating animals or foreign languages, I could give rhythm and modulation to a vocal score that I then used as a base from which to work with the text. The logic that allows me to place a hoarse, hard sound of pretend German onto a text spoken in Italian remains personal.

The exercise of particular vocal techniques like yodelling, tremolo, guttural and the production of harmonics, has not only been interesting as exploration, but above all in the adaptation of these effects to a text, maintaining the variations and at the same time the comprehensibility of each word. Labial, nasal or guttural sounds, sounds that don't use the vibration of the vocal chords, sounds with the mouth closed, musical tones that surface only in the vowels, or sequences of consonants, have to find a translation through equivalences that allow the text to be understood.

The vocal action of the fog that embraces a whole city helps me find a warm and enveloping voice. I used the intonation of invented Chinese for a question in *Doña Musica's Butterflies*: 'Chuang Tzu, the philosopher, had dreamt of becoming a butterfly; or was it the butterfly that dreamt of becoming Chuang Tzu?'

In order to fix a vocal score to be used as subtext, I can also make an improvisation. Starting from a theme, I improvise freely with the voice, then I repeat and, to memorise, I record or identify detailed images. After I have fixed the sequence of tones and vocal qualities, I reproduce the same variations applying them to the text. In this process it helps me to sing the text first and then to speak it. 'There is the silence of the old, so loaded with wisdom that language cannot express it in comprehensible words to those who have not lived': from this phrase I decide to improvise on sunrise. This association comes to me because I think of the wisdom and age of nature that cannot be explained in words. My voice creates the mist that precedes dawn, the first feeling of light and the sun that rises, shines and warms the fields. I repeat the tonalities of the improvisation first as a song, then with the words distributed on the different vocal actions. At the end I repeat the text, remembering the improvisation but without making the tones evident.

A vocal score that is to be applied to a text can also be fixed on the basis of other kinds of vocal improvisation. For example, with Edgar Lee Masters' poem *Willard Fluke*, I take the word 'weighed' from the first lines ('My wife lost her health until she weighed barely ninety pounds') and improvise vocal actions in reference only to that word. From the next lines 'then that woman, whom the men called Cleopatra, came along', I choose 'came' to improvise other sounds. Finally I use the sounds to say the whole poem. I could also proceed in another way. With the same poem in mind, I could improvise freely. Subsequently, on the basis of my memory of the improvisation, I interpret the text. It is repetition that allows my body to memorise and maintain the structure and quality of the improvisation, so I can adapt it to a text and present it to the director. Improvisation and repetition integrate so I can remember by letting my body think for itself.

I can also use the articulated interpretation of a text, different from the one I have to say, to fix a vocal action and employ it as subtext. I read the text as a grandmother's fairytale, a television programme, a football commentary, a school lesson, a declaration of love, a boa slithering up its victim, a sword duel, a ball playing in the waves of the sea, a gazelle bending over a stream to drink . . . I create a vocal score with a succession of people and characters, imitating the voices of the seasons, rivers and waterfalls. Applying this vocal score to the text, I can use different fragments in the different parts. With the sounds of a boa I might find many ways of whispering the words. A labial waterfall sound might turn into spurting or stammering consonants. A guttural sound that imitates a pig might result in a swallowed or regurgitated text.

Imitation of the vocal quality of Sardinian or Corsican shepherds allowed me to find the voice of my character Mr Peanut. I started simply reproducing their way of singing, then maintained the same characteristics while speaking a text. Later I gradually removed the guttural sound to achieve a relaxed croaky voice. It felt as if I had moved the guttural sound from the top of the palate back towards the inside of my throat. Mr Peanut talks with the variations of this cavernous voice. His comic or dramatic dialogues inspired me to develop his raucous voice, passing from one technique to the other and alternating very low relaxed tones with high intense ones.

My voice has a natural tremble. At times I try to control it; on other occasions, instead, I enjoy pursuing its wavering movement, for example when accompanying the modulations of Indian songs.

If I use vocal techniques with strong fluctuations of pitch and spectacular effects, applying them to a text requires a process of gradual reduction. For the voice to be persuasive and the text comprehensible, for the monologues or dialogues to have acceptable characteristics even if they are removed from the everyday way of speaking, it is often necessary for me to reduce the form of the vocal score maintaining only its essence, image or the memory of the starting point.

Melodies and music as subtext

To use a melody to speak a text is one of the ways I have found of drawing singing and speaking techniques closer together. I choose some melodies and graft the text onto them, respecting their rhythm and tonalities as much as possible. I lengthen a vowel or insert pauses to adapt the metrics of the text to the song. Not all melodies are suitable for this process, but I do not know how to identify a musical rule on which to base the choice. I follow my intuition; I try things out and eliminate the melodies that don't fit. I can choose cheerful music for a dramatic text or a melodious song to reinforce the images of a poem. I choose songs that attract me.

After singing the text, I gradually let the melody fade away. I change the projection of my voice, without sustaining the tones for their melodic span, especially at the end of the words. On repetition, I let the musical notes fall away more and more until I have the feeling that I only touch them for a fraction of a second. At the end the melody remains as a kind of memory that nevertheless dictates the inflections and rhythm of the text. I can always return to this musical subtext by singing the melody again. Once the song is absorbed into the way of saying the text, the music is no longer recognisable to the listener and the text also assumes other melodic characteristics for me. I find this process particularly useful when I translate dialogues and monologues from a performance into the language of the different countries we tour.

In the exchange between music and text, I have also found the opposite process useful: to recognise a melody in speech. The musician Michael Vetter would ask me to say a sentence and then repeat its intonation until I had fixed the melody by ear and was able to transform it into a musical phrase. I use this procedure to work with people who think they are not able to reach a certain note, or who imagine that the spoken voice has only a few possibilities for variation. The musical tones can be recognised by associating the notes with the sounds of birds or animals, with drawings or hand movements.

In speech the notes are not sustained; they change rapidly and in fractions of tones that our musical ear is not used to distinguishing. The influence of the harmonics that permit us to recognise the difference between one vowel and another is not usually heard as music, but simply as the variation of inflection, timbre and colour in the voice in association with the meaning of the words or the emotional state of the speaker. The exercise of passing from the spoken to the singing voice helps me better understand its musical structures and possibilities as I venture more and more into the ever widening and mysterious territories of voice.

Music is an important reference for me. I mould the text as if it were a musical composition, exploiting the melodic structures of each vowel, the glissando and interruptions, the impact of each consonant. The music is not necessarily harmonious yet it gives me great freedom to find variations that also awaken the emotional level of the text. The variation of harmonic tones within the same note increases the possibility of shaping a single syllable or word.

Musical composition also helps me feel how to build the sense of a sentence, the harmonious rhythm of a poetic text, the rhyme in a long monologue, the vocal variations in a whole performance. With changes of interval or tone I mark the punctuation, the passage from one phrase to the next, I underline meanings, I give the sensation of making a pause in the flow of words. For this I need to be able to pass from one vocal timbre to another without a break, as in a physical action I must know how to pass from walking to running without hesitation.

At times I improvise freely with the voice, without following principles, rules and references, or searching for results that need to be remembered and fixed. These are happy moments, difficult to repeat. After a river of impetuous and frail, exaggerated and introverted sounds, I finish quietly with T. S. Eliot's poem about mermaids and the effect their singing has on those who listen to them. After all kinds of variations, the text said with simplicity contains and suggests the potentialities of everything said previously and of what might come later.

7 The character

Identities

In an Odin Teatret performance, the spectators see me portray characters. Sometimes these have received names only at the end of rehearsals; I have not built them intentionally and they have surfaced from the montage of actions I have created using other references. In fact, my actress's material can be constructed from improvisations or compositions on themes that don't have anything to do with a character, but the combination of all my physical and vocal scores, woven into the text and the actions of the other actresses and actors, accompanied by particular music, create in the spectator the impression of a character. But the work on character can also be the point of departure for creating scores, providing information and stimuli. I invent and compose how a character walks, sits, speaks, or I use a character for historical research that inspires me to build physical behaviour.

I can create a character by investigating its psychology and past, the historical environment to which it belongs, or finding its postures and the different ways in which it moves. There are many points of departure from which I can discover how a character behaves. I search for clues that allow me to take the first steps: I look at sketches and paintings, listen to music, decide on colours and props, I choose walks, imitate people, remember events, illustrate a story, use the image of an animal, think of a biography or of an emotional incentive. I retrieve concrete references, translating the themes, biographical information or personality traits into a personal language that helps me proceed. It will be this particular way of being together with the costume, way of speaking, meaning of the words and surrounding situation that then make a character emerge in front of the spectators.

Odin Teatret's performances remain in repertory a long time and I have not played many characters during thirty years of work. Some exist only in the performance for which they were created; others continue to live independently from the framework within which they first saw the light. There are characters with which I have said something and others that made me say what I didn't know I knew. There are characters with which I cohabit for only two or three years and others that have accompanied me for twenty-five years.

The characters that survive the performance are those that have an identity independent from the performance for which they were conceived. They have their own way of moving, gesticulating and speaking, and can intervene and interact in the most varied situations, emigrating from their original performance to install themselves in other contexts. They are characters that I have created by thinking directly about their behaviour. The characters that disappear with the performance are often the result of a process in which the improvisations and compositions had themes and interests separate from the character to be portrayed, and in which the character is the result of the montage of my actions in a given circumstance, not 'someone' whom I have tried to manifest directly.

In the creation of characters from nothing as in the interpretation of a character whose role already exists before rehearsals begin, there needs to exist for me something mysterious that I don't control. This enigma keeps my relationship as an actress with my characters alive even after years of playing a performance, and allows me to discover new facets of a character's temperament and personality each time I play.

In the early years, when approaching a character, I devoted a lot of time to the costumes. I chose the material, drew models and sewed. Once the costume was ready, I spent more hours washing, ironing and adding small details. Ribbons, hair clips, rings, stockings, lace . . . were all elements that helped me find the roots of a character by starting from its exterior appearance. My first costume at Odin Teatret was violet, a colour that is said to bring bad luck in theatre and film. It was used only once when I performed on stilts. Then I made a striped skirt in the shape of a cluster of leaves, a black velvet dress bordered with white lace, a pair of orange cotton trousers and top decorated with green ribbons that were inspired by training clothes.

In addition to the characters belonging to full performances, I created occasional figures for street interventions or unrealised projects. One of these accompanied the clown performance parade. On small green stilts, my clown wore a long silk skirt that hid me when I lifted it over my head. With her I started to use femininity, charm and joy as features of a character.

In the early performances, while I focused only on 'functioning' on stage, the costume had a great influence in deciding who I was. I wore a full Mexican dress of black lace for *The Million* (1978–84). I had worn it while training and had discovered that the acrobatic dance I did with Tage Larsen was enhanced by the wide skirt. I proposed the dress to the director and it was accepted. In the performance I didn't think of character, but how to keep my balance while I danced at speed, how to play the trombone in rhythm and tune with the other instruments and how to chant the texts that the director had entrusted to me. *The Million* started as a performance based on Bertolt Brecht's life and works and I was cast as Mrs Peachum, Polly Peachum's mother in *The Threepenny Opera*. This name stayed with me for the performance that became *Brecht's Ashes* (1980–4). When we recognised the separate identity of the two performances *The Million* and *Brecht's Ashes* –

on which we worked almost simultaneously – the Mexican suit dress stayed for the former and the character's name for the latter.

In *The Million* I danced barefoot, as I had in training. I would not have managed to dance in the same way with shoes on. To justify the fact that an elegant character was barefoot, a scene was added deliberately so that I could take my shoes off. At the end of the performance I stood beside Marco Polo, a traveller priest who had become a distinguished gentleman in tails. I held his triumphant sword and smiled at the spectators. Still my expression was not influenced by how my behaviour might be interpreted by the spectators. At that moment I focused only on making my smile shine through my eyes in a similar way to how, halfway through the performance, during a funeral procession, I tried to make a tear fall by breathing through my eyeballs. I imagine that my character seemed romantic, naïve and submissive towards the dandy who made me circle through the air in a breath-taking and hazardous dance. This was the consequence of the montage and not an intentional objective of mine.

It was only on the day I read the programme for *Brecht's Ashes* that I noticed Ilse Koch's name in the list of characters. This is how I discovered that I had another role in addition to Mrs Peachum. A childhood friend of mine was called Ilse and she had told me once about other women who had the same name, so I happened to know that Ilse Koch was the wife of the Nazi commander of the Dachau extermination camp. But I could have played this character for the spectators without knowing who she was. At that time, it was not my historical knowledge that steered the evolution of my behaviour on stage but the interpretation that the director gave to my actions by relating them to the historical circumstances in which Bertolt Brecht had lived and struggled.

In *Brecht's Ashes*, one of my first productions with Odin Teatret, my own wishes didn't count much. I felt so encumbered by the narrow dress, nylon stockings and high-heeled shoes chosen for me. My presence was so different from that of the easy movement made possible when wearing training clothes. In an attempt to deal with my awkwardness, I was given some leather trousers and then finally I found a pair of Japanese trousers with wide flaps, similar to riding breeches, and some boots with laces. I watched the others in order to learn and sometimes I was able to use the suggestions they gave me. I remember that Else Marie Laukvik encouraged me to curl my hair, using an old hairdressing iron that was heated on the fire lit by the Cook (Silvia Ricciardelli's character). I took advantage of my character's high rank to resolve a personal tension with another actor and I invented a scene with a truly realistic slap. For the whole performance I was supposed to smile, distant and proud: a real torture.

My character in *Brecht's Ashes* found its true nature long after the performance's opening night. There was a difficult scene for me: I went up to Katrin, the mute daughter of Mother Courage, played by Iben Nagel Rasmussen, and demanded that she give me her scissors. The scene was in silence and I felt all the attention focused on me. Eugenio Barba asked Katsuko Azuma, ISTA's Buyo Kabuki dancer collaborator, to help me. After her intervention, I put on my boots in the morning training hours and worked on placing resistances and very small breaks in the different phases of a footstep. The concreteness of this task helped me accept who I was in *Brecht's Ashes*: I started to smile from within, while discovering the pleasure of malice.

This lesson changed the costume's function in the performances that followed. It was no longer just a covering but a dress that helped me change and reveal the inner secret of a character. Since then a character's depth depends for me on its humanity and vulnerability. I aspire to create a stage persona impregnated with contradictions, desires and tenderness.

For *The Gospel According to Oxyrhincus* (1985–7) we worked with what we called 'marble', sequences of actions created in pairs by improvising with an object: a chair, a ladder, a bowl . . . In pairs, we fixed actions and reactions while together holding an object that acted as a bond between us. For example, I held two legs of a chair and my companion the other two. I turned the chair upside down and my companion was forced to follow me, then my companion pulled the chair towards her and I had to shift, and so on. When we knew the sequence in all its smallest details, we repeated it without the object. We often had to go back to the object to check that we had kept all the right tensions. We had to verify that the stick had not become elastic, that the chair retained its dimensions, that the hands were holding a bowl and not a carpet. Once the precision was guaranteed without holding the object, we repeated the sequence alone, without a companion. In this way we had individual physical material that could be elaborated and included in the performance.

My character, Jeanne d'Arc, moved on stage using these re-elaborated scores, but frustration and an improvisation were necessary to find her essence. The improvisation (with the double theme: 'Aliosha Karamazov in front of the old monk Zosima's stinking corpse; a jug of water that falls from the table but has not yet broken on the floor') gave me her voice and a feeling of suspension and excitement. I said the words quickly using a very high tone, as if I were talking to the angels. The frustration, resulting from the impossibility of being as 'mature' as the 'old' members of the group, gave me the idea of being a rebellious filly. I dreamed of having a real horse in the performance. I imagined training it as in a circus and riding it to the theatre every morning. I had even inquired as to how to transport it on tour. This wish became the point of reference for the construction of the character.

The director had given us the task of preparing a scenario for each character. I mixed historical fact from the story of the Maid of Orleans with episodes from the legend of King Arthur and the Lady of the Lake, Morgan le Fay. I prepared a montage of scenes with Christoph Falke, the assistant director, on the basis of my scenario. We concentrated in particular on how to show Joan's death at the stake. Additionally, for the crowning of the King of France, we introduced a comic scene similar to a Kyogen in a Nô performance. I improvised the text and actions for this scene in a completely different style

The Gospel According to Oxyrhincus
Julia Varley as Joan of Arc
Photo: Jan Rüsz

from what I was used to. For the first time, while writing the scenario and combining texts, my rebellious young spirit was getting in touch with the excitement of dramaturgical montage.

One day, after the exploration with the 'marble', the director gave us costumes. He had hidden them behind a screen and, in an order dictated by drawing our names at random, each of us went to choose one piece of clothing at a time. That same day, Eugenio asked us which character we wanted to play. Silvia Ricciardelli chose Jeanne d'Arc, I spoke of the filly. When Silvia left the group, Jeanne d'Arc's role was passed on to me even though the rebellious young horse kept on spinning in my head.

I decorated my dress and hat with the pieces of a bridle. I made a face mask from which a small crucifix hung under my chin. I made a yellow tunic and bandaged my ankles in the same colour adding some spurs. I tied my hair in a ponytail wrapped in a ribbon like a show horse. I used a stick and a white shirt stained red for Jeanne d'Arc's banner with a crown of arrow heads used by the Yanomami, an Amazonian tribe. I placed a plastic heart on the shirt. It lit up with a heart-beat rhythm and red fringes came down from it, as if they were trickles of blood.

In contrast, Kirsten Hastrup, the anthropologist I played in *Talabot* (1988–91), was the result of improvisations and compositions based on my recollections of a recent trip to India and Thailand and on my interest in solving vocal problems. Retracing in my mind the meetings and images of the exotic places I had seen, I made an unconscious connection to the theme of the performance: people who had chosen to leave their country to live and work elsewhere.

We began rehearsals for *Talabot* in a house by the sea in Chicxulub, a village in Yucatan, in Mexico. In the morning we all ran and trained on the beach. Then we gathered to rehearse in the biggest room in the house. At our request Kirsten Hastrup had written some hundred pages about her life and each of us had the task of staging three episodes from them. We also prepared 'knots' – images saturated with contrasts – for each of our characters. In the pauses between rehearsals I prepared my own material that I presented to the director when I felt confident. The soul of my character sprang from an improvisation that was not used in the performance. For the first time I dared sing in my slightly hesitant and trembling voice, accompanied by simple physical reactions that illustrated a landscape of undramatic, but intense memories.

It was clear to me that I could not copy Kirsten Hastrup's way of being: a Danish university professor who lived and taught in Aarhus. It seemed foolish to think of imitating her way of walking, looking and speaking. I took only the costume idea directly from a detail she had related: she always wore a suit at her lectures.

Talabot
Jan Ferslev, Julia Varley
Photo: Jan Rüsz

Talabot
Julia Varley
Photo: Jan Rüsz

In the performance my character based her behaviour on a montage of actions fixed in reaction, or as accompaniment, to my voice. Then the skirt, the high-heeled shoes and lipstick helped me contain the forms I had found into smaller almost realistic movements, acceptable for a woman who studies, quarrels with her father, graduates, works as an anthropologist in India and in Iceland, has four children, gets divorced and falls in love again. Eugenio suggested that I could give birth to my children from my head like a Greek divinity and I succeeded in hiding some feathers in my hair, three blue and one pink. These led me to the nest that I tore apart in the divorce scene.

'My' Kirsten Hastrup lived only in *Talabot*; her existence was tied indissolubly to the actions of the other characters in the performance, to the world that was created for the hour of play, which included the fish and beer thrown over me, the shells that I crushed with my feet, the dry leaves with which I covered the floor and the dark mask made of a mixture of thyme and basil with which my anthropologist plastered her face while she sank into the identity of the 'other'. The character emerged every evening from a succession of actions and reactions connected and woven to those of my colleagues and to the intimate memory of my travels far away from theatre.

Anyone who knows Odin Teatret is also familiar with Mr Peanut, the skull-headed character that was born on stilts for *Anabasis* (1977–84). He is one of those independent characters that refuses to die with the original performance, takes possession of their destiny, decides for themselves and leads me toward situations, texts and new performances that I no longer determine. Mr Peanut has travelled the streets of the world and forced me to make my first 'solo', *The Castle of Holstebro* (first version 1990–7, second version 1999–). Dressed as a woman and without stilts, he dances in *Ode to Progress* (1997–) and he appropriated for himself the final scene of *Doña Musica's Butterflies* (1997–), another performance in which I am alone on stage. The solo performances have housed my most persistent characters: Mr Peanut and Doña Musica. They have become emanations of my personality, alter egos with whom I improvise and tell stories. They deserve a chapter of their own.

It is not only the visible results that count in the interpretation of a character, but also the discarded mistakes and blind alleys encountered along the way. Of this subject Daedalus – a character from *Mythos* (1998–2004), who has taught me the importance of entering the labyrinth in which there are many roads to follow, even if there is only one way out – will speak later.

Mr Peanut

Mr Peanut is one of Odin Teatret's archetypal characters. A tall, heavy skeleton hanging from a long stick accompanied Odin Teatret's first street parades in 1976. Then he took the form of a child's skeleton attached to a drum until 1977, when a skull was placed on the head of Tom Fjordfalk, one of the stilt-walking actors, in *Anabasis*, the performance whose 'army' of actresses and actors marched across village and city roads to climb up towards the sea. Tom christened him Mr Peanut because of the shape of his head and to recall a rich peanut farmer who was also president of a big nation. In those years Mr Peanut was strong, hard and aggressive. He was scary.

In 1980 Mr Peanut changed personality. In order to avoid playing the big drum in *Anabasis* any longer, I was prepared to confront my vertigo and try out taller stilts. Mr Peanut became more elegant: his black tails were adorned with white gloves, an embroidered shirt and a handkerchief of red silk around his neck. His legs were covered with feathers. I had inherited him from Tom and his head was now fixed on mine.

Mr Peanut danced as my female clown had previously and moved his curious hands at a fast tempo. 'Death' wiggled his bum for fun. Mr Peanut is not death for me. Only once, during a visit to an old people's home, did I worry about the literal meaning of his features. I imagined that the hairless skull, toothless mouth, skinny face and hollow eyes would resemble the people I met there too much. But, while I skipped about and joked with the elderly, the reaction was of hilarity and amusement.

With Mr Peanut I introduce myself. With Mr Peanut I have spoken at a lecture on semiotics, I have studied Theatre Anthropology at ISTA (International School of Theatre Anthropology); I have done a striptease in the streets; I have danced samba, waltz, candombe; I have visited newspaper headquarters, beaches, supermarkets, libraries, churches, television studios, factories, swimming pools, hospitals, airports, fountains, markets, schools, theatres, museums, prisons . . . In many cities Mr Peanut has stolen hats from policemen, glasses from teachers, ice creams from children; he has admired women's breasts; he has been received by ambassadors and ministers, by the powerful and by those who submit to their power.

Mr Peanut has gone two hundred metres underground in a mine in Wales; he has improvised to reassure the suspicious anti-guerrilla soldiers at the airport in Ayacucho, Peru, and followed a religious procession in a village in the Andes. He has slipped on the snow in Sweden, hitchhiked in Salento, danced in Hamburg's port district, in the Fabrika in Bologna with its squatters, with the communist campaigners of the Feste dell'Unità in Italy and the Catholic activists of the *poblacioneses* in Chile. He has protested against an attempted coup in the Plaza de Mayo in Buenos Aires, had his tails burnt by the Abruzzo Dancing Doll's fireworks, has played hide-and-seek with the Balinese Rangda, has been attacked violently by a terrified woman in Oslo, had his head broken by the army in Chile, founded a club in Blaenau Ffestiniog, Wales, with children who all walk on stilts like him, has been stopped in a peremptory way in New York's East Village by a police officer who wanted to take his photograph, sold a Barong (a Balinese 'dragon' mask) at a horse market in Lampeter and bought a hen at the goat market in Mejdal. He has danced accompanied by tambores, tablas, gamelan, shamisen and rock orchestras. He

Mr Peanut meets local authorities at the Moneda Palace in Santiago de Chile, 1998

Photo: Tony D'Urso

Greeting children in Holstebro
Photo: Fiora Bemporad

Mr Peanut on stilts with Doggy (Jan Ferslev), the White Angel (Iben Nagel Rasmussen), Otto (Kai Bredholt) in front of soldiers from Holstebro's barracks, during the Festuge (the festive week), 1991
Photo: Torben Huss

In a slum near Santiago de Chile
Photo: Tony D'Urso

On the Brooklyn Bridge in New York
Photo: Tony D'Urso

has played football in Montevideo, ridden an elephant in Munich, learned to play children's games on the beaches of Yucatan and there, on the sand, he also learned to fall. He went to the dentist to have a new tooth put in at the military hospital in Cordoba. He participated in more than twenty years of barters with Odin Teatret, mixing with the *burakumin* of Osaka and the girls of Barcelona's *barrio chino*. When he returned to Raquira, in Colombia, where Odin Teatret had made a barter some years earlier, the people thought he had brought the rain that fell and made him offerings: guava and avocado.

Mr Peanut is curious, lively and friendly; he likes to be taken for a walk around the towns among people he doesn't know. He doesn't have many illusions, but he is stubborn and continues to come out of the box in which I keep him to wander around the world. He is protected by his height, which distances him from people. For years he has been the identity behind which I could both reveal and hide myself. In *The Castle of Holstebro* I chose Mr Peanut once again to speak for me. He asks questions, thinks, and tells secret thoughts out loud. In this way, through him, I dialogue with myself.

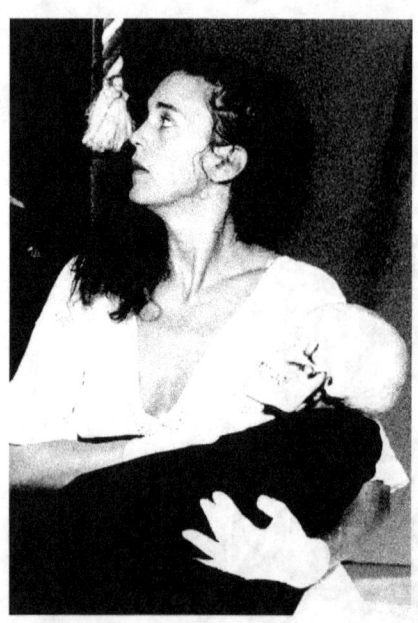

As a baby in Julia Varley's arms in *The Castle of Holstebro*
Photo: Fiora Bemporad

Mrs Peanut in *Ode to Progress*
Photo: Francesco Galli

The butterfly in *Doña Musica's Butterflies*
Photo: Jan Rüsz

On Julia Varley's head
Photo: Emidio Luisi

As a bride in the final performance of the Holstebro Festuge (the festive week) in 1993
Photo: Fiora Bemporad

For a second version of *The Castle of Holstebro* I wrote him a letter.

Holstebro, 24 February 1999

Dear Mr Peanut,

We have travelled together a lot during the past fifteen years. We have visited different continents, spoken different languages and met many different spectators, though we know that it is possible to make a voyage in one's own mind and around one's own room. Now we have moved hand in hand into this intimate space surrounded by the ocean. We will invite each spectator into this castle that fits in a home, where the voice is so soft it can tell about the hidden beats of the heart.

Of course you could not enter this space with your long wooden legs; you would never have got through the door! Therefore now, after being a giant, you look like a dwarf in your short trousers. As we get older instead of growing we get smaller and smaller.

Together we found a piece of coral in the ocean: 'of her and of his bones are coral made'. Our wish has been fulfilled: the girl dressed in white and the man in tails with a skull head are one and the same. In the secret chamber of *The Castle of Holstebro II* we travel towards each other as never before.

Lots of love,

Julia

Doña Musica

One of the threads of *Doña Musica's Butterflies* is the dialogue between the character, the actress and Julia, without the possibility of clearly distinguishing between my different identities. The director also introduced himself into the dialogue by enhancing a sense of humour that is usually considered to be mine.

In the novel *Wind in the West* and in the performance *Doña Musica's Butterflies*, Doña Musica speaks of herself as a character:

I am Doña Musica. I am a character from a performance, *Kaosmos*. My name was inspired by a character from *Le Soulier de Satin* by Paul Claudel, a princess who whispered 'who does not know how to speak, should sing!'

How was I born? Did the actress give me life? Or did I, a character, reveal the actress? Did the actress mould her energy so as to transform it into Doña Musica? Or did I, Doña Musica, modulate the actress's energy? These questions won't lead us anywhere, because a character is a tendency, a tendency to exist, just like those particles that leap and dance in an atom.

While the characters, the actors and the director were intent on the creation of *Kaosmos*, my actress – Julia – was reading a popular science book, *The Tao of Physics* by Fritijov Capra. Julia had underlined some passages which pointed towards the secret of what she wanted to do in the new production: infinity, to be and not be, flowing and changing, the shadow, what cannot be known and understood, the dance and the dancer who are one and the same. Julia was surprised by the wisdom of modern physics which seemed to rediscover the knowledge of ancient Asian philosophies. She wanted to translate these abstract concepts into the concrete behaviour of a theatre character – these abstract concepts which revealed truths that she was not able to grasp.

Listening to a Japanese melody, a present from Kanho Azuma to Julia, I took my first steps. I discovered how to move my arms, my physical postures and the many possible head positions. I understood where to place my weight and where to hide my strength. Accompanied by this music, my voice found the intonations for the reality of theatre fiction.

But the director was not satisfied. One day he would ask me to slow down, the next to move even slower and the next to be faster. To please him I contrived to behave in a way that disguised the rhythm. If rhythm is given by a succession of beats, which is to say the slower or faster succession of intervals contained by a beginning and an end, my secret was to proceed without beginnings or endings. This also allowed my actress to put on stage that flowing and becoming of which she had read.

At a certain point in the process of creation of *Kaosmos* the director told the actress that her role was the Doorkeeper. This Doorkeeper, in a novel by Franz Kafka, prevents a Man-from-the-country from being admitted to the Law. The director's briefing was to make realistic scenes and an elderly character, while my actress was thinking of infinity, of how she could make a character similar to the sea gone with the sun. So the actress worked on the elderly character. Julia quickly wrote down her first associations: wrinkles, wisdom, sadness, slow steps, small steps, remembering the past, not remembering, without fear, teeth falling out, eyes that don't see, longing for beauty, black teeth, rigid joints, life disappearing, shrinking, Isak Dinesen, falling, suffocating, rereading the same book, gangrene, colostomy bag, amputation, deafness, shrivelled hands. For each association the actress found equivalent physical actions. Many associations came from memories of Julia's grandparents.

Years before the director had said to the actress: 'I would like you to create a very old character.' Julia bought a wig and found in her father's attic a nightdress in black silk and a silver embroidered Arabian cape. One day she got dressed and made her face up with grey and white to surprise the director. She wanted him to see again his grandmother with her long loose white hair, that image of little girl and old lady that he had described in his book *The Paper Canoe*. The costume – from the texture of the clothes to the hairdo, from the shoes to the jewellery – is one of

(Above and right) *Doña Musica's Butterflies*
Julia Varley
Photo: Jan Rüsz

Kaosmos
Torgeir Wethal, Julia Varley
Photo: Jan Rüsz

Doña Musica's Butterflies
Julia Varley
Photo: Jan Rüsz

the character's most obvious traits, something which transforms and is transformed. So I worked on the costume: dark veils and lace, a pair of high-heeled shoes covered in cloth as if they were the bound feet of a Chinese woman, a costume which would make me tall and thin like Kazuo Ohno's Argentina.

Doña Musica reminds me to add another piece of her text:

> All the words we use to describe experience are limited; they are not features of reality, but creations of the mind, parts of the map, not of the territory. In modern physics the universe is seen as a dynamic, inseparable whole. The infinitesimal atom and the whole universe are engaged in endless motion and activity, in a continual cosmic dance of energy.

And then she continues to paraphrase what I don't know how to explain:

> In narrating I have used the first person: I am Doña Musica and I am not. I am the actress and I am not. I am Julia and I am not. I am and am not. I go forwards and backwards in time, just like those particles which leap and dance in an atom. In *Le Soulier de Satin* Claudel makes his Doña Musica say: 'through chaos there is a sea of darkness at our disposal'. Chaos is the art of building complexity from simple elements. Chaos creates forms, information and order; a hidden, mysterious, paradoxical, unforeseeable but undeniable order, which obliges us to see again. In chaos a small cause can have great consequences. It is called the butterfly effect: the wing beat of a butterfly in Japan can provoke a hurricane in Denmark. Or as the poet had already disclosed:
>
>> Wind in the West
>> And fallen leaves
>> Are gathered in the East.

Dramaturgy according to Daedalus

Daedalus, my character in *Mythos* – presented by Odin Teatret for the first time on 1 May 1998, in Holstebro – made me think of dramaturgy as a labyrinth. A long time before I knew the theme of the performance and the character I was going to play, Daedalus had begun leading me into this maze.

A cassette tape arrived by post from Brazil. It was a gift sent to me by someone who had seen *Kaosmos*. On one side of the tape were a few sonatas by Heitor Villa Lobos and on the other a concert that used bird songs and jungle sounds as a starting point for developing a chant interpreted by a woman. I had always liked Villa Lobos and the music inspired by nature also attracted me: the female voice was similar to my own and offered me subject matter for research. I listened to the tape so often that its sounds began to sink into my system.

I knew gold would be my colour. I had found a gilt feather in a shop in Holstebro and bought it. Showing it to Eugenio Barba, I told him that it was an element for the next performance. I was sure of this, although I didn't know why.

The path Daedalus was leading me into was seductive: at a distance it looked mysterious and it was easy to get lost once on it. I would be forced to defy closed roads, to turn back and start the journey all over again. On the way I would meet elements from my imagination – sirens and monsters – and old acquaintances. Once inside the labyrinth, my main concern would be to find the way out, to reach a conclusion and finish the process. The red thread of the plot, the theme and the theatre life of the character, kept breaking. Logic seemed to disappear and the only alternative was not to give up – to continue to move forwards or backwards. When everything seemed lost, a new clue would appear that prompted me to start marching again.

At Odin Teatret we do not always have faith that the performance we are putting together laboriously will make an impression on the spectator, but we take our doubts into consideration only when we are close to the exit. In any case the spectators who see the performance may feel immersed in a labyrinth and only recognise what they have explored a long time after the experience.

For myself, I have defined the actress's dramaturgy as the instrument that helps to organise scenic behaviour, the logic with which actions are chained together and the technique to make 'real' actions in a fictional world. As an actress I have trained myself to lose the division between body, mind, imagination, senses, feelings and reason, to act physically and vocally on the spectator's senses. As I have already said, during rehearsals, the importance and priority of the different phases of my dramaturgy change depending on my interests at that moment and on the stage of development. Building presence, creating stage behaviour through improvisation or composition, memorising results and repeating them, interpreting a text or a character, elaborating and repeating performances – each of these phases has its own dramaturgy.

I would like next to consider dramaturgy in more general terms than those of an actress and enter the complex dramaturgical logic of a performance, *Mythos*, but from the restricted point of view of only one of its characters, Daedalus. The first step is to find the entrance to the labyrinth.

First steps

While travelling in Bali, I became fascinated by the flowers that adorn the statues and the dancers' costumes, and by the rich colours of all the decoration in the streets, temples and villages. While in the tropical regions of northern Australia, as I crossed a bridge over a swampland, I was impressed by the enormous variety of animal sounds and bird songs. I listened and tried to repeat them: impossible. Those sounds reminded me of my Brazilian cassette tape. I started to mix the sounds of imaginary birds with my attempts to produce harmonics with my voice. Chance works for me when I collaborate with circumstances: sometimes the point of departure presents itself accidentally.

I had learned some rudiments of the techniques of harmonic singing a month earlier during a workshop with Michael Vetter, Stockhausen's German collaborator. My interest in harmonic singing had arisen after listening to a recording of music from Mongolia. It seemed to me that I could hear the sound of a high whistle together with a male voice, even though the notes on the record cover explained that it was the double song of only one person. I could not understand how it was possible to produce such a sound. I searched for other references and so came to know about Tuva singing, David Hykes and his Harmonic Choir, and Michael Vetter. Later Vetter's music remained as a background accompaniment to my physical training and the harmonic singing disappeared like many other acrobatic exercises that I absolutely failed to do, while I followed other paths to grow as an actress.

I wanted a character that would come from 'nature', not 'culture'. I worked for a whole night to prepare a costume composed of a carpet of flowers. I was afraid that the flowers would wither before I could show it. I only managed to prepare two shields of pink and yellow daisies that I placed on my back and chest. I painted my mouth in a thin black shape to reproduce the image of a beak. Waiting outside the room where all the actresses, actors and director would meet for the first rehearsal of *Mythos*, I was embarrassed and excited. A poncho covered my suggestion of a costume so that it would not be revealed before entering the space that had been prepared secretly during the previous two weeks. Everyone was informed that the words of the next production would be taken from the twenty-five volumes of the poetic work of Henrik Norbrandt, a contemporary Danish poet, and that the theme was the funeral of a song (*The International*) and the burial of a myth.

The group's actors knew their characters: Oedipus (Tage Larsen), Thersites – the cowardly soldier of the *Iliad* (Torgeir Wethal), Orpheus (Jan Ferslev), Prometheus (Frans Winther) and Guilhermino Barbosa – a soldier who marched for 25,000 kilometres across Brazil with the rebel battalion led by captain Luís Carlos Prestes (Kai Bredholt). The actresses were still ignorant of their characters.

I turned to stone when I entered the room and saw the stage space that the director had prepared with a stage designer and Tage, one of the actors. It was a Zen garden: nothing was alive there; it was a long extended area of grey pebbles and some rocks, an icy and powerful space.

We sat on the benches around the raked gravel and the stones that had been placed asymmetrically and perfectly, while the director spoke about the themes he wanted to touch on in the performance. He gave the actresses the names of their characters: Medea (Iben Nagel Rasmussen), Cassandra (Roberta Carreri), Smyrna (Isabel Ubeda) and Clytemnestra (me) – all female criminals. We all started to improvise in the space. My colourful flower costume was completely out of place.

The character 117

Whatever movement we made in this landscape of stones was excessive. It was as if our presence was out of place. For each new performance Eugenio has always searched for a starting point full of obstacles that force us to find new solutions. This time it seemed to me that he had gone too far. I felt dispirited; I was a long way from the Balinese and Australian tropics, and I was cold. The next day I came to rehearsals wearing a woollen suit and a fur hat, and the following with a leopard-skin coat, inherited from my aunt. But my courage and defiance finished there.

Months of technical and building work followed. We moved towers and stones; we experimented with lighting effects and to find floors that could withstand the trampling of the gravel. Every experiment demanded hours and hours of preparation because the room had to be cleaned first using spades and wheelbarrows to make heaps of the seven hundred kilos of pebbles on the edge of the space, before redistributing them again. Clouds of dust were raised. We wore masks over our mouths and labourer's overalls. We asked ourselves how long our lungs could last. We ordered various kinds of gravel to test colour and solidity. We washed the gravel and passed it through sieves to reduce the dust. The men of the group were active, available to solve technical details, while we women – often alarmed by the weight of all the elements used – often observed all the activity from the benches.

Greek myths did not captivate me much, and the figure of Clytemnestra even less so. I would have preferred to have a male character to distance myself from Doña Musica, from the long black dress and high heels of the previous production. When one of the actresses left the group, which changed the balance of the characters since there were now fewer females who had committed a crime, the director proposed that I should play Daedalus. I immediately recognised the possibility of flying like a bird and of translating the theme of the Greek myths into the world of 'nature' in which I was interested. I accepted. Smyrna had disappeared; with time Prometheus became Lucky from *Waiting for Godot* and finally Sisyphus; at a certain point Thersites was called Ulysses without the actor having any warning and without the change in name having any consequences for him.

The builder of the labyrinth

During the months of rehearsal we worked with Michael Vetter and Natascha Nikprelevic, the Vietnamese musician Trang Quang Hai, and four musicians from Mongolia. Each morning we practised harmonic singing and adapted fragments of Henrik Norbrandt's poems to Mongolian melodies. We wanted to create a 'mythical' sound, which came from another world, a non-human timbre and at the same time to sing with a rhythm that would urge us to dance.

I read all I could find on Daedalus and decided not just to represent the character, but to present the context to which Daedalus belonged. Instead of following the logic of a person, my dramaturgy in the performance (and consequently the material I proposed during the rehearsals of *Mythos*) referred to all the situations and people with which Daedalus had been in contact, however indirectly. The labyrinth, the Minotaur, the god in the likeness of a bull that emerges from the sea, Pasiphae, Ariadne, the thread, betrayed love, Theseus, the quail, the machine for the coitus between woman and animal, jealousy between artisans, mechanical dolls, the string in the snail, the power of Minos, Icarus's flight, the journey to Sicily and Sardinia, the sun that melts Icarus's wings, the island in the Aegean Sea, the spring dance – these were all elements I referred to and that I wanted to present in synthesis through my character.

I have never thought of Daedalus as man or woman, but as the builder of the labyrinth, a worker and a parent. At the centre of the myth of Daedalus was the Minotaur. The thread was the element that helped me orientate. The most common visible attributes in all the images of Daedalus and of his son Icarus were wings.

I built my own Minotaur. As the animal's leg I used a two-metre-long rain stick bought in Colombia that I painted gold; a white rabbit skin was the body; a big hand with lean fingers sculpted by a Balinese artist from the root of a tree represented the head and horns. I hung a golden rope on the fingers. Different references came together in this composition: the sound of rain denoted nature, the wood evoked the construction of the coitus machine, the white fur Zeus, the cut hand and crown the attributes of power. The supernatural and mythical being that was neither human nor beast was also inspired by the sculptures I had seen in Turin's Egyptian Museum.

In Holland, in a haberdasher's in Utrecht, I bought metres of golden string in different sizes and widths, and a long roll of rooster feathers. In Korea I found a small bell-cup with a cover that resonated harmonically. I first wound twenty metres of string into the cup and then let it unravel freely so that it fell magically onto the floor following its own tangled itinerary. I sewed the roll of feathers in a V shape and found a way of attaching what looked like wings to my arms. In this way other references and ideas were transformed into tangible elements: the bond between Ariadne and Theseus, the shape of the labyrinth, the harmonics, the hidden secret, the constructed wings, the bird and once again the colour gold. From this universe I received inspiration to create material and scenes.

During a break in a workshop, I went to Amsterdam with Eugenio to visit Van Gogh's Museum. At the exit we came across four Asian men who were playing and singing in a nearby square. Their clothes helped us identify them as Mongolian. They had a strange string instrument that could neigh like a horse, and a kind of mandolin. The songs followed the pressing rhythm of a gallop. The 'whistle voice', the harmonic singing that alternated with a soft, low, growling voice, could be clearly heard above the rest of the music. One of the men, making use of majestic gestures, at times declaimed texts in which we could distinguish the words 'Chingiz, Chingiz Khan'. He was the one with whom we tried to communicate as he spoke a little German and Russian. His name was Palamshav Childaa. We managed to persuade them to come to Holstebro, after many telephone calls to and meetings with their local Dutch hosts, and having put pressure on the Danish Embassy and Home Office in order to receive an immediate entry visa for them. They at once charmed us with their generosity, cheerfulness, and musical and vocal ability. In five minutes they learned the melody and text of a Danish song, while we needed a whole week to manage merely to approximate the rhythmical variations and vocal effects and to write down a few lines of their song about the Altai Mountains.

Palamshav was also a dancer. One day he showed us some folk dances from Mongolia. I saw a bird fly. The arm movement and the steps that augmented in pace represented the daily actions of people who ride, use a whip and lasso, hunt and hold reins. But the rapid lifting and lowering of the shoulders, and the arrow hitting a bird that refuses to fall, seemed to me to be the essential movements of flying. That would be Daedalus's way of moving.

I recorded some of Palamshav's dances on video and then for a month, helped by his ever-smiling image, I devoted myself to learning the steps and postures of those Mongolian dances accompanied by the driving rhythm of their music.

Music and text

One day, while working with Michael Vetter and Natascha Nikprelevic, we improvised for a long time using only one word. It was really incredible to discover the huge variety of ways possible to say a few syllables. I worked with the word 'minotaur'. Later the Minotaur became a central element of the performance, but not in the shape of the sculpture stick that I had built, nor as sound, but as the long vibrant snake of goat nails hanging in the space over our heads. Thanks to Michael Vetter, I had discovered that there is a whole world to explore within a word or a syllable, and that it is possible to sing harmonic melodies that would be difficult for me even with a normal voice.

The director had given me three texts; one of them was composed of fragments of Henrik Norbrandt's poems. I tried to apply the harmonic singing technique to the words. For one text I used an extremely high pitched voice, where my harmonics were limited in number, but strong. In another text I used the lowest and most relaxed voice I could reach. I interrupted a third text with bird sounds aided by the harmonic effects of some mouth and tongue positions. I had fun improvising for a long time mixing the sounds of birds, monkeys and frogs. I let the director listen to these improvisations, refusing to fix them into a consistent vocal score. I wrote other texts myself starting from what I had read about Daedalus. Other actors of the group, especially the Scandinavians, concentrated more on Norbrandt, proposing some of the poems they liked most. Many of my texts disappeared completely or were reduced in length, to the extent even of keeping only the vocal articulations that change the vocal harmonics. I worked on other texts by grafting them onto a montage of Sephardic songs, the Jewish songs from Arab Spain.

It was difficult to reach a coherent musical dramaturgy in the performance and to overcome the fragmentation of the different melodies from Mongolia, Corsica, Sephardim, which had been added to the original compositions by our musicians and the vocal improvisations of all the performers. The sound of the gravel, which created the 'sea' or the 'labyrinth', helped us find this unity.

Strings and feathers

The first idea for costumes came from two glossy jackets that the director had bought in an expensive shop at the Santiago airport in Chile. These were shown to us with other objects such as a deer cranium and lama foetuses that he had found during a journey across Bolivia and the north of Argentina. In other shops in Utrecht and Italy we bought evening dresses, coats, hats and wigs. Two sets of skirts and jackets had been made for me while I stubbornly continued to follow my own image of a craftsman dressed in overalls and gold to create my costume. Only when I managed to complete my own proposal, by adorning it with many metres of the string I had found in Utrecht, were the trousers and golden jacket finally accepted.

In fact Daedalus's costume is what is left from an enormous amount of work around the labyrinth. Starting from the idea of the tangled string that fell from the Korean bell, I had suggested a labyrinth made of rope held at the extremities by some of my colleagues that would serve to trap the revolutionary character Guilhermino Barbosa into the timeless landscape of myth. I imagined that the origin of the labyrinth was in Daedalus's mind and, to make this idea concrete, I made a hat of plaited rope that slowly freed itself to make the labyrinth.

Many metres of rope were necessary to make this labyrinth so I wrapped more plaited string around my neck, adding it to the hat. To help me find the point from which I could start uncoiling it, I hung the ends of the string on the stick that was my Minotaur. The technical solution to this and the preparation that the dozens of metres of cord required, kept me busy for two or three hours a day for many weeks. The rope also formed the labyrinth that suddenly divided into four parts to capture and pull Guilhermino Barbosa in like a wild animal to be tamed. I wanted to introduce the subject of the labyrinth right from the beginning: I worked on a scene with another actor whose musical instrument was pulled by the rope, accompanied by harmonic singing and an Italian *tarantella* song. I also created a gigantic spider's web and a rain of strings that extended from the centre of the performance space.

From one day to the next the director got rid of all these scenes. The string and cords were no longer present in the performance. They were left only in Daedalus's costume, to make the hat and the decoration around my neck and at my wrists. The entire dynamic of the labyrinth scene changed into an invisible dramatic force and the rope was only used to pull off Guilhermino Barbosa's clothes and leave his naked corpse exposed.

During rehearsals I had created the rope labyrinth and Roberta had suggested the image of the captured animal and the instant pulling off of the clothes. Jan had drawn a labyrinth in the gravel by allowing the red carpet to appear from underneath with the help of the snowplough that we normally used to clean the space at the end of rehearsals. The carpet made the string more obvious than the gravel did. Consequently I had to dig a labyrinth following the string's path. When the string finally disappeared from the general montage in the performance, all that was left was the labyrinth created by the contrast between the carpet and the gravel. My Minotaur stick then became both the sceptre of power and, by adding a small spade and fork at the opposite end of the sculpted hand, Daedalus's building tool. The hand was placed directly on top of the rain stick and the white fur, now redundant, taken away. The drawing of the labyrinth also indicated Guilhermino Barbosa's tomb, and the sceptre became the element that guides the ritual that converts history into myth.

At the end of the process I felt that it was not worthwhile to work so hard. All the material that I had spent hours, days, months developing had been cut. The scenes I had proposed with less thoroughness, the transitions and solutions that changed my position in the space were what remained. I consoled myself by thinking that the wastage might be used to build another performance in which string could have the main role.

Two years later, during a meeting with the whole group, the director explained that my efforts, which he had considered a mistake from the beginning, had allowed him to discover the dynamic structure of the performance. I was satisfied: even though my actress's work had disappeared, I had contributed towards the building of the dramaturgy of the performance as a whole. I also realised that Daedalus's consistency as a character depended on all my eliminated work.

I also believe that the wings I made for Daedalus helped change the dramaturgical direction of the performance. They were beautiful and I absolutely wanted to introduce them into the montage, even though the director insisted that his wish was to save them for a final scene. I did not trust that this would happen and I knew that any material that was not included would soon be forgotten. So I persisted to the point of disobedience and during each run-through I introduced the wings at some point. I kept the feathers rolled up in my arms like a baby cradled by a parent, then I unwound them round my head like a shaman's headdress and at the end I put them on by fixing them to my arms. This prop was technically very difficult to master: the transformations always took too long and occasionally I remained caught up in a tangle to the director's evident irritation.

With Daedalus's wings appeared Icarus, the son, and slowly the criminal action of these mythical figures, so central at the beginning of the process, receded and the focus became the relationship between these characters and

Mythos
Frans Winther, Julia Varley
Photo: Tony D'Urso

their children. Idealism, the hope for a better world, the struggle to change reality and the future were made manifest through sons and daughters: children to be killed, sacrificed, put to death, forgotten, placed one against the other.

The cry of the parent who searches for Icarus; the scene I created to present his fall into the sea from which only the song was kept; the bird movements and rhythms I had learned: all this contributed to making the absence of the children visible. And one day Icarus's wings were put on the revolutionary soldier Guilhermino Barbosa. In this way another performance 'knot' was tied bringing together not only the destinies of Medea, Oedipus and Daedalus, but also that of the Brazilian soldier who marches to safeguard dignity. The characters met in the labyrinth. From there, armed with wings of wax, they tried to fly away to reach the sun of freedom. The parents, those responsible, would survive, but what legacy would they leave?

Crete

I absolutely had to go to Crete, where Daedalus had built the labyrinth. The performance was almost complete so the journey would not give me new material to use in the montage, but I felt that I owed it to my character. I had to see the labyrinth, the place where it is said that the Minotaur was enclosed and where Minos's wife had made love with the white bull, the uncontrollable god. It was strange to arrive on the island at the same time as German tourists and see bars and restaurants called by names we knew from the work on our performance: Mythos, Labyrinth, Minotaur . . .

I searched for traces of the labyrinth in Minos's palace in Knossos and in the other Cretan palaces; not so much by observing the position of the walls, but in the marks that the dance steps and rituals of the past had left on the stones, in the Mediterranean landscape and the objects exhibited in the museum. I discovered the power of matriarchy in the rooms of the priestess, in colours left on the walls and in the statue of the woman with naked breasts holding two snakes in her hands. I perceived the laborious passage to patriarchy in the inverted bull horns, the battle between religion and politics, the extremely well-cared-for bodies in the paintings. Artistic value and magic were to be found in everyday objects, in the dolls and a small toy swing, in the jewels, vases and small clay cups that had been crafted with the care and insight of an artisan. The quality and variety of each of these fascinating objects from the past made the abundance of mediocrity with which we live today so very evident. I recognised the same value that we try to give to our work when creating a performance at Odin Teatret in the perfect irregularity of the form and decoration of the small cups, in the attention to detail and in the simple imperative of the object.

Spring was just starting to make itself felt, as I toured the island in a rented car with Dorthe, a painter friend. The dolphins, the blue and turquoise colours, the quality of the stone in Crete were both 'nature' and 'culture'. Things that had been created by human beings had the same congruity as the sea, as the trees on which the first flowers were appearing, as the sky, as the rocks and the wind. The big coin with indecipherable marks exhibited under glass in one of the rooms in the museum manifested the fascination of what cannot be grasped: the attraction of the labyrinth. In Crete I became aware of the secret that Daedalus had whispered to me: dramaturgy starts with the capacity to explore beyond what is evident, taking care of all hidden details.

A chain of reactions

In *Mythos* the story does not evolve in a logical way, with relationships of cause and effect between the characters, but rather flows contiguously from one character to the other.

One scene starts when Ulysses gathers amputated hands into piles around the stones, while a blue light blinds the spectators like the glare of the sea. Ulysses says: '*Of the sea from last summer only the reflection of the sunset is left. Of the reflection only the faces and of the faces only their waiting.*' Daedalus cries '*Icarus!*' and throws himself on the hands, as if in search of his son among the waves of the sea. All the characters sing: '*The sea . . . in front of us . . . full of secrets . . .*' while Sisyphus plays his viola. Orpheus and Oedipus wander through this landscape of stones and severed hands. As he continues to rake the hands into the blue-lit gravel, Ulysses comments: '*I am afraid that I am a house inhabited by many people who never tire of going round at night sweeping, and that dust fills my body instead of blood.*' Cassandra echoes him: '*I see his bones on the seashore.*' Daedalus picks up a feather from underneath one of the stones and sings: '*The weight of your skeleton tells me every night the height of the mountains I fly over in my dreams*' and then, seeing the winged soul of Guilhermino Barbosa carrying his own lifeless winged body in his arms, startled he cries: '*Icarus?!*' While Guilhermino Barbosa continues his march, Cassandra sneers: '*You taught him the art of flying. You didn't teach him the most important thing: the art of falling.*' Daedalus embraces Guilhermino's knees and whispers: '*Cursed be the impatience which has filled your pockets with sleepless nights and dreams that scream like a child being born.*' Guilhermino frees himself from the embrace to continue advancing undaunted. Daedalus picks up the feather: '*I saw a child on the seashore. Ulysses, I thought it was mine. He shook his head as if to say: don't use me once again in your dreams.*' The feather falls to the ground accompanied by the sound of sad twittering. Daedalus kneels to bury the feather in the gravel while Oedipus laughs scornfully: '*Blind yourself. Tear out your eyes so you will see history only in the light of your memories.*' Daedalus leaves uttering a lament of bird sounds. Ulysses uncovers the feather with his feet, picks it up to put it in his hat as a decoration and tells the spectators: '*In Italy they are smarter. There they eat the small songbirds so they don't wake you early in the morning, and above all don't shit on the cars!*' Daedalus looks on Medea in terror as, with two lama foetuses visible on her shoulders, she advances attracted by Orpheus's song: '*I call out to love and despair, to madness and insight. I call out to her everywhere where I have not been.*' Medea strangles the foetuses, buries them in the gravel and abandons them: '*Be naked small children, and calm. This is the guest we awaited so impatiently, you and I, the guest who soon will separate us and take us home to ourselves.*' Ulysses enters with the rake to add the foetuses to the heap of amputated hands.

The characters remain isolated in their torments and in their world, though they participate in weaving the associative and narrative threads of each of their stories and at the same time of a larger story that transcends them. If I follow only Daedalus's point of view, I might interpret the scene as the search for Icarus after his fall into the Aegean Sea, and recognise in the big stone under which I find the feather the island where Theseus stopped or where Ariadne was abandoned. But I do not think of this during the performance even though it is interesting to discover other meanings in what happens because of my actions. I might see Icarus's soul in the winged soldier, the anger of the gods at the human longing to fly in Cassandra's predictions, an alternative to exile and running away from Crete in Oedipus's choice of blindness, the interlocutor for the parents who refuse to understand in Ulysses's shrewdness, the corpse of the son lost at sea in Medea's foetuses, victims of the ideals of my youth in the severed hands, the fallen Berlin Wall in the stones or infinite illusions of a better future in the gravel.

The performance narrative is carried by passing from one character to the other in a complex interlacing: montage and simultaneity. Cassandra warns at the same time as Daedalus searches, as Orpheus and Oedipus pass through the space like animals in a cage, as Sisyphus plays and Ulysses rakes. The spectators can be disoriented by this simultaneity of actions, but the director indicates which threads to follow in this skein of diverging directions. The director's logic moves through contiguous territories. It jumps over walls dividing parallel stories and opens up the passage from one closed road to the next through a sequence of often associative and rhythmical relationships, connections that can be words, objects or lighting effects. Ulysses mentions the sea in his text, Daedalus searches for his son Icarus in the sea, Icarus flies like a bird, Guilhermino's soul has wings like an angel, Cassandra speaks of the art of falling, the feather falls, and Ulysses amuses himself with an image of birds who shit on cars.

The simultaneity and montage impose credibility when they are rooted in the actions and reactions between the actresses and actors. The organic, living, relationship follows the principles of action and reaction. This relationship is not only established through ways of looking and an exchange of lines, but rather through a spider's web of actions and impulses. This requires a long time to develop, especially when it takes place between solitary characters like those in *Mythos*.

The organic logic is dictated by an intricate chain of physical, vocal and musical actions, and by a constant dialogue between the performers and the space in which they move. When Torgeir (Ulysses) finishes his text and the blue lights come on, Jan's (Orpheus) accompaniment changes tonality to start the collective song about the sea. Julia (Daedalus) cries 'Icarus!' and Torgeir starts to rake, Iben (Medea) and Roberta (Cassandra) continue to sing, Frans (Sisyphus) plays the viola in a different rhythm, and Jan (Orpheus) and Tage (Oedipus) enter the space. The thud of the stone falling silences everyone; only the fine vibrato of the viola and a whispered text are heard. Roberta sings, Kai (Guilhermino Barbosa) advances to the rhythm of the song and the last note provokes Julia's fall and the embracing of Kai's knees. Kai starts walking again and Julia picks up the feather from the stone and searches for the stream of light to illuminate it, while directing her attention towards Torgeir who stands on the opposite side. After the feather has fallen and been covered with the gravel that makes a sound like waves on the seashore, Tage starts his text. Julia turns towards him and follows the rhythm of his words with small impulses of her body and the bird sounds. Meanwhile Torgeir waits for the precise moment when the text ends suddenly to leave the stone on which he has been standing precariously in order to slide towards the feather and take hold of it. Torgeir's abrupt arrival makes Julia stand up and the rhythm of her exit corresponds with Iben's entrance.

Through this precise rhythmic modulation of actions and reactions it is possible to establish bonds and allow meanings and stories to emerge. The director discovers how to give the spectators clues about the narrative thread by working on what we call the organic level of dramaturgy, on the microscopic and continual elaboration of tiny details. The actress's material and actions, the relationships and new contexts that are created during the process, indicate which path to follow to find the way out of the labyrinth and these have sensorial and interpretative consequences for the spectators and the performance.

Daedalus watches from a distance in one of the scenes I like most in this creation of meanings by contiguity: Ulysses has just finished commenting ironically on Guilhermino's revolutionary song '*And if the hands are yours, what they do is also yours*' when Medea, calling for her children, appears with her hands red with blood. Daedalus is in the dark; nobody sees him as, shaken by the dance movements, he tries to escape from the labyrinth.

Wings of wax

It is the spectators who must fly free of the story, the characters, the montage, the dramaturgy and of the performance itself. Ariadne's thread, which leads the spectators' eyes through the scenes with the invisible power of actions, must disappear.

Entering a labyrinth, getting lost, meeting the unknown, finding an exit, flying away are images that belong to everyone. In these kinds of experiences myth still has a function: it is a common recognisable reference. Daedalus has helped me to understand the dramaturgy of *Mythos* and accept that the Greek myths speak of a contemporary reality.

In the performance the spectators should each be able to find a personal coming and going, recognise what they have believed and perhaps still believe in: experiences, stories, myths, fantasies, ideals and dreams. Daedalus has persuaded me that today we are still able to fly, even if our wings melt in the sun. But, after all, is it so bad to fall into the blue Aegean Sea?

The puppet character

During a session of the University of Eurasian Theatre in Scilla, south Italy, in 2002, the sculptor Fabio Butera showed us a puppet, the construction of which he was still improving. The puppet had an attractive face and a fascinating simplicity of movement. In search of unpredictable directions that might interrupt and reinvent the habits and experience of previous performances, Eugenio Barba asked Fabio to build me a puppet that was a replica in miniature of two of my characters: Doña Musica, with her long white hair; and Mr Peanut, with his skull head. The new puppet would also have a third face, beautiful, charming and young, like that of the original model. I didn't know if I was interested in working with a puppet, but I said nothing. After all, it is good that the director engages in finding inspiration for one of his actresses.

For *Andersen's Dream* (2004–), all the Odin actresses and actors had to prepare one hour of resource material and choose one of Hans Christian Andersen's tales to stage. In a meeting at the end of 2001, Eugenio had spoken of further themes that might be pursued: Africa (a continent not so well known to Odin Teatret); an old people's home and its inhabitants; the slave route and the oasis of culture that it had produced – jazz, the blues or samba. Then he imagined the Little Match Girl from Andersen's fairytale dressed as a young Palestinian woman.

To begin practical work on *Andersen's Dream*, I chose some African music and some postcards with images of old people. I had bought the cassette 'Ladies of Jazz' and the complete works of Hans Christian Andersen in English. In the rehearsal room I danced freely to the African songs. One of these provoked me to move my arms and body in a way that made me think of a woman defending herself from people stoning her. I learned some blues and some songs from Egypt and Azerbaijan, and every day I fixed one of the postcards and one of Andersen's tales in a physical score. What I thought was a character began to emerge from the repetition: a rather simple person, happy but desperate, whom I had seen on a television programme about Kosovan refugees.

I had been to Germany for five days to research the potential of vocal improvisation with Michael Vetter. I worked barefoot on the beautiful Persian carpets in his study. To help me find variations, while improvising with only one sound, syllable, word, position or musical tone, my mind took shelter in the patterns of the carpet. Back in Holstebro I bought a small Persian carpet to keep me company. Kneeling on it, I improvised with sounds made only of air and breath, while lighting matches and allowing them to burn out, recalling the images of cigarette smoke that I had studied with Michael Vetter. Dogan, Holstebro's Kurdish carpet seller, offered me another smaller carpet, telling me with a knowing twinkle in his eyes that only silk carpets can fly.

The puppet with its three heads was also in the rehearsal room with me. I sometimes devoted myself to her, but the endless technical problems of working her tired me. I had to solve how to keep the puppet's support attached to my shoe, how to hold and light matches with her hands, and how to change the heads. These difficulties distracted me from the more important task of animating the puppet, deciding how to hold and manoeuvre her arms, how to move her head and use the particularity of her flexible support leg, how to walk and make her walk, how to sit and make her sit, how to get up and make her get up, how to breathe with her.

One day, while I was trying to make the puppet fly, she doubled up. It seemed as if she had broken. I got a fright, but nothing had actually happened. Another day, I dressed the puppet in a chador and placed her on her support on the small silk carpet. The black cloth of the chador emphasised the expression in her eyes and she began to speak to me. I started to address

Andersen's Dream
Scheherazade, Julia Varley
Photo: Fiora Bemporad

the actions and texts of the fixed score to her. I understood that the puppet had become Scheherazade for me. From that day the chador became the motivation for making the puppet dance. I had to expose and uncover her veiled life, free her from immobility and find her voice, liberate her from the black shroud and give her colour.

I made Scheherazade a new dress with the fabric I had purchased in the bazaar in Damask, during a tour in Syria. In an alley behind the Great Mosque I found a shop that sold camel wool shawls woven and embroidered by hand by Palestinian women. They were very expensive, but irresistibly beautiful. I bought one to make a cape for Scheherazade. In Syria I added to my collection of music from Egypt and Azerbaijan, cassettes by the Lebanese singer Fairouz, and then I spent a year learning songs in Arabic.

Dressed like a princess and holding a box of matches between her fingers, Scheherazade has taken me by the hand into the world of fairytales. I devoted myself to containing my acting vitality within minute, delicate and fleeting movements. I had to dispel any trace of my broken footsteps, the concreteness of my weight, the tension of the scores and sequences, in order to transform the relationship between our dissimilar presences into a continuous magic flow. I had to understand how to move her, how to pour my life into her without retaining it only within me.

I fixed small actions: the way Scheherazade touches, prays, combs her hair, greets, applauds, undresses, calls, and says yes and no . . . I needed hours and days to understand how to make these simple gestures. I searched for a delicate voice, like a light breeze, placed slightly above my own. A shy little giggle filled the pauses needed to change the position of her hands, to tilt her chest or make her kneel.

During rehearsals I tried to see through her, to let my eyes look through her eyes before going out into the space to win the spectator's attention. The director wanted me to look only at her, so that the spectator would only see the puppet, but I rebelled against this destiny. I didn't want to end veiled behind Scheherazade. I had to discover our separate lives, while remaining, sister-like, behind, underneath or beside her. I looked at her to learn from her beauty and poetry, from her flirtatious and playful desire to amuse herself.

Now in the performance *Andersen's Dream* I am Scheherazade's sister and I sit close to her on the flying carpet. A veil of clouds protects us while we fly like Chagall's lovers, telling fairytales and observing the problems of the world from afar. And the character is a puppet.

8   The director

Meeting a director

My autonomy as an actress has a counterpoint in an inclination to support and oppose, collaborate and compete, meet and clash with the director. I find this approach necessary to keep our creative relationship alive and fertile.

I arrived at Odin Teatret at a time when Eugenio Barba only occasionally followed his actresses' and actors' training, and my meeting with him happened when we had to prepare a performance. That is the reason why I didn't list Eugenio among my teachers in the brief review of my apprenticeship, even though I have learned an incredible amount from him. My dialogue with Eugenio started when I met the director, which is to say the person who observes, watches over and examines my accomplishments as an actress and who has the last word in deciding how these are presented to the spectators.

In Denmark, for a long period when I was first in Holstebro, Eugenio and I kept our distance. My presence imposed on his horizon yet another person who needed attention, seduced by one of his actors, an unexpected guest whom nobody welcomed and whose reason for staying on nobody understood. He was annoyed by an article for which he held me responsible that had appeared in the *Quotidiano dei Lavoratori*, an Italian newspaper of the revolutionary left that had criticised the subservient relationship of some Italian theatre groups to Odin Teatret. For Eugenio it was gratuitous and destructive criticism of people who wanted to learn through imitation before finding their own way. The article had been published during Odin Teatret's tour of Italy when I first got to know the group. It coincided with discussions in the Italian political and theatrical milieu on grass-root groups and Third Theatre. I was not responsible for the article, but I very well knew the reasoning that had produced it. Despite being in Denmark and physically distant, I didn't want to disavow my old comrades even if they accused me of betrayal. I had abandoned them at the difficult political moment of ebbing enthusiasm, in the years after the police had evacuated the Santa Marta Social Centre whose beginnings and first achievements we had shared.

Consistent with his disagreement with the way I had been introduced to Odin Teatret, Eugenio ignored me until the day I got married, thus demonstrating my intention to live in Holstebro. At that point he was convinced that I was not affected by a passing infatuation. I had already demonstrated my interest by working hard for many months, but Eugenio takes time to accept people. Our true dialogue started years later, after I had made two performances and won my place in our group with the perseverance that accompanies the inevitable loneliness of professional autonomy.

When I started my priority was to learn and rebuild my existence as an actress. I addressed myself to those who could help me in my first steps. I believed I did not have the right to disturb the director: I had nothing particular to say to him. It was only on Iben Nagel Rasmussen's insistence, and encouraged by Tage Larsen, that I spoke with him one day before deciding if I should return to Milan or remain in Denmark. I remember that he gave me a smile that showed his teeth while I tried to explain my confusion, but his eyes remained cold and indifferent. I expressed my doubts about my wish to remain at Odin Teatret. I was afraid that this dream hid a form of laziness and lack of determination in facing the difficulties of the world around me. Eugenio told me that to remain at Odin Teatret one should either be professionally very good or a particularly treasured person. It was clear for me that if I wanted to stay I would do it against his will. Tage supported me in this battle.

Two years passed before I had the chance to work alone with Eugenio. Rehearsals for *Brecht's Ashes*, the performance on Bertolt Brecht's life and artistic activities, were beginning and everyone had embarked on the process of creating characters for the performance. Sitting on a chair in a corner of the white room, Eugenio asked me to work with various parts of my face following the principle of introversion and extroversion. He explained that I could dilate or compress different parts of my face, open my mouth to the maximum while I half closed my eyes, widen my nose while knitting my forehead, tighten my lips and wink, and so on. I was petrified and I don't know how I managed to move a single facial muscle. The freedom guaranteed by the director's distance during my first stay at Odin Teatret had been replaced by an awareness of Eugenio's influence and authority in the group. I felt totally unprepared in front of him and he frightened me.

Some time later he gave me my first theme for an improvisation: a brief text on a small piece of photocopied paper. He asked me to read it in silence, focusing on the verbs. I didn't realise that emphasising the verbs was a strategy to help me find actions. Once again fear prevented me from understanding. The improvisation was recorded on video and I remember the long and excruciating effort of repeating every movement while looking at myself on the screen. I was ashamed of how I looked and unsuccessful at memorising the sequence. The material from this improvisation was never used in the performance, although Eugenio worked on it for a long time with the intention of introducing it into a scene with other actors.

During rehearsals for *Brecht's Ashes* the director sculpted me like a stone, as if I were a being without any personal autonomy. He would say: 'Lift that foot, shift your weight; step with your left leg rather than the right . . .'

He would introduce difficulties that didn't exist and that I hadn't expected. I was surprised by how much his suggestions influenced my physical behaviour. His patience was the guarantee that each actress and actor would be present in the performance giving of their best.

Another improvisation was used for a text by Nietzsche. It was my second improvisation since joining Odin Teatret. I had memorised every step and the different arm movements, and I knew the exact number of actions. I repeated the external forms while going over in my mind the images that had triggered them, convinced that the precision that was demanded obliged me to repeat in the same way each time. It was hard for me to envisage that I could change direction or add some steps; I simply strove to accomplish obediently what the director had asked me to do. Eugenio was preoccupied by the complexity required to weave together and develop relationships and narrative structures with eleven performers. During the long hours I spent waiting, sitting in a corner of the room, I focused on how he worked with the others, trying to grasp his logic. It was as if I had to learn a new language.

For *The Million*, the performance about Marco Polo that we worked on at the same time as *Brecht's Ashes*, Eugenio intervened directly in my work only when the fear apparent in my face during an acrobatic dance with Tage started to diminish, and also to fix the melodic intonation of a poem. I remember that Tage, who had been an Odin Teatret actor for seven years, complained about the small amount of attention the director gave him. What right did I have to claim more consideration?

In those early years, Eugenio used me in pedagogical situations to demonstrate that dedication was not enough to produce a convincing stage presence. My example was useful in explaining how many years of work were necessary before signs of 'life' appeared in a performance. I understood that my only possibility was to continue along my way and let the results materialise of their own accord. To serve as a guinea pig was a privilege, because it was a chance to learn from working with the director. Others would have liked to be in my shoes. I exorcised the humiliating aspects of the experience with a pinch of irony, and avoided getting needlessly upset.

When Eugenio returned from the first session of ISTA (International School of Theatre Anthropology), held in Bonn in 1980, he wanted to share some reflections on improvisation with members of our group. I improvised on the theme 'That branch of Lake Como' (the well-known sentence that begins Alessandro Manzoni's novel *I promessi sposi*). Working with me with endless patience, the director altered every one of my actions by a few centimetres. He tried to inject life into my movements. Iben protested because she considered unfair such cold manipulation of material that had meaning for the actress. But I was thankful to be submitted to that long, tedious and technical operation. The process of relocating the direction and size of my actions helped me gradually to recognise the physicality of my training. I became aware that I had to use this same physicality when improvising and performing. It had taken me four years to understand with my whole body what I can now explain in words in a few minutes.

Small rewards counterbalanced the director's rare and specific comments. During a tour of Peru, in 1978, Eugenio organised impromptu public scenes with the group's younger generation, while the others rested before the evening performance. We presented clown sketches in the streets, invaded newspaper offices, made parades to greet authorities and acquaintances. Eugenio encouraged me to develop my inventiveness on small stilts while I improvised among the tables of a cafe or around journalists' desks.

One day, during a rehearsal of *Brecht's Ashes*, he smiled with amusement as he put on my head the hat belonging to Mackie Messer, the character who at that moment was playing chess with Bertolt Brecht. He told me that I was free to do and fix whatever actions I wanted. I received my first compliment from Eugenio when he told me that it was right not to readjust the skirt of my costume after picking up a prop that one of the other actors had lost during *The Million*. I had been at Odin Teatret for four years when, after having seen my training, he commented: 'There is nothing that disturbs me.' For him this was huge praise.

The second production usually represents an important evolution for an actress at Odin Teatret. It is the threshold beyond which the relationship between actress and director grows deeper. *The Gospel According to Oxyrhincus*, in which I played Jeanne d'Arc, was this threshold for me. I created my character's materials in collaboration with Christoph Falke, the German assistant director. I regularly rehearsed with Eugenio on Saturdays and Sundays, when the others rested at home. I was getting divorced and work was my salvation. In the rehearsal room I forgot about what was happening in my life, I enjoyed myself and my tearful swollen face would transform with a smile. The director cut and reassembled my material in a different order to the one I had established with Christoph. The logic of what I had created changed little by little as it was included in the general structure of the performance. I kept the motivations and stories that had guided the creation of my first montage to myself. Eugenio and I exchanged only the words necessary to decide on the required alterations or the elaboration of new proposals. Our 'whys' were enveloped in silence.

Working with a director

It was in 1988 with *Talabot*, the next production, on the life of the contemporary Danish anthropologist Kirsten Hastrup, that I decided not to worry about 'functioning' in the director's eyes.

Come! And the Day Will Be Ours had been a performance about the meeting between the *other* – the Native Americans – and English Puritans who ventured into the unexplored New World as pioneers after having left their country to escape religious intolerance. *Brecht's Ashes*, taking the biography of the German playwright and poet, dealt with the theme of enforced travel, having to flee from one's homeland for political reasons, and of the exile's meeting with the *other*. However, *Talabot* was the story of a woman who chooses to leave her own culture and becomes a foreigner of her own will, in order to study the *other* as an anthropologist.

My task was to give life to Kirsten Hastrup on stage. With this character and performance I believe I succeeded for the first time in proposing material that inspired Eugenio as a director.

Before starting rehearsals again in January 1988, I travelled for three months far from theatre and the people who knew me as an Odin Teatret actress. The distance gave me a different perspective on my professional problems and the journey stirred an autonomous creative curiosity in me.

Eugenio immediately accepted the first costume I suggested for *Talabot*. He worked for a long time on one of my improvisations in which I sang in a way I considered not so 'Odin-like'. During the creation of this performance, for the first time I felt confident in my translation of the director's tasks into concrete proposals about props, scenes and ways of speaking the text. It was as if his words had changed for me. They no longer represented threatening authority, abstract theories, reproach and the effort to push me to attain results at any cost. The same words were now solid and concrete entities that provoked immediate and free reactions in me.

After *Talabot*, my solo performances further developed my autonomy and consequently a different relationship with the director. But I had to persist for three years before Eugenio agreed to work on *Doña Musica's Butterflies*, which I have played since 1997. While I propose themes and material for my solo performances, the group productions usually originate from the director's ideas or from some necessity that he recognises in the group.

Perhaps precisely because of their origin, the solo performances bind us in the creative dialectic of actress and director, enveloped in an expressive patina that encourages the spectators to believe that the concerns, moods and humour emerging from the montage are mine alone. In fact I would say that my personal expression manifests itself exactly because of the director's input. I create the performance almost entirely by myself, but it is the director who provides the finishing touches that lift the result to an altogether different dimension. His experienced external eye, the difference between our personalities, his perspective on my motivations and his professional rigour, all these support and encourage me to shape and weave the dramaturgical structure of the performance with efficacy and greater precision. His thoroughness, the demands he makes and the constant repetition grant me the freedom to take risks during the process because the director takes responsibility for the choice of what the spectators will see. The director's nervous system excises any dramatic inertia and intervenes in the tempo/rhythm. He doesn't allow uncertainty and is unforgiving of weakness and indecision. He opens unexpected prospects for my proposals, clothing them with the force of suggestion and multiple meanings. Above all, we struggle together to come across solutions that are out of the ordinary for us.

Reacting to what he sees, Eugenio may change very little of a scene I have presented, or he may distort, mix or even cut most or all of it. If my material evokes associations, images and an assemblage of conflicting information in him, he will start from there to build stories and scenes. I have rarely seen him create a scene starting only from an idea.

It was at the beginning of the rehearsals for *Brecht's Ashes* that I understood that Eugenio was the first to sacrifice his ideas if they didn't work in practice and that he was a director who built above all upon what was offered to him by his actresses and actors. Eugenio had imagined a prologue in which a young man visits a wise man asking to be accepted as his disciple. The pupil arrived with a sack of wheat on his back as payment. But the sack had a hole and the wheat fell slowly into an empty pan creating what Eugenio called a 'theatrical silence': a hardly noticeable sonorous flow making time perceptible to the spectator. After numerous attempts, Eugenio couldn't achieve the effect he wanted and the scene was cut. On the other hand, the problems that Else Marie Laukvik, one of Odin's founding actresses, gave him by proposing scenes unrelated to the developing dramatic structure, stimulated him to contrive unexpected solutions.

The language that the director chooses in order to communicate, comment and impart tasks changes according to each phase of the process. At first Eugenio makes a long oral improvisation leaping from one topic to another: a programme he has seen on television; a book he is reading; anecdotes and

Eugenio Barba, Kirsten Hastrup, Julia Varley
Photo: Tony D'Urso

personal recollections. He shares with his actresses and actors the questions he is asking himself and which impel him once more to create a performance. His observations and thoughts establish interesting starting points and references for me both in a professional and personal sense. His explanations and his vocal intonation simultaneously create a protective feeling and a spirit of adventure that incites us to start the journey towards the new performance. Later, during the rehearsals, our language becomes technical. Eugenio uses simple words and gives straightforward tasks, drawing on a work vocabulary that we share. He makes no reference to an interior world or psychological justifications. Even if he does allude to them indirectly, he does not mention personal motive. We know that our inherent tacit areas operate better when they are not revealed as concepts.

When I present a scene, Eugenio reacts and intervenes while always respecting the dynamic essence of the action: the impulses and tensions in the torso. He protects what I call the 'heart' of the action because he wants to safeguard its life on stage. The movements of arms and hands and facial expressions can be meaningful in the story I follow as an actress, but often they are only one-dimensional for the spectator. They don't offer evocative potential and ambiguity. It is often these expressions and gestures that Eugenio changes, reworks or simply takes away.

I became aware of this basic characteristic of Eugenio's way of working while collaborating with another director in 1990. Miguel Rubio – the director of the Peruvian group Yuyachkani with whom I had undertaken a study project – asked why I refused to allow him to modify one of my actions. I tried to explain that what he suggested drew me away from the substance of the original impulse. He wanted me to preserve the arm position while the torso contradicted the original movement.

Eugenio asks me to change the 'extremities', to make actions less apparent and obvious. He often eliminates the excess details so that the scene becomes more enigmatic. He adapts the physical actions to a text, preceding scene or theme or uses the actions as a contrast or digression. He creates other contrary or complementary stories parallel to my original ones. But he does not change the dynamic heart. He respects the essence, which is to say that nucleus of impulses that exists even when all the external glitter and superficial covering has been eliminated.

If the stage life is protected, and the organic quality of the actions secured, I experience a broad rainbow of feelings, rhythms, memories and associations. In this way the spectators are induced to believe in my performance, even if they don't understand it. When what the spectators see awakes in them a sensation of life, my inner life is safeguarded as well. I feel that a director like Eugenio allows me to preserve what is essential to me. It is difficult for me to describe what this is. I can only say that it is something as fluid and impalpable as water and that it is contained in the breath of every cell of my body. It is carried by the concreteness of a particular muscular tension in tandem with a compelling vision that wishes to make a mark on history.

It is a whirlpool of energy, a slow stream of perseverance and a waterfall of a million molecules that think for themselves.

Many scholars and students ask me how Eugenio works as a director. The complexity of his performances, the way he weaves different stories together, the emotional charge that his montages manage to achieve, his dramaturgical imagination, all demonstrate a rigorous professional and intellectual preparation and a conspicuous creative gift. Frequently, however, one of his particular qualities is overlooked: his perspicacity in intervening in the chain of impulses and reactions that build the actress's organic behaviour on stage. The result of these interventions persuades the spectators to 'believe' in Odin Teatret's formalised acting style. It seems strange, but the meanings and emotions, the perspectives and questions that surface in the spectators' minds are also the consequence of the director's minute, intricate and patient elaboration of the impulses in the actress's actions and of their imperceptible montage into a spider's web of other reactions and impulses.

The first result for which Eugenio searches is the theatre 'life' of the action, its quality of stage presence, which at Odin Teatret we call 'organicity' or 'organic effect'. If such an effect already exists in my proposal, he will pursue a new vitality by connecting my proposal with other characters, with the space, an object, a light, a costume, a piece of music or text. In an analogous way, if he recognises a particular suggestion in a poem's dynamic, meaning and

Theatrum Mundi rehearsals
Eugenio Barba, Julia Varley as Mr Peanut, Torgeir Wethal lying down, Kanichi Hanayagi, Tjokorda Raka Tisnu as Rangda
Photo: Fiora Bemporad

rhythm, he will try to relate it to an action on stage that provokes complementary reactions. During rehearsals we spend months in search of this 'life' and its conflicting tensions. The greatest part of the director's attention, effort and patience, in collaboration with the actress, is devoted to what in books and Theatre Anthropology lectures is called the 'pre-expressive' level, although in our practice we simply call it rehearsals or run-throughs. Eugenio is ready to seize meanings, associations and potential developments that emerge from the thousand details in the scores. He chases and shapes them, mixes them with the theme or a preliminary text, while always justifying to himself the choices he makes, the cuts he imposes or the suggestions he asks us to pursue.

Towards the end of the process the director takes on the responsibility of protecting the spectators and assumes the right to make the final decision. Concentration on the 'pre-expressive' level does not guarantee the quality of a performance, but it is of great help in infusing a persuasive power that makes it acceptable to the spectators, especially when the story seems difficult to decipher or is narrated in a foreign language.

During a Festuge (festive week) in Holstebro
Nando Taviani, Eugenio Barba, Julia Varley as Mr Peanut
Photo: Fiora Bemporad

The hardest phase is when Eugenio abandons the actress's perspective and assumes the spectator's point of view. A lot of material is eliminated. Whole scenes, that I have worked on for months and am particularly fond of, disappear. New texts or unfamiliar objects are introduced and I must be able to integrate and justify them. Many observers are perplexed when faced with the director's power. The interruption and fragmentation of the actress's logic seems to be limiting rather than enriching.

I believe that my creative freedom expands through the meeting/clash with the director who imposes limits, doesn't accept the obvious and insists on digging deeper and deeper. He encourages me to go to the core and concentrate on my personal process. The dialogue with Eugenio's way of thinking and reacting, and with the overall dramaturgy of the performances in which I act and for which he has ultimate responsibility, has enabled me to discover my own dramaturgy as an actress and realise that this has an influence on the director's decisions.

My collaboration with Eugenio has continued for more than thirty years with periods of greater or lesser incomprehension and difficulty. This long-lasting collaboration with the same director forces me not to repeat myself. I am spurred on to find new solutions and tasks. Dramaturgy becomes a fertile battleground. Mutual knowledge gives us both more trust and autonomy. As a director Eugenio is the main point of reference for my work as an actress: he knows where I come from, where I am today, and he confronts me with the necessary and useful challenge of surprising both myself and him with where I will go next.

The surgeon and the mountaineer

Since 1990 I have accompanied Eugenio Barba on many workshops for directors, listening to the stories he repeats to tackle basic questions on directing and montage and to explain his personal technique. The first workshop was held in Cardiff, in Wales, and was followed by more in Italy (Bergamo, Fara Sabina, Scilla, Bellusco, Palosco, L'Aquila . . .) and in other parts of the world (Philadelphia in the United States, Puangue and Santiago in Chile, La Sarraz in Switzerland, Coventry in England, Buenos Aires, Mexico City, Cairo, Taipei, Brasilia . . .). Every time the initial catalyst was a question: is a pedagogy for directors possible? Does a knowledge exist that is valid for every director and can be transmitted as a technique?

Theatre Anthropology, according to Eugenio Barba's definition, attempts to give performers useful advice on how to acquire stage presence and find valid working principles beyond style, experience and personal aesthetics. Through the dialogue with participating directors and the relation of their own experiences, the challenge of these workshops was to enquire whether objective technical principles existed for the craft of the director. Eugenio pointed out that his work as a director focused on three autonomous levels of dramaturgy: narrative, organic (or dynamic) and evocative. In the workshops he concentrated on organic dramaturgy and its relationship with narrative dramaturgy. He omitted evocative dramaturgy because, as yet, he didn't feel ready to offer general principles.

For me the workshops were an opportunity to identify my specificity as an actress. They were a welcomed opportunity and another field on which we could meet and clash, implementing the dialogue between actress and director. At each workshop Eugenio told simple stories that I have noted down. I admired his ability to present these stories in a different way every time, as if he wanted to squeeze from them a meaning that still evaded him. The stories were supplemented by comments with which I agreed, or by suggestions for directors that revealed a way of thinking with which I was acquainted only through a tacit practice. Eugenio's stories – some of which are presented below – are a testimony of expectations and difficulties, ideals and subterfuges that accompany us in the daily routine of our professional lives.

> When Christopher Columbus arrives on the coasts of the Americas it is difficult for him to describe his discoveries in the letters he sends to the Spanish court. To convey the astonishment of a strange new world he is forced to make comparisons with what is known. He speaks of trees more luxuriant than the oranges of Seville, of flowers more perfumed than the roses of Malaga, of fruit sweeter than melon but shaped like a big thorny apple – a pineapple.

One should not aim directly at the target. Illustration and tautology are enemies, something that in Scandinavian is called *smør på flæsk* (butter on fat). To reach an end that surprises us, the most fertile path often begins from the opposite direction.

> When hunters want to shoot a bird in the air, they don't aim directly at it, but point the rifle a little further forward. If I want to go to Jerusalem, which is to the south of where I am right now, I start by walking to the door that is to the north. I set out in the opposite direction to reach my destination.

The director chooses suitable language to communicate with the actress. Evocative or neutral words, their intonation, whether whispered or spoken out loud, said with a smile or seriously, the choice of poetry or prose – all this has emotional and rational consequences for the actress and influences her reactions. The manner of introducing the theme for an improvisation or of speaking of events belonging to a wider shared context needs to provoke the actress's imagination and memory and open up a range of personal options. The actress has to receive information that stimulates her to make concrete actions (hence the importance of active and transitive verbs), but that also leaves her absolute freedom to develop the opposite sense of the theme. The theme creates a framework that contains oxymora and contrasts, and above all empty spaces that extend the horizon of the improvisation instead of limiting it to illustration of the text or of the director's task. The theme of an improvisation builds a space similar to a house with doors and windows from which the actress can escape. The theme of an improvisation is not in direct relationship to the performance, but can be connected with it associatively. It can be a laconic or evocative word or sentence, or the verse of a poem that the actress unravels, or a story that introduces a complex situation.

> During an ISTA session devoted to improvisation Katsuko Azuma, the Japanese Nihon Buyo dancer, was asked to give an example of how she improvised. We were uncertain as to how she would solve the task because, in her tradition, dances and performances have been fixed and passed on in the same form for generations. Katsuko repeated three times a scene about a monk who sees a ghost, asking us at the end if we had noticed the variations. To all of us the scene seemed identical every time. We begged her to repeat it. Again she asked us if we had seen the differences, but to her surprise we confirmed our incapacity to ascertain any change, however minuscule. She repeated it again and once more we didn't observe anything. Finally she explained: 'The first time the ghost appeared five metres away from the monk, the second time ten metres away and the third thirty metres. The focus of my eyes changed accordingly.'
>
> Kanichi Hanayagi, another Nihon Buyo dancer, gave a similar example. Before starting a scene that takes place in a cherry orchard he decides what season it is and whether the imaginary trees around him will be in bloom or covered with snow, green or bare.

At the beginning the actress needs a solid foundation to lean on, even though we know that the final form will depend on many other factors. It is the organic aura of the actress's actions that decides the life of the performance. An actress's actions are like bricks.

> If we want to build something we need bricks of good quality. Then we can decide to build a mosque, a bank, a hospital or a brothel with those same bricks.

In the first phase of work the actress improvises and creates material. She feels that the director's trust in her is total. Her work is not judged and complete freedom of action is guaranteed. In the second phase the director improvises on the basis of the elements fixed by the actress. The director cuts, adapts, models and kneads the material without the actress criticising or requesting explanations that the director is probably not yet able to give.

The director improvises making a montage of the actress's material while being aware of Poincaré's theorem on the instability of matter: when more than two influences overlap the result is mathematically unpredictable.

> Some French ethologists were investigating the language of crows to study their behaviour. After many months of patient observation and recording they discovered that the crow's caw is in fact an aggressive and threatening call to defend its territory and keep other birds at a distance. This apparently useless discovery later turned into an effective procedure adopted by farmers. They placed a recorder that regularly repeated the crow cawing to keep the birds away from their fields.

When exploring, we do not know in advance what the final result will be, nor how it will be used. At the beginning of a creative process we concentrate on the preliminary tasks to be solved without foreseeing their outcome. Strange and sometimes confused questions and suggestions provoke our curiosity and induce us to make digressions along the way. It is important to know the technical principles that underlie the process, but it is unproductive to anticipate what the performance that is growing will be. We must know *how* to proceed, *how* to sense the next step, *how* to detect the clue that will orientate us and above all *how* to wait actively, by doing.

In preparing a performance the point of departure can be a text, a story, a theme, a core of questions. In the first phase of the process, the director protects and motivates the actress who is free to follow the meandering of her own associations, the eccentricities of her imagination and wishes, to produce all her clichés and mannerisms. Only in a following phase does the director assume the spectators' point of view. He demands more and more from the actress, he evaluates and chisels her material and cuts, carves, shortens and condenses it in order to prioritise coherence, distil ambiguity and emphasise the story's conflicting elements. Following circumstances triggered by chance (serendipity) sometimes scenes evolve where everything seems accidental and gratuitous. The struggle to tame chaos can lead to unpredictable discoveries. Creation doesn't depend on inventing something new, but on identifying unknown connections and revealing unexpected relationships. The actress has to know how to deny the action at the same time as executing it in order to make the spectator vigilant.

> I am riding my bicycle. In front of me a man, also on a bicycle, pedals, his concentration tightly focused. All of a sudden he lifts his right arm. He doesn't extend it as one normally does before turning right, but bends the arm forward at the elbow – and in fact he doesn't turn right. A little later the man, still with his head down, clearly points up with his left arm. I look in that direction and see a bell tower. It seems to me that this cyclist is a bit strange and that his signalling is rather unusual. I increase my speed and overtake him. He is speaking to a child in front of him. His behaviour immediately becomes coherent to me.

The first and second scene of a performance need not be comprehensible, but the third one must allow the spectators to say to themselves: 'Ah! This is why they behaved in that way!' In the course of a performance there may be fragments and even long scenes that cannot be grasped conceptually, but the spectators lose interest in what they are watching if their state of mental and emotional apathy lasts too long. It is crucial to maintain the spectator's attention – hence the importance of organic dramaturgy.

> If you see someone in the street looking up at a balcony and really seeing something, you will also stop and look up. If after some seconds nothing happens, you move on.

Theatre is the art of telling through physical and vocal actions and its first imperative is not to be boring. The director should be able to convey the entire complexity of the performance in one sentence, but at the same time it should be impossible to articulate the experience of a performance. Theatre offers an opportunity to reveal stories that are enigmas, and enigmas that throw light on our experience. The technique consists of *how* to tell, keep alive and lead the attention of the spectator, *how* to build the succession of events, suspense and surprise for the spectator. The montage of materials in a performance follows the living logic of oral storytelling, which doesn't respect linearity of space and time. The montage of actions functions like a crotchet hook: we operate on the form to create holes as a result of which patterns become visible.

> If you describe your brother to someone else, your story will jump forwards and backwards in time, it will go from physical description to remembered events, from friends you have in common to ways of dressing.

In theatre, precision is synonymous with necessity.

> A surgeon who operates on an eye cannot make an incision a millimetre slightly to the left or to the right. The precision of the cut is decisive: it blinds or gives sight back. Unfortunately, our profession is the only one that doesn't involve legal sanctions if we are inaccurate.
>
> On one occasion, the carpenter who helped us build our theatre came to see one of our performances. On the way out he commented that he had understood very little, but that he had appreciated the actors' work. It was well done. He had noticed the attention to detail and the finish of the actions, qualities that are rare nowadays but were at one time taught to artisan apprentices.

Theatre is the art of letting the spectators hallucinate. At first the spectators see a tall or small, blonde or dark, chubby or slender actress on stage. Her hair is loose and she is dressed in white: she personifies Ophelia. At the end the spectators should be moved by a young girl invaded by a madness that is, in fact, pretence.

There is a difference between metaphor and symbol. In theatre the art consists of building metaphors through the real actions of the actress. The spectator's hallucination happens because of the metaphor, and not because an action or an object symbolises something else. The action is always literal to the spectator. The actress's art consists of transcending this literalness.

> One day I took my three-year-old son to see a performance for children. An actor had taken off his sock on stage and put it on his hand while moving his arm like a snake. My son asked me why the actor had removed his dirty sock from his foot and was waving it about with his hand.

Actions are made fascinating and persuasive by their organic quality. The spectators 'know' even if they don't 'recognise' what the actress is doing. Their attention is kept by *how* the story is narrated, rather than by what is told. Theatre is an organic relationship between two living beings, the spectator and the actress. The relationship changes radically at a distance of more than seven or eight metres; at that point the small changes of tension in the actress's body are no longer perceived by the spectator. All five senses together with the sixth kinaesthetic sense participate in the intellectual and emotional experience that a theatre performance offers in the here and now.

> When another cat enters the room my cat reacts, although it continues to sleep peacefully even if a tiger appears on the television screen.

In theatre the most effective language is that of the body, and it is made up of impulses that act on the spectator's nervous system. The actress expresses emotions through physical and vocal actions.

> I had recently emigrated to Norway and I didn't know the language. On the tram I always tried to decipher the body language of the other passengers. I wanted to understand, when they moved to make a place for me, whether they did it out of kindness or to keep me at a distance.
>
> The great Japanese sword master Musashi taught his pupils that, confronted with an adversary, they had to focus only on becoming one centimetre taller.

Two distinct conventions exist in theatre: stage behaviour that resembles everyday life (the convention of verisimilitude) and modified or stylised behaviour that recreates on stage a sense of life through actions that are 'real' but not realistic (the convention of formalisation). Verisimilitude aims at stage behaviour that is recognisable in our everyday existence, while in a formalised (codified) genre the behaviour is the result of artificial composition (classical ballet or different kinds of Asian classical theatre).

> Looking at a classical ballet performance, not only do we accept the unnatural behaviour of the ballet dancer, but we begin to think that all human beings should walk in a way that annihilates weight and gravity.

The actress's actions should transmit a sense of life to the spectator. This means that they must have an organic effect. This can also be obtained by remaining faithful to the starting point, for example when deciding to move on tiptoe in classical ballet. Different impulses, rhythms and tensions reveal a coherence that respects the complexity of the starting point. Coherence persuades the spectator even if the actress's behaviour is unusual, because the spectator perceives the real – although hidden – motive that supports the choice that has been made. When coherence is lacking, formalism appears: form without information.

What is alive and organic, indissolubly contains its opposite: the actress should deny the action and the director should deny the literal meaning.

> If I throw a needle, a handkerchief and a heavy dictionary on to the floor, and then go to pick up one of the objects, even before I bend down the tension of my fingers reveals which object I intend to take. To fight against this predictability I lean towards one object but pick up another at the last moment. Or I take one object as if it had the form and weight of another.
>
> Meyerhold was the first to think something unthinkable: to conceive physical actions separately from the words that accompany them. When observing two people chatting at a bar from a distance, their behaviour and reactions, although small and contained, reveal the kind of relationship they have.

There are performances in which both the actress and the spectator know the story, others in which only the actress knows the story, others in which neither knows it. When the tale is known to the spectators, their attention is captivated by *how* it is told and by the network of events that happen at the same time and independently from the story. The interpretation of a performance is given by the quality of information present in the scenes, and not by the narrative content. The efficacy of an actress is revealed by her ability to be real and ambiguous, to move from the literal to the metaphorical.

> We presented a clown performance to the Yanomami, an indigenous Amazonian tribe. There was a particularly amusing spaghetti scene. The indigenous people didn't understand; they were troubled by our laughter and looked at us with apprehension gripping their spears and arrows more strongly. They had never seen spaghetti before.

In contrast to drama, humour is not transcultural. There are experiences common to all human beings: being loved and accepted; feeling betrayed or humiliated; witnessing the death of a person we love or a birth; believing in something to the point of self-sacrifice ... A performance that enables the spectators to relive these experiences moves them despite any strange stage convention, style or alien cultural reference. For some spectators theatre is necessary because it evokes these moments. The conventions may be unknown, but dance and song often succeed in touching us because they allow us to establish an intimate and personal bond with the performance we are watching.

> If a dog entered this room my first impulse would be to leave. I am afraid of dogs: I was bitten twice in Latin America. But knowing that in this country dogs are not aggressive and don't have rabies, I would be able to keep the impulse to run away under control. However I would start sweating, my heart would pound and I would go red in the face because of uncontrollable automatic reactions. Then – since I am Eugenio Barba standing here in front of you and you consider me to be a master, I cannot show my panic. So I would go up to the dog and stroke it.

Emotion is a complex reaction, which manifests itself through a multiplicity of reciprocally contradictory impulses. The actress should be able to make perceptible this behaviour, in all its contrasting motivations: legs move in one direction, hands in another, the eyes smile, the mouth cries.

> In *Elective Affinities*, Goethe describes the relationship between two cousins, a young girl and a grown-up. The girl is sent to boarding school. When she returns home ten years later, she runs up the stairs to the door of the house and kneels to embrace her older cousin's legs. The older cousin, embarrassed, asks the girl not to humiliate herself by prostrating before her. The girl looks up surprised and explains that she hugged her legs to experience again the feeling of warmth and safety that she remembered from her childhood.

Interpretation depends on one's own biography and every spectator embodies a personal point of view. The director works with these different points of view. The actress must know that the effect that her behaviour provokes doesn't correspond to the stimulus that gave birth to her actions.

> When I speak to you, I don't want to express something. I am only concentrating on making my words as clear as possible. I am interested in passing on some information to you, yet a part of me would like to be out in the sun reading a book. The tone of my voice creates an intimate or distant space which attracts or rejects you.

There are two centres on stage: one is geometric, the other dynamic. The dynamic centre is provided by the actress. The director plays with the spectator's perception alternating the relationship between the geometric and dynamic centre. Every time an actress makes an action the spectator's perspective should change. The voice, with its musical quality and range of intonation, its timbre and colour, plays with the space and continuously alters the sensorial perception of the spectator. Organic or dynamic dramaturgy affects the spectator through the actress's physical and vocal behaviour, independently from the meaning of the text.

Newspapers supply fast communication: the headlines immediately explain the content of the article. Poetry is slow communication; the information is condensed in unique verbal images that need reading over and over.

In order to create density and metaphor, it is useful for a director to be acquainted with the rules of poetic composition. Theatre is the art that inspires the spectator's imagination through density: it uses a maximum of compressed information in a lapidary form.

Richard Schechner speaks of performances that are like banquets in which the spectator can choose from many courses and of performances that have a fixed menu.

If the performance takes place on a stage that the spectators can't take in in one glance, they are forced to choose where to look, thus creating their own dramaturgy and montage. Every detail of the performance has a reason for being. Some spectators focus on actions that others overlook. The more information a form contains, the more density and complexity is created, and the more premises are given for the experience of life in theatre. The spectators develop their own story from the received stimuli. The director must know the reason for every detail of the performance, and for mistakes that have not been corrected.

An imperfection is always left in the most elaborate and beautiful Persian carpets. Muslims know that only God is perfect.

The director strives to demand the utmost. She or he is the repository of rigour, a quality that the spectators don't need to have. The director should be a creative and competent manager, an effective pedagogue and an imaginative leader, setting an example by working twice as hard as anyone else.

Mountain climbers in a team know that they are all responsible for each other's lives. Every climber is aware that the peak can only be reached with humility: this achievement depends on every single step, on how a foot is placed and on the encouragement given to those who become tired.

The land belongs to those who work it. The performance belongs to the spectator who knows how to make it productive.

The performance is a complex organism because it is made up of different levels of organisation: organic, narrative and a deeply subjective evocative level. Although the different levels are inseparable in the final result, during the process one needs to proceed without mixing them up. Both an organic and a narrative level are present in the physical actions; a sonorous and a semantic level in the vocal actions.

The organic or dynamic dramaturgy arises from the interaction of all the impulses that have an impact on the spectator's nervous system. The dynamic dramaturgy determines 'organicity' – synonymous with life – and the breath of the performance. The behavioural synchrony – the link between all the smallest physical impulses and the accompanying words – is the foundation that supports the organic dramaturgy. The aim of life is to stay alive; the aim of the dynamic dramaturgy is to have an organic effect on the spectator. The intention is not to create meanings, to convert to socialism or to pray to one of the many divinities.

The narrative dramaturgy is often provided by words that need to become the Word. The evocative dramaturgy touches the intimate realm of the spectators arousing a different resonance in each of them. It represents the moment of truth. A spectator can be made to react on the spur of the moment. It is difficult to devise a performance that provokes delayed reactions, acting slowly like a tropical parasite or a scorpion's poison.

    I.   You will work with constraints and ought to know how to exploit and give them value.
    II. You will address one, several or all of the spectator's nine senses.

During the most recent workshops, Eugenio considered compiling some 'recipes' and 'commandments' for directors. He dreamed of writing a manual of directors' techniques. So in May 2000 at Teatro India, directed by Mario Martone in Rome, Eugenio and the directors who participated in the workshop agreed upon the first two commandments.

The discussion became animated when a kinaesthetic, a medium (as in spiritualism), a historical and an intellectual sense were mentioned in addition to the five human senses, and when the verb 'narrate' was replaced by 'address' or 'tell'. All the participants agreed that the director's creativity has more to do with constraints than freedom and that the director operates in the three intersecting fields of organisation (social), organism (structural complexity) and 'organicity' (being in life).

    Meyerhold was betrayed by his actors.

I conclude this compilation of stories for directors with this sentence, often repeated by Eugenio. It reveals an aspect of the complex relationship between actress and director, in which trust and distrust, love and intolerance, unity and detachment co-exist.

The peasant and the cook

It was as an actress that I assisted Eugenio Barba in the directors' workshops where I collected the stories I have called 'The Surgeon and the Mountaineer'. As an actress I represented a different point of view: that of the person who moves in space and acts with an embodied knowledge. I associate this point of view more with the work of a peasant or a cook. During the workshops this approach prevented Eugenio's advice and words from becoming the 'Barba method', and stopped the confidence with which our experience was presented giving the impression that it is easy to reach results. Giving body to words, in the material sense of the term, I showed that a deep truth contains its opposite, and that a rule that is valid in one situation is inefficient in another. I had to demonstrate results to the participants and at the same time indicate the work and the way of thinking that precedes them, disclose some of the difficulties and still astonish, be both available and convincing. As an actress, I often had to contradict the director. From the conflicting and complementary information that we provided together, the workshop participants could draw the conclusions that were most helpful to their work.

Odin Teatret's pedagogic activity has primarily been dedicated to the performer's work. The occasions focusing on the specific skills required to compose a performance are rare. Eugenio started giving workshops for directors after more than twenty years with Odin Teatret when the group's performers were already autonomous masters both in creation and training.

The teaching in workshops is suffocated by lack of time. It requires verbal explanations and practical shortcuts that replace the hours, months and years necessary to assimilate and mature direct experience. The performing principles that have been implicitly incorporated after many years at Odin Teatret, are explained, analysed and exemplified during the workshops in just a few hours. The knowledge that was passed on to me through months of tacit practice becomes an understanding that is only conceptual. A more emotional place is reached when technical questions are put aside to speak about motivation.

In the directors' workshops the words reflected reality askew because they had to clarify and make accessible complex and hidden processes. As if they were the presuppositions on which the work is predicated, the words explained conclusions that have been understood at Odin Teatret only after long practical experience. During the workshops ways of proceeding were reconstructed verbally as if at Odin Teatret we were aware from the very beginning of how to reach certain results. Eugenio answered the participants' questions. I often shook my head and then added another point of view.

The workshops started from knowledge that the participants had read in books. It was difficult for them to imagine that this had not always been so. They couldn't envisage that the work language we use every day to communicate as actress and director at Odin Teatret is completely different. Our concrete work helps us to find unexpected theatrical solutions; the reflections that acquire the value of theory are written subsequently. In everyday practice Eugenio often behaves without considering his books, almost as if they were written by others.

In a workshop we tend to explain, while during rehearsals at Odin Teatret we rarely discuss. We try to let our actions dialogue without revealing our intentions and aims. Disagreements are resolved by making alternative proposals. Only those not accustomed to the persuasive power of actions would attempt to solve problems through words. During the workshops the participants want to clarify their intentions by speaking, while Eugenio needs me as actress to demonstrate without comment.

I have directed some performances and am aware that the kind of energy I use as a director is completely different from that I draw on as an actress. I know how much effort is necessary to transform a shapeless mass into tangible energy that can take off and fly. As actress I sleep at night because problems resolve themselves through action while rehearsing. As director I remain in my bed with my eyes open imagining the endless consequences of my suggestions, while potential solutions run around in my head. The director's responsibility is heavier and, as director, I have become aware of the difficulties that must be faced in order to lead performers and compose performances.

It is not always the director who determines the course of a performance. I organised the first Transit Festival in 1992 on this theme. I had noticed how, within the Magdalena Project network, many women had started directing after having been actresses and how many actresses had produced performances on themes vital to them, forcing their male directors to follow. I was searching for a word to describe the element that drives a performance, which is sometimes associated with a person, sometimes with the group and sometimes passes from one person to another. I chose 'conducting' in the sense of the passage of energy in electricity. The themes, stage solutions, character creation, text montage are not always the responsibility of one person called the director, but are 'conducted' during the process by a *collective mind* and organism. In fact the 'conductor' moves among the different components engaged in the process, to disappear at the end so that only the performance remains as a living entity.

After many years at Odin Teatret I have learned to recognise intuitively what our director is hoping to achieve. At the same time, as an actress, I know that it is more rewarding to follow a personal associative path rather than attempt to materialise directly someone else's visions. In creative work, resistance, contiguity and divergence are more helpful than conformity. Eugenio explains to the workshop participants that when he gives a theme for improvisation, it is better if the actress does not know the director's aim or intention because she might illustrate the theme, thus running the risk of tautology and being one-dimensional. This was true for me in the early years.

When I started I was helped by the fact that the themes of the improvisations were not directly connected to the theme of the performance. With time, however, I learned that a literal reading can be an incentive to pursue unusual solutions as well. If my only choice is to illustrate, I need to know how to hide that illustration and make it unrecognisable. Through association I enrich or transform the theme or text with unrelated material. The workshop participants wondered why it was necessary to distance oneself so much from the theme. Eugenio and I both answered that this helps us discover what we don't know and that this procedure often characterises research in both science and art.

During the directors' workshops I exerted myself and sweated. Eugenio gave the participants the impression that he was the director who retains power and makes decisions. They wanted to protect me from him and help me. They asked how I reacted to being manipulated by the director when my improvisations and materials were cut, changed and reassembled. Those observers didn't recognise that I was being offered the opportunity to give the best of myself by the director's demands. Contrary to appearances, a director who insists on the impossible, in order to ensure the quality of what the spectator receives, strengthens my autonomous identity. I don't need to worry about the final result, about what the spectators will see and understand. I can concentrate on my own work. Released from having to observe and judge myself from the outside, I can pursue the disordered threads of my interests and needs, in an attempt to let my actions say what I cannot explain in words.

When I direct, it is the actress's way of thinking that prevails in me. I build on my experience, on my knowledge of the sense of an action, even though I am sitting on a chair and observing. Some directors work with what they have previously imagined. Eugenio works with what he sees in front of him. Faced with the actress's improvisations or material, he is able to transform his reaction into an action that develops unexpected perspectives. This has taught me both to be concrete as an actress and, when I work as a director, to guide patiently, allowing a plurality of meanings and details to emerge slowly from the material presented to me by the performers.

The University of Eurasian Theatre, Eugenio Barba and Sanjukta Panigrahi, Fara Sabina, 1993

Photo: Fiora Bemporad

The director observes from the outside and intervenes to guide the actress who is a different and separate person from her or himself. It is not the director's body that is active in space, but her or his ability to see and offer inspirational comments for the other person to enact. The director uses her or his own body intelligence, senses and memory to evoke images, and needs to know how to choose words or silences that communicate these instructions. I have always experienced the director as the antithesis who helps the synthesis materialise. Eugenio speaks of his actresses and actors as his alter ego, an extension of himself with whom he can improvise and project himself in space and time. Through our collaboration as actress and director we succeed in reaching a representation of reality that contains conflicting aspects. To me as actress and Eugenio as director the same situation appears different. Instead of this being an impediment, it is an incentive to work together.

As an actress I create from myself. This doesn't mean necessarily that my actions on stage are rooted in psychology or in my intimate self, but that I begin from my body, from my own being on stage. Even if I ignore my ego and consider only the effect of what I do, as an actress I see a reflex and listen to an echo of what I have initiated directly. In order to make an action, I transmit information to myself, directly, within my body and with my own senses; I let my physical intelligence lead me without interference. Passages happen without external explanations; intelligence is already immediate action, faster than light: it is a process that is difficult to explain in words, because it is wordless.

In representing the actress's point of view during the workshops, I keep searching for examples of women who might help me introduce the value and particular intelligence of incorporated actions into theatre history. It is an effective and not objective intelligence, but it reveals some truths to me; however my effort is still unsuccessful. Eugenio explains that one of the technical levels consists of *how* to tell: you can narrate like Dostoyevsky or Joyce, Proust or Tolstoi, Marquez or Balzac ... Faced with a list of male names, at times I feel tired and think that the struggle is futile. Then I start to dance and find the energy to continue once more.

It is useful for me to imagine that my cells have a memory and intelligence, and that my whole body thinks. The director explains that an actress should be like the waves of the sea or flakes of snow so that every action is different and rich in detail; or he maintains that an actress should radiate in all directions like the sun. As an actress I know that if I succeed in being sea, snow and sun, it is because I concentrate on what helps me to become sea, snow and sun unwittingly.

The body's mind stores experience as knowledge. The course it follows is illogical and reacts quickly, changing in a process similar to intuition. As an actress I have learned to let my feet think, I am 'animal', but this does not mean I have less soul, mind and imagination. I also try to use this particular way of thinking when I direct and in my everyday life. I live with both points of view.

9 The performance

Replica and difference

When I am working on a performance I don't feel as though I already have something predetermined to say and that I only have to find how to say it. I have a starting point, a pretext, some questions or concerns that initiate a process at the end of which I will discover what I have to say. Sometimes I become aware that I have expressed something particular because of a spectator's way of looking at me, or hugging me and crying after the performance. In those moments words are superfluous.

It is not easy to give advice on how to make contact with our hidden motives and personal needs, our creative engine and the submerged world of rules and disorder. Experience helps us trust the logic of our associations and discover the structures within which these can act freely. The level of my actress's dramaturgy that is not to do with technique is concealed in the shadows. There my need to make theatre joins my paradoxical ambition to leave a mark of my own on the course of history.

Coming from an amateur theatre, not provided with tools of the craft, I was stunned when on one of my first days at Odin Teatret I was asked to buy three bells at a price that seemed exorbitant to me. I was even more bewildered when the director decided not to use them because they were not suitable for the street performance he was rehearsing. I wondered what this behaviour meant in a so-called poor theatre. I understood it when I saw another company's performance, which had technical lighting effects, movable curtains, a floor that revolved and shifted in different directions, while accompanied by a recorded soundtrack. Ping pong balls and paper plates were the main performers. When the performance finished I couldn't remember the faces of the actresses and actors. They had been swallowed up by a technical apparatus that was stronger than them.

I think that the richness of poor theatre is the work of the actress, the freedom to devote time to process and to consecrate personal resources to creation. This wealth does not respect any particular moral code and is only justified by what the performance necessitates. The accounts finally balance: the bells were later used in two other productions, *The Million* and *Brecht's Ashes*.

I am really happy when I am working alone in the rehearsal room. This usually happens during the holidays, in the period when a new performance is beginning to take shape. The theatre is empty and I can stay as long as I like. I sing, invent costumes, play with props and create sequences of actions. A feeling of euphoria comes over me where nothing is obliged to make sense, or be believable or effective, and yet meanings and stories pop up in my mind and in and out of the space. I really enjoy the solitude of research, of being at the beginning of a process that is not yet geared to results, when the only rudder is the special way of thinking that I have learned as an actress.

Theatre is my way of establishing relationships. I don't necessarily connect visibility to materiality and invisibility to spirituality in order to obtain stage presence. The energy and motivation that dictate the actions that the spectators see and hear are concrete for me because they constitute the breath of my body's cells. I am aware that I want to provoke a different understanding of my actions in each spectator and that I aim to share an experience rather than to represent. Every day theatre teaches me to deal with personal truths and not with something that is objectively right or wrong.

During rehearsals it is the performance that decides what is necessary and what is redundant. It walks on its own legs and chooses for itself. The performance tells stories, some of which are clear, others to be deciphered. It always demands slight variations and I adapt to its development.

At Odin Teatret a performance remains the same night after night, without being identical. It also grows as a result of the reception given by spectators. As actress I try to be precise, decided, whole, present in the here and now, even though I know how and when the performance will end. I discover new details and dance with the attention of the spectators, attracting and rejecting it. I strive to give the spectator the feeling that every evening the performance is rich in variations, even if it is the same. Only the director is aware of the minuscule changes.

Some spectators, when they come back to see one of our performances again, comment on the changes they have noticed. In reality the scores and scenes are identical. This sense of difference is due to a total mastery of the score and the freedom the actress experiences after repeating the performances many times. The first showings of a performance don't yet have the assurance that is achieved after months of being on tour and having to adapt constantly to different rooms and acoustic conditions. In the fully developed performance a person who seems insignificant and of average height in everyday life can acquire a special kind of beauty, a transparency that simultaneously reveals and conceals a secret. The huge amount of time dedicated to rehearsals, confined in a room that seems to have run out of oxygen, is justified: the reward is a performance with its own life that travels around the world to encounter spectators. It is around the performance work that the whole of Odin Teatret really comes together.

At Odin Teatret time is measured by performances. They remind us of what happened at that period. With *Anabasis* I officially joined the group;

with *The Million* I learned to play the trombone; with *Brecht's Ashes* I worked for the first time with a director; during *The Gospel According to Oxyrhincus* I got divorced; to prepare *Talabot* I travelled alone to Asia for the first time; *Kaosmos* gave birth to Doña Musica; *The Castle of Holstebro* was created when I fell in love again after a long time; *The Rooms of the Emperor's Palace* was presented to close the second theatre group meeting in Peru; in *Ode to Progress* Mr Peanut put on women's clothes; *Mythos* began after a trip to Australia, *Inside the Skeleton of the Whale* with a meeting in which I wept from exhaustion and *Andersen's Dream* after having been to Egypt and Syria; *Doña Musica's Butterflies* was rehearsed in hotels in Spain and Italy, and in Odin Teatret's white room; *The Great Cities under the Moon* reminds me of the celebrations for our group's fortieth anniversary; I bought the first costume for *The Echo of Silence* in a shop in Copenhagen's pedestrian street; rehearsing *The Dead Brother* I broke a projector in Grotowski's theatre in Wroclaw; *The Whispering Winds* belongs to the period when I managed to explain clearly the difference between movement and action; *Text, Actions, Relationships* was made to meet Tage again and to confront a classical text; *The Flying Carpet* when I knew how to run through thirty years of performance in fifty minutes in public.

The performance is a ceremony, a fixed structure that returns and represents itself in the same way every day, recreating an identical space and time within which energies, stories, meanings, senses and needs come together. The spectators seem distant: they take away whatever they require for themselves. The capacity to establish a dialogue with them does not come from paying attention to their demands and tastes, but from my own concentration on the actions and motivations, situations and questions raised by the performance. Generosity – one of the qualities I appreciate most in an actress – consists of a rigorous and minute preparation for a potential experience, through coherent actions that aim to touch the senses of every one of the spectators. The performance is a way to make the spectator creative through stimuli offered by the actresses' and actors' presence on stage.

My preparation for a performance is a sequence of personal rituals. I repeat simple actions: I iron my costume, put my props in place, go through my texts quietly, get dressed, brush my hair and put some make-up on. I need to recognise the people and energy in the room as identical every time: just before the performance, I don't like being disturbed by external noises, by voices with which I am unfamiliar, strangers or unexpected problems. I am ready about five minutes before we begin. I wait standing or sitting if the costume permits. I feel empty and sleepy. At the end of the performance I just feel tired. I take off my sweaty costume and my make-up, I brush my hair again, collect my props and put them away every night in the same way. I don't like meeting spectators immediately after the performance. I am careful not to ask them what they think of what they have just seen, as I respect their right to react freely. Both before and after the performance I need to be alone and in silence.

Preparing for *Talabot* I painted my nails and warmed my voice up by going over my texts and songs. After the performance I took a shower to remove the thyme from my face and the smell of the fish and beer that had been thrown at me during the Iceland scene. Before *Mythos* I stretched my muscles by lying on the set's red carpet, and brushed my hair and put on my costume in the performing space. At the end I was the only actress to remain hidden on stage with the technicians who saw the spectators out. Doña Musica, whose make-up is complicated, waits instead for the audience to enter before appearing from the dark, and at the end exits to hide while the spectators applaud the figure of death who has taken her place.

Each time we have a new production we return to the cities Odin Teatret has visited in the past to meet our spectators once again. The performance spaces that we reconstruct with exact measurements in theatres, squares, churches, gyms, markets, museums, schools and jails in different countries, allow me to feel at home and recognise what surrounds me. Today I can say that my everyday existence is on tour. I live a nomadic life, even though I have a home in Holstebro where I keep my washing machine and a garden that I enjoy caring for. My family, friends and Odin Teatret's spectators are spread out all over the world. I travel within a network of people and theatre groups like ours, a complex of personal and professional contacts that we fight to protect and keep alive.

As a child I saw fairies in the refraction of light bulbs that had just been turned off; I enjoyed recognising the shapes they left on the walls, ceiling and my closed eyelids. Later I began telling stories to myself at night, pursuing the shadows and figures that my eyes perceived in the dark. I knew that I could not stop, because if I did the spell would be broken. I have rediscovered this pleasure in making up improvised stories with one of my godchildren, Meg Brookes. She gives me a title and, without hesitating, I invent. In 1977, for *Brecht's Ashes*, I felt unprepared for the creative work of a performance. Tage, who was my teacher at the time, told me I should trust the stories I glimpsed in the dark. I still follow his advice today, in 2005.

At the end of the fourth Transit Festival I was sitting with some 'grandmothers' of the Magdalena Project (Brigitte Cirla, Cristina Wistari Formaggia, Dawn Albinger, Deborah Hunt, Geddy Aniksdal, Gilla Cremer, Gilly Adams, Jill Greenhalgh, Luisa Calcumil, Maria Ficara, Sally Rodwell, Teresa Ralli, Ya-Ling Peng). I was drinking champagne and laughing with the women with whom close bonds of collaboration have united me since 1986. We were celebrating the freedom of not having to feel responsible any longer. We had passed through the childhood phase of apprenticeship and the adult phase of teaching.

In Montevideo, during a supper in a restaurant with the whole group, I received the silver spoon that Roberta Carreri has made the traditional gift for those who have stayed with Odin Teatret for twenty-five years. We had just finished a performance of *Mythos*. Among the spectators was Daniel Viglietti, the author and composer of *A desalambrar*, the song that

Guilhermino Barbosa sings in the performance, translated ironically by Ulysses, and that I used to shout as a young activist during the demonstrations and popular fêtes in Milan. I was once again in Montevideo when Atahualpa del Cioppo, the great theatre artist who founded El Galpón, came to compliment me after *The Castle of Holstebro*. I felt ashamed: just before the performance I had thought how tired I was and that my motivation to continue was getting weaker. He made me aware that motivation can also be a gift conveyed by the spectators.

At Holstebro, during a seminar on Indian theatre and dance in 1977, I was sitting at the feet of Shanta Rao, full of admiration, listening to this dancer who had not respected the rules and had become an exemplary teacher. In Ayacucho in Peru, during a tour in 1988, I looked with respect at Daniel Quispe and his group who, despite military and terrorist feuds and attacks, continued stubbornly to make theatre. After thirty years at Odin Teatret, I intuitively perceive the course that runs from the source to the sea. It is a fluid channel between being woman and actress, between events and coincidences, technique and motivation, craft and politics, process and consequence, personal necessity and social urgency, that continues to carry the foundations of my experience: stones of water.

Visiting Pablo Neruda's home in Piedras Negras, Chile, 1988
Jan Ferslev, Naira Gonzáles, César Brie, Lena Bjerregaard, Torgeir Wethal, Richard Fowler, Roberta Carreri, Iben Nagel Rasmussen, Eugenio Barba, Julia Varley, Poul Østergaard

Photo: Tony D'Urso

Odin Teatret's thirtieth anniversary in Holstebro
Torgeir Wethal, Kai Bredholt, Iben Nagel Rasmussen, Frans Winther, Pushparajah Sinnathamby, Jan Ferslev, Ulrik Skeel, Mariana Skeel, Eugenio Barba, Rina Skeel, Julia Varley, Else Marie Laukvik, Louise Andersen, Patricia Alves, Isabel Ubeda, Tina Nielsen, Sigrid Post

Photo: Fiora Bemporad

10   Faces, words, landscapes

In 2003 I received a letter that reminded me of the years when the Teatro del Drago would meet in a garage in Milan and, with Marco Donati, Clara Bianchi and others, I thought that theatre could help change the world:

Dear Julia,

It is a very hot evening in June (35 degrees); I am wet and sticky from head to toe. Tomaso [Marco and Clara's son] is on the balcony with three friends. They are studying like mad, from nine in the morning until midnight, every day, to prepare themselves for their imminent exams. A brief pause for supper (lovingly prepared by Clara, who is still incredulous that her son is studying so intensely) and then back to Kant, the nebulas, integral calculations, a little Virgil and the history of the right wing movement. They met at their theatre group and they have been together ever since. This year they played the *Oresteia* (a two and a half hour long performance). Tomaso was a kind of aedo [story-teller]; he connected the scenes between an Agamennon with a little bit of hair under his nose and the Erinyes (extremely good). Now and then the four of them talk of continuing to make theatre together, as the experience was too intense to be only a digression. I look at them with satisfaction and am moved. This is immortality, Julia; to see oneself reflected identically and differently at the same time in a story with which we are already familiar, with an actor who resembles us, and a friend of the protagonist called Giulia, in a parallel story that I decide after consideration not to tell them in order to see whether it ends as we already know or whether it is able to keep some surprises. Similar stories but never exactly the same, I say to myself as I keep on looking out of the window to enjoy the sight of them: twenty-year olds, beautiful, with energy to give away.

A big hug,

Marco

PS. Some good news: Berlusconi has lost the regional elections. Are my fellow countrymen returning to reason? Has it all been just a bad dream?

* * *

I landed in Sarajevo on my way to Mostar in August 2002. The war had ended, but not long enough before for it to be forgotten. One of the boxes containing props for my performance had not arrived. I received my first Bosnian money from the local Lufthansa office at the airport with the promise that the luggage would reach me the next day.

The organisers in Mostar had sent a car to fetch Ana Woolf (an Argentinian actress), Philip Doolan (Odin Teatret's Irish technician) and me. The driver spoke only a few words of English. I was very tired after an intense period of work and slept most of the way while the landscape changed from the green hills covered with pine trees around Sarajevo to the dry rocky mountains surrounding Mostar. We were driving towards the sea following rivers and lakes. Many construction sites and brand-new little houses could be seen around Sarajevo. As we approached Mostar the signs of war became more apparent: burnt walls and empty windows were all that was left of houses where families had lived once.

In Mostar we stayed in a new hotel on the main street. Sitting at a restaurant table, I faced the ruins of the old Neretva luxury hotel on the other side of the river of the same name. From my bedroom window I observed the shattered walls and a tree growing out of the window on the second floor of the remains of a house. The historical centre of town was not far away, I only had to follow the road that had been in the middle of the crossfire: on one side the Serb or Croatian army, on the other the Bosnian resistance; on one side the Orthodox Christians and on the other the Muslims; on one side the rich and on the other the poor. Along this road not one single house was standing. I noticed I was walking on some coloured tiles – the floor of a kitchen that was no longer there.

Amin Joha Hadzimusic and Sead Djulic came to welcome us. Sead – whom I soon learned to call Sejo – is the director of the Mostar Youth Theatre (MTM), founded in 1974, and of the Alternative Academy and International Theatre Festival, which is held every year in August. Joha is an actor who started as a young boy in the Youth Theatre and is now also the director's assistant and interpreter owing to his fluent English. They explained our schedule: a workshop, performances and work demonstrations. Other workshops were going on at the same time. The participants came from all over ex-Yugoslavia and from other European countries. Many of the original inhabitants of Mostar had moved elsewhere.

Mostar was famous for a bridge that connected the two parts of the historical town. Young boys used to dive from the bridge to show their daring. Tourists came from all over the world to admire its shape, which rose to a gentle point in the middle. It was built in 1566 by the architect Hajruddin at the time of Suliman the Magnificent during Ottoman rule. Postcards were on sale everywhere depicting the bridge. Alongside them were others showing the bridge being destroyed during the war, with 'don't forget' in red over the images.

One evening Sejo and Joha took us to see the site of the old bridge, which a Unesco project was then trying to rebuild. Some soldiers from the UN Peace

Corps were taking snapshots of the big blocks of stone that had been fished out of the water. I stared up at the mountain with the gigantic cross that overlooks Mostar. From there the Croatian army controlled the movements of the inhabitants. From there they shot at the legs of people going to collect water, so that others would come out to help them and more people could be killed by the snipers. From there they bombed the bridge. The commander who gave the order had been a theatre director. He had even worked with the Mostar Youth Theatre staging Brecht plays. Ana Woolf couldn't believe it. Sejo commented calmly: 'Now he lives in Zagreb; he is a wealthy businessman.'

I looked down at the flowing water of the river and the stones of the demolished bridge. I thought of the paradox of the bridge being destroyed by a theatre person and remembered all the times that the importance of theatre was revealed to me precisely in situations in which hope, social community and a normal daily life no longer seem possible.

The water flowing sometimes peacefully and sometimes impetuously in the river beneath the then non-existent Mostar bridge was a source of inspiration for a speech I made subsequently at the Festival Voix de Femmes in Belgium. Every two years, this festival brings together female artists and singers with the mothers, wives, daughters and sisters of the 'disappeared' from different countries. The festival is dedicated to cultures in resistance and is both an artistic and political achievement. Its special identity comes from the mixing of two worlds that would not normally meet. African, Asian, European and American voices fill the festival hall with their songs, music and rhythms while spectators dance, and declarations and testimonies from African, Asian, European and American women remind us of history's harsh reality.

I know of the tragedy of the 'disappeared' from my frequent tours to Argentina, Chile and Uruguay and because I have directed a production on this theme, but I always thought of it as a phenomenon confined to distant countries. The presence of mothers of Belgian children kidnapped by paedophiles, the sisters of men taken during the wars in ex-Yugoslavia and wives of Kurds imprisoned in Turkey reminded me that all this happens just round the corner from comfortable and civilised Denmark where I live.

The festival director, Brigitte Kaquet, used the image of a bridge to explain the relationship that the women who sing and the women who weep for their family members were establishing. Politics and theatre were nourishing each other, pain finding a voice in song, hope and struggle inspiring artists to persevere.

The image of Mostar's bridge being destroyed by a theatre director made me think that we should not build bridges between art and politics, between women struggling for justice and women struggling to create, between theatre and life. We should link these worlds differently. Bridges are made of stone; they are fixed and thus can be destroyed. Living connections are made of flowing elements. Affection, memories, gratitude, resentment, compassion, yearning, aspirations, the inability to forget, reconciliation, factual as well as emotional information pass from one person to the other, from one experience to the next, like the water of a river that goes from green mountains to rocky seashores, bathing opposing banks on its journey.

Personal engagement, human relationships, the sound of voices and the expressions on people's faces remain to give meaning to a shared resistance. The flowing element changes ceaselessly; it cannot be pinned down or described, in the same way that it is hard to measure the personal and historical consequences of these women meeting at a festival. They only leave traces in the subterranean history of theatre.

* * *

After ten years of absence, Tage Larsen returned to Odin Teatret in 1997 to play Oedipus in *Mythos*. He had left us in 1987 to create his own theatre group. Having left Odin Teatret he had to fight at first hand the battle to get funding, to resolve the conflicts of internal company dynamics and measure himself against the difficulties of theatre creation and production. In those ten years he also honoured his love for Shakespeare.

Tage was my guide during my first years at Odin Teatret and I consider him one of my masters. On his return, the first thing we did together was a work demonstration using a text from Shakespeare's *Othello*. We wanted to show a procedure that interpreted classical text starting from physical actions. Tage felt the need for a demonstration that put the accent on process instead of result and on the relationship between at least two people on stage.

Tage's absence from the group means that I have now been at Odin Teatret longer than he has. It is strange to be 'older' than my teacher, to discuss with him the importance of the relationship with text, props, music and between actresses and actors; of rhymes and intonations, of the freedom of improvisation and the capacity for repetition. The experience is common, but the time that we didn't share has created a vocabulary that we imagine to be different. It is unusual to find myself in the position of inspiring my trainer. The teachings that I now receive from this bond are different, although Tage remains for me the most solid example of a grounded actor.

Tage began making amateur theatre in the village where he grew up. He has often spoken to me of the film *Les enfants du paradis*, with Jean Luis Barrault, that turned his vision of theatre upside down. He remembers rehearsals for *My Father's House* (1972–4), on the life and works of Dostoyevsky, his first performance at Odin Teatret, for the commitment of someone who desperately wanted to belong to a group. He was a mason. Manual jobs still give him the stability and concrete support that he needs to create actors' material and characters. Among his idols are Marilyn Monroe, Marlon Brando and the Rolling Stones.

When I first got to know him, Tage played the violin in *Come! And the Day Will Be Ours* and a set of glass bottles in *The Book of Dances*. We started music lessons together, he played the trumpet and I the trombone. He still perseveres with music that now includes dedicating himself to an electric bass guitar. Tage also taught me Danish, despite which we still speak English to each other.

In 2001 I organised the third Transit International Theatre Festival, in Holstebro, on the theme Theatre – Women – Generations. The performances, workshops, meetings, debates and demonstrations were devoted to the transmission of incorporated theatre knowledge and to choices of ways of exchange between different generations of women theatre practitioners.

Iben Nagel Rasmussen, the teacher, and Maria Mänty, one of her students, presented a demonstration in Odin Teatret's white room. I was happy to be able to offer such a concrete example of the relationship between master and pupil to the other invited guests and participants. The difference in wisdom, precision and control was material, palpable, evident. Iben moved very little: every action was essential and necessary. Maria moved about quickly, displaying commitment and vitality: she was good, but she showed that she was. Iben would observe attentively, using just a few words to give instructions. Maria concentrated on performing the different exercises to illustrate to us in the best possible way the results of their common process. Iben resembled a tree trunk saturated with nourishing sap. Maria seemed like an energetic filly intent on dissipating its strength. Iben's backbone contained years of secrets, Maria's showed tensions, oppositions, directions, principles, actions. Iben *was*, without anxiety. Maria *wanted to be*. It was a moment of magic clarity.

Teaching has always been a priority for Iben. She has stubbornly pursued this need first at Odin Teatret by adopting a group of pupils that she called 'Hugin', the name of one of the crows that flies ahead of the mythological god Odin. Then she created the groups 'Farfa', 'The Bridge of Winds' and more recently 'The New Winds'.

Iben has always been particularly careful to make her students autonomous through research essentially dedicated to training. At first she taught exercises that she had invented and practised herself, later she chose to remain outside to observe, guide and give advice while her pupils invented exercises and principles themselves. The 'samurai steps' (different ways of walking with very bent legs, the weight towards the ground and the strong energy of a Japanese warrior), 'slow motion' (passive decelerated energy that moves like seaweed in water), 'green' (active energy retained by resistance as if advancing through porridge), 'the wind dance' (a collective dance characterised by a light double skipping step that follows the rhythm of the sound of breathing) are some of the characteristic exercises that she uses with her pupils. They can be encountered in numerous variations disseminated around the world. Iben, besides being a master, is the founder of a tradition.

Masters make the words of their teacher their own. Ingemar Lindh had totally absorbed the words of the philosopher of the body Etienne Decroux and, like him, he sang when executing mime *études*. Ingemar's face was full of wrinkles and he had a beard. He spoke Swedish, English and Italian, but only French when it had to do with corporeal mime.

He explained the *entraînement isométrique*:

> You must grasp eternity in an instant. A painting is active the whole time. Why didn't the painter wait for the action to go on five more minutes? The difficulty consists in not doing; to be immobile doesn't mean to be dead. *Isométrique* means to engage the muscles as if making the action, taking the intention all the way, exactly to the point when it is most dynamic and about to explode. This moment is exhilarating because it is compressed.
>
> Imagine blowing up a balloon; at the beginning it expands a lot, but it is not as interesting as when the pressure is at its maximum and the balloon is about to explode and only moves fractions of millimetres. An unexpected halt resonates in the space. When you say something important you stop: also when I think I am still, but active. When you are frightened of the dark and you hear footsteps, you don't move but you are in turmoil.

Ingemar was fascinated by the *prière* (prayer) that he considered to be his teacher's most abstract yet concrete figure. He also explained that the *prière* applies the causality principle of a sausage: when you squash one side everything comes out of the other. He clarified a rotation movement: 'You borrow Christ's nails to turn on your feet and remain in the same position.' Then he illustrated the counterweight: 'You jump upwards to go down, like children with the pump handle.'

Ingemar repeated:

> When you put your socks on you don't think about them. We are more honest in our minds than in what we say. I want to see not only the action, but also the intention. The essence is given by the way of being. The actor is only a bad copy if the essence is not there. I am because I act in a certain way. The less we move, the more we become essential and every time we move it must make sense. We don't repeat a movement many times in order to learn it, but to reconstruct it from different perspectives, to know it from inside and out, from left and right, to be able to execute it at any moment. Both in simple and complex actions an opposite always exists. Pleonasm is used by traditional theatre because of the belief that the meaning of things comes from the things themselves. We need to be in contact with what we feel, with a double hidden motivation, because drama cannot exist in absolute harmony. Also the exercises function as something other than oneself, with a separate identity of their own that we need to appropriate. Life is a sequence of accidental events; the daily practice of exercises helps us grasp chance signs like a radio receiver.

For each step, when the foot lifts from the ground, Ingemar recalled the image of a ski jump: 'The moment of take-off is magnificent! What danger! What freedom!'

Patricia Alves, a Brazilian transplanted to Denmark, was Odin Teatret's tour manager from 1993 to 2006. She assumed the fundamental role that had belonged to Agnete Strøm in the 1960s and to Leif Bech in the 1970s. It was her job to protect the performances from outside. Like a master, taking care of the smallest details, she gave a creative and human face not only to the work of organisation but to the meeting between our group and the people who had invited us.

* * *

In 1991, just as the first Gulf war had broken out, I was on tour in Chile with *The Castle of Holstebro*. I took advantage of a gap in the schedule to travel to the north of the country and see the Atacama Desert: an arid stretch of sand and salt; waves of white, coloured by dust, shining in the sun.

I arrived in Iquique by plane and rented a car. The first stop was at an abandoned miners' village. Wandering along its empty streets, I found myself in front of an immense wooden theatre, full of chairs and the ghosts of absent spectators. The floors creaked, the doors hung from their frames, the sky was visible through the ceiling and the wind whistled across the stage. It was spooky. I imagined performances that had disappeared leaving no trace. Now inhabited by the wind, the building was the only witness.

Driving towards the mountains, through sand and whirlwinds, I noticed the gigantic geometric drawings left by the ancient inhabitants still visible on the hills. Were they signs left for visitors from space? Signals for orientation? Sacred symbols? They were certainly very important messages, indecipherable today.

The car had to climb to three thousand metres while the carburettor protested. Because of the lack of oxygen, I approached Atacama's highland with jumps and puffs. Another van with the same problems had given up, so I picked up four men on the way, which made the climb even slower.

Inca mummies were exhibited at San Pedro de Atacama's museum. They had been buried in terracotta vases, curled up in a foetal position, the women enveloped in elaborate embroideries. I discovered the *quipu*: bundles of strings with tiny knots in different places, composed of threads of various consistencies and colours, joining and separating, long strings and short, some thick, some thin. The knots were as assorted as those used by sailors, knots over knots, simple and complicated. A text explained that the *quipu* were the Inca culture's computers or books: they stored information. Each knot had a meaning depending on its position, the amount of woven threads and shape. They were fascinating.

I was confronted with concrete images of how human beings pass on experience: the empty theatre, drawings on the sand hills, mummies and *quipu*. Outside I was surrounded by salt. The horizon was an endless lake of solid white on which pink flamingos were strolling.

It was in the Valley of the Moon, on my way to San Pedro de Atacama, before catching my first glimpse of the pink flamingos on the lake of salt, that a true silence shook me. I have worked for years on the theme of silence and have trained myself to listen to it, but never before had I experienced such a complete absence of sound. Nothing moved, nothing lived, nothing grew; even the sky seemed still: only rocks, stones, sand, brown, yellow, grey, gold, red, black. No plants, no animals, no green, no cactus, no ants, no people. Not even a drop of water. The sign saying 'Valle de la Luna' and the rented car reminded me that I was still in this world. Around me only barren, mute, dry mountains and plains.

I climbed up a hill – slowly because the air was thin – only to find a view of more sand and stones. I walked carefully along a ridge looking down at the golden crystals, at dark dust, at holes and spikes, at the flat and circular movements of the cliffs. With fear I breathed in the enormous landscape of silence and, as if by magic, I could perceive its hidden, imperturbable, ancient and enduring life.

Some time later in Brazil I visited a *terreiro*, the sacred house where the Afro-Brazilian Candomblé religion is practised. Stones planted in earth by initiated members indicated the 'foundation' of their religion. Helped by the humidity in the air and from the ground, these stones grow. It is true, they grow! They sprout and grow out of the earth where they were planted years earlier.

Knowing that a little humidity is enough to infuse life and that stones can grow changed the silence of the Valley of the Moon in my memory. It became a potential universe of voices and sounds, of music and songs. The rocks and sand became beings charged with secrets. The immensity of nature that surrounded me became an impressive horizon of wisdom. Life was waiting hidden in stillness. That silence made me think of the actress's inner being, of the secret that is not revealed, of the life that the spectator perceives although the actress does not display or show it.

* * *

Beside my grandfather's garden was an orchard that belonged to somebody I did not know. The best way down to the river at the bottom of the hill was along a path that crossed the orchard. It was a nice walk, in the shade of apple and plum trees, but I felt uncomfortable each time a grown-up decided we should go that way. As a child I was always respectful of 'no trespassing' signs, I did not like entering private property, I hated being in the wrong place and breaking rules. I preferred to conform and go unnoticed. I did not trust officials and policemen. I would try to persuade my mother not to climb over gates, explore cemeteries, enter closed doorways and peek up other people's driveways. Like my father I imagined that there was a bull in every field, that spirits would appear in the cemeteries and that nasty fierce dogs would defend their masters' grounds. In Italy where the countryside is mostly fenced in and in England where it is not, I preferred to go for walks along roads that were clearly public.

At the same time I did not want to conform to social rules: I was shy, I disliked conversation and parties, I hated discussions and arguments, I did not like what was considered proper behaviour. I felt embarrassed if my mother spoke to people in shops and on the streets, while I myself enjoyed being cheeky and disrespectful with friends. As a foreigner I could get away with most of my antisocial attitudes; being a stranger was a privilege.

Against all expectations, leaving university and ski-racing behind, I joined the world of theatre. I entered a territory where going against the rules is considered creative, travelling is a daily routine and being a foreign element in society is accepted. In theatre opposites meet and actions count more than words. Here I could live on the borderline without contravening the law. Theatre taught me to recognise paradox as the norm and to think differently, in a way often considered conservative by the revolutionary and revolutionary by the conservative. Theatre requires me mentally to jump over gates and trespass all the time; it incites me to be a vagabond and move on from the places I know.

From the garden of my grandfather's country house in Devon I could see the Tamar River making its way among the hills down to the sea. I was fascinated by the tides that emptied and filled the river bed alternating water and mud. I looked at the moored boats sitting upright on the water in an arrangement dictated by the wind and currents, and then saw them leaning sadly on their sides waiting for the tide to return. I would go with my brothers to inspect the dark water that hid crabs and seaweed. My brothers fished with string to which they tied small pieces of lard while I waited for the tide to take the river out to the sea so I could squash the bubbles of air in the mass of seaweed lying on slabs of stone by the shore.

I still carry in my purse a stone I picked up there. I left another stone that belonged to the Tamar riverbed in Humauaca, in Argentina, in exchange for a seed. I swapped that stone with the group El Baldío as a good luck token for the construction of a new theatre in the thin air of the Andes. Thus my childhood accompanies me to the other side of the world.

* * *

Jill Greenhalgh is the founder of the Magdalena Project: she organised the first festival in Cardiff in 1986. She was an actress with the group then called Cardiff Laboratory Theatre. In their last performance she had interpreted the biblical character of the Magdalene. Dressed in red, with long loose hair, Jill had a transgressive manner, vibrating with anger and insecurity.

We had been together two years earlier, in the summer of 1984 on Lake Bracciano in Italy, when we started dreaming of a new meeting among theatre groups. We were participating in an event during which six European

168 *Faces, words, landscapes*

companies collaborated in a performance directed by Tage Larsen. It was the lunch break. We decided that we would not invite complete groups to the next meeting, but only the most interesting people we liked. We immediately agreed that these were the women. At that time, the women showed more curiosity and initiative in the meetings, and also greater magnetic power on stage. Jill invited to Wales thirty-six actresses and some stage designers who came from all over the world. In so doing she threw into the water the first stone whose succession of waves and ripple effects – the Magdalena Project – is still expanding today from New Zealand to Colombia, from Australia to Belgium, from Singapore to Italy, from the Philippines to Argentina . . . Jill and I are close: we dedicate ourselves to planning activities together and to interpreting the development of the Magdalena Project. We have very different characters and often act as a complement for each other.

During the first Magdalena festival, we worked all together on a performance in a former potato factory. The spectators were supposed to pass through three rooms. In one of these a Czech actress had to introduce a scene called *The Magic Circle*. Just before the performance began, the actress had a crisis and refused to carry out her task. Panic! Jill started to cry desperately: she could not do this to her! The actress immediately returned to reason and Jill

Holstebro, Denmark, 1987
Elin Lindberg (Norway), Anne-Sophie Erichsen (Norway), Brigitte Kaquet (Belgium), Netta Plotski (Israel), Michelle Kramers (Switzerland), Lis Jones (Wales), Beatriz Camargo (Colombia), Julia Varley (Denmark), Mela Tomaselli (Italy), Geddy Aniksdal (Norway), Jill Greenhalgh (Wales)
Photo: personal archive

turned towards us with a radiant smile. Jill's weeping was an example of effective improvisation at its best. I will never forget it.

Jill has given me another important lesson. She has taught me to respect the limits of time, even if they go against my needs in the moment. During another meeting of the Magdalena Project in Cardiff, Jill had assigned every workshop one hour to present their work publicly. To give every participant in my workshop the possibility to show her sequence I went over the agreed time. I thought it right to respect the democratic principle of giving space to each woman. In reality I was enthusiastic about the process we had shared and that I wanted to show. The consequence was that another group had less time. Jill pointed this out to me. Since then I endeavour to combine my concentration on a task with attention to what is happening around me.

* * *

In 1978 I travelled outside Europe for the first time. We landed in Ayacucho in the Andes. The aeroplane we boarded in Lima had remained suspended in the air for a long time because of a technical problem. We had been called back to the capital and had then left again after a small man in yellow overalls on a ladder had given a couple of turns of his spanner to one of the motors. We could hear the sound of chicks coming from the captain's cabin. They had been stored there because the airplane's baggage container was full of boxes of theatre costumes and props.

Suspended in the air I had been afraid: I had gripped hold of Iben Nagel Rasmussen, who was sitting beside me, while I stared at Tage Larsen and Leif Bech who had stopped talking and gone quite pale. Arriving in Ayacucho, though, I only felt the fascination of the strong landscape around us. The airplane's wings seemed to touch the mountains as we prepared to land on the runway that appeared suddenly on top of the plateau in front of us.

We walked to town from the airport. There was no public transport. In 1978 there had been revolts all over the country in protest against the rise in food prices dictated by the military junta. A state of emergency and curfew had been declared. The civil war, which would see Sendero Luminoso and the Peruvian army fighting violently for twenty years, was just starting. We noticed soldiers hiding behind bushes. Burnt tyres and broken glass littered the road. Children, women and men looked impassively at us. Our white faces didn't dare smile at the dark faces we met. The people wore black hats and stripy brown ponchos. We felt useless and out of place. At the hotel where we stayed, our jeans were ironed and we were served coca-leaf tea to give our lungs respite from the altitude.

We had arrived in Ayacucho to take part in an international Third Theatre Group Meeting organised by Cuatrotablas and its director Mario Delgado. The meeting had gathered theatre groups from all over Latin America who were curious about Odin Teatret's way of making theatre and suspicious of its motives. We decided to follow the Meeting from outside and, while the

In the central square of Ayacucho, Peru, 1978
Nando Taviani, Leif Bech, Else Marie Laukvik, Julia Varley, Francis Pardeilhan, Tom Fjordfalk, Roberta Carreri, Iben Nagel Rasmussen, Tage Larsen, Eugenio Barba, Torgeir Wethal, Torben Bjelke, Silvia Ricciardelli, Peter Elsass, Ester Nagel, Toni Cots

Photo: Tony D'Urso

Latin American groups were closed in the seminar space exchanging techniques and experiences, Odin Teatret concentrated its efforts on being visible in the town.

The next day, wearing our street performance costumes and carrying our musical instruments, we went to the market. In such a poor country I was overwhelmed by an opulence of colours: jungle flowers, mountains of oranges and carrots, woollen and cotton skirts, seed necklaces, juicy and bloody meat, hats decorated with ribbons, hand-woven ponchos and carpets, plastic and jute bags, terracotta plates and Inca Cola. Under the sun and in the thin dry mountain air, everything shone and seemed closer. The dark faces surrounded us.

'*Toca! Toca! Toca!*' Play, perform, dance: a request, an order, a necessity. Our instruments came out of their cases, the stilts started to move more confidently. Surrounded by hundreds of people we started to improvise. Suddenly what we did – theatre – was important, useful, attractive.

We were taken along a path following the shouts of people inviting us into a labyrinth of tiny streets, squares and stairs. For the people at the market, the most amusing scene was when the police stopped us and we were taken to the police station: what we did was forbidden. Many people followed us and everyone laughed at Tom Fjordfalk who could not pass through the door on his stilts and at Iben Nagel Rasmussen who put her drum with its coloured ribbons on a table full of official papers. Eugenio Barba apologised to the police officers: we didn't know that we were not allowed to perform, we were Danish, we were only showing our folk dances, we had been sent by the Queen of Denmark ... We were admonished. They explained to us that it was forbidden to assemble people on the streets or to play instruments in public: Peru was in a state of emergency.

The next day, still dressed in costume, but this time carrying the stilts on our shoulders, in silence, walking in pairs at a permitted distance from each other, we went to take a souvenir photograph under the town monument in the main square. We were recognised and invited to give a performance in a *barrio* up on the side of the mountain, where a different law was in force, where *gringos* and police did not dare go.

Our stilts danced in a small, steep, cobblestone square and our clowns played several scenes in front of a hut where, in response, a band with damaged instruments played under a Madonna carrying a Child with indigenous features. There we saw the Scissor Dance for the first time: a complex foot dance with acrobatic jumps accompanied by the rhythm of the two metal parts of a pair of scissors continuously knocking against each other.

Around us people laughed and applauded, their faces and teeth were dark, and they ceaselessly invited us to drink. First I was offered *chicha* (an alcoholic drink made from maize), as a sign of friendship, and then, from an unlabelled bottle that I could not refuse, a liquid clearer and thicker than water. It was handed to me by the old, wrinkled hand of a small, thin man, who had danced while playing the flute and beating the drum, his smile brown from chewing coca leaves. The drinks passed continuously from mouth to mouth fuelling the festivities. I was not a white, foreign and (supposedly) rich woman, a *gringa*. I was orange and green like my costume, which I didn't take off until we left for Lima in the doorless bus that the theatre group Cuatrotablas had managed to obtain from the Peruvian Ministry of Culture.

One of Tony D'Urso's photographs shows me on the bank of the river in Ayacucho wearing my orange and green costume, with a pair of sneakers and holding my trombone. I am talking to a young girl with a heavy load on her shoulders wrapped in a poncho typical of the Andean regions. She had been to the river to wash clothes: she was fifteen years old and had three children. A little earlier we had sat on the bank of the icy water in which she beat and rubbed the clothes. She had asked me if it were true that in my country a pill existed that prevented women from having children. I don't remember what I answered.

* * *

Meeting by the river, Ayacucho, Peru, 1978
Photo: Tony D'Urso

During a tour in Cuba, I was taken one morning to a tobacco factory. It was a big room with about two hundred workers, mostly women, sitting in rows at old wooden tables all facing in the same direction like a school. They made the famous Cuban cigars for export. I call it a factory because there were many people working together, but it had no modern features and there were no machines in sight.

Teatro Escambray, a group from Santa Clara province, presented a dramatic reading on the life of José Martí there, in the tradition that decrees that twice a day someone reads a story to the workers. I had difficulty in following the performance as my attention was totally captivated by the women working.

On each of their tables were piles of tobacco leaves and two wooden blocks into which were carved a line of holes in the shape of half cigars, that fitted together when put on top of each other. Each table had a shelf on top and some of these bundles of completed cigars tied with coloured ribbon. The women worked at different rhythms and were at different phases in the making of their cigars. Each worker went through the whole process of producing a cigar, perched on her stool on top of which some had put cushions. Some of the tables were decorated with photographs, newspaper cuttings and small pictures.

Gradually I understood the order of work. First the workers took a bundle of the larger tobacco leaves and folded, rolled and shaped them. Then they cut a longer leaf into a special moon shape using a small sharp piece of metal and rolled the leaf around the embryonic cigar. They cut away the straggling ends. Some bits would land on the floor as the women quickly wiped their table with their forearms; other bits would end up in a container placed behind each person's chair. What began to look more like a cigar would be put into one of the holes in their boxes. When all the holes were full, the women put the lid on and placed the box under pressure. Many boxes were piled up on top of each other under a weight tightened by a press. The women left their chairs, opened the press, turned some of the boxes upside down, put new boxes in, operated the wheel that closed the press again and returned to their places with another box filled with pressed cigars. They obviously recognised their own boxes, although I could not figure out how. They turned the cigars round and put them back under the press. Finally they chose some special leaves, which seemed to me to be more elastic and wet, to finish the cigars, rolling them around one of the ends to make a closed tip. Sometimes the cigar was licked and put into the mouth to give the finishing touch. Then the cigars were tied in a bundle with a piece of wide string that had been distributed beforehand by a stern head of department.

It was hot. The room was open onto the street on two sides, but the big ventilators on the ceiling did not move. The women, mostly dressed in shorts and sleeveless T-shirts, were of all ages and shades of skin colour; some had red or blonde hair, some had green or blue eyes. Many of them were good-looking and had curious and lively faces. The presence of foreigners and of a Cuban actress who had been on television enhanced their animation. At times they chatted with their neighbours, at times they listened to the story, looking up and smiling, at times they seemed lost in their thoughts. They never stopped working. Their hands knew exactly what to do. Some of them had young apprentices sitting behind them who learned by watching.

A woman came with a metal cup of coffee, which was passed down a row of workers. Everyone took just one sip. They answered questions willingly. Some of them worked from six in the morning, some of them had worked in the same factory for thirty years. They earned a certain amount for each cigar they produced.

I observed them in this steamy room smelling of tobacco and admired their *real* work: a repetitive action with no personal meaning except earning money. I wondered about their lives. 'We are *guajiro*, peasants from the province.' Most of them had never even travelled to the capital, La Havana. They rolled dozens and dozens of cigars a day to make a living; fell in love, got married, had children, and worked to maintain their families. Participating in local politics could be a way of making living conditions better. The rest of the world was experienced only through television.

Before leaving the factory I accepted a gift with a smile: a cigar. I keep it as a reminder of my privileges: I learn and enjoy myself even in the effort and fatigue of overcoming the daily constraints of the theatre craft; I travel and choose my own schedule and can vary my activities; I work hard, because the profession I have chosen has a meaning for me.

* * *

María Cánepa, a well-known traditional actress, was recalling the brutality of the 1973 military coup in her country, Chile. At that time the news of how Pinochet took power had distressed many people in Italy as well. While I interviewed her, María's voice made me relive the indignation, sadness and need to protest that had made me and Teatro del Drago make an agit-prop performance in Milan. María's memories mixed with mine. Her passion touched me and, sitting with the recorder in my hand, I had a lump in my throat. I had to let others know her words, to convey the values contained in the sound of her voice.

> In 1968, all kinds of social reforms reached Chile from Europe. The theatre followed suit politicising itself and presenting plays that reflected the conditions of the working class. Salvador Allende's presidential victory had made us dream and after the military coup d'état we sank into an abyss of despair. It was like permanently walking hand in hand with death. I lost my husband. Pablo Neruda's death was also very painful.
>
> Salvador Allende was buried in Valparaíso, under military escort; they only allowed his wife Trencha Busi to accompany him. The funeral was organised secretly, at dawn, to avoid any tribute by the Chilean people to the president who had meant so much to their country.

When the coup happened, on 11 September 1973, Pablo Neruda was in hospital in Santiago. He managed to hear Allende's last message. Despite the gravity of his illness, he was aware of what was happening. His desolation quickly aggravated his state of health. Twelve days later his heart stopped beating. That same evening, while his wife Matilde was with the Poet, the military invaded their home on the hill of San Cristóbal, they opened the water supply and flooded the house, smashed doors and windows, destroyed furniture and personal belongings, burned books and objects. It was raining and cold. Matilde decided to organise the funeral wake in this house exactly as it was, to show the dictatorship's horror to all those who came to take leave of Neruda. The young people of his party made a picket to watch over the coffin. My husband, already sick, went to pay homage and say farewell to the Poet. He returned home shaken by what he had seen. Priests – among whom was our friend Mariano Puga – diplomats, humble people and students participated in the procession. All were silent, pervaded by an immense anguish. The Chilean people were crying. I had always imagined that we would sing *When the Poet Dies* to him, when he died. Instead he was buried in a borrowed grave. Later Matilde moved him to a modest niche so that she would be able to lie beside him when she passed away.

There was no longer any respect for significant personalities and for what they represented. At that time there was no respect for anything at all. But theatre continued to be the voice of those who could not speak.

In Chile, between 1973 and 1989, theatre was a small and precarious island of freedom. The regime didn't close all the theatre venues to avoid international comment: after all a performance involved only a very few people. Theatre didn't have the strength to fight against repression directly, but it could guarantee a parallel culture as a space for meeting, memory and dialogue.

María worked in the *poblaciones*, the poor districts of Santiago. She gave 'harmless' courses in diction; teaching women to speak out loud and encouraging them to express themselves individually. The rules of diction and voice placement, the reading and writing exercises became a small gift that subsequently allowed her 'theatre students' to participate in the meetings that their imprisoned husbands could not attend. They spoke of the impossibility of finding work, of their children, of schools. They were extremely grateful because they had overcome the fear of speaking out in public.

In 2001 I invited María to the third Transit Festival in Holstebro, dedicated to generations in theatre. María, who was eighty years old, came accompanied by her second husband, the fifty-year-old director Juan Cuevas, and presented a poetry reading with poems by Pablo Neruda, Gabriela Mistral and Nicanor Parra. María read in Spanish – the only language she knew – standing behind a lectern. She wore an elegant suit. Her only preparation consisted in going to the hairdresser that afternoon.

After the performance a twenty-year-old Australian girl told me with glowing eyes: 'Now I understand why my grandmother always used the best tablecloth and plates for Sunday meals. From now on I want to make theatre with this same approach.'

* * *

Sanjukta Panigrahi died in 1997. She had contributed to the foundation of a tradition of Indian classical dance, the Odissi. She danced on stage and in life as a little girl and a warrior. With just one pirouette she knew how to go from representing a snake to behaving like a god, from being a furious elephant to a maiden decorating herself with garlands of flowers. On stage, in her white costume or dressed in vivid colours, she always managed to surprise me with the mischievous expression in her eyes that accompanied complex rhythmical sequences of dance. In the performances of Theatrum Mundi, the ISTA (International School of Theatre Anthropology) ensemble, we shared the rare experience and subsequent wonder of a dialogue among different performance genres underpinned by a similar artisan's logic.

At Odin Teatret, after her death, we built a *varde* (cairn) and tower in her memory. The *varde* is a heap of stones, about one metre high, that in Norway as in Scotland marks the way across moors and mountains. We erected Sanjukta's *varde* in the garden in front of our theatre in Holstebro. The tower is at the back. It contains an octagonal room with big windows, furnished with a carpet and a sofa. We use it for important meetings and particular work sessions.

To build the *varde* we wrote to all the people who had known Sanjukta asking them to send us a stone. For months our postman couldn't understand why Odin Teatret's post had become so heavy. Packets of all sizes arrived from every part of the world. They contained pebbles, fragments of rock, semi-precious stones, tiny sculptures, pieces smoothed by sea waves or covered with seeds and lichens.

During the first meeting of the ISTA artists after Sanjukta's death, we listened to her husband, Raghunath Panigrahi, sing to the sunset on a solitary beach at the North Sea. After returning to the theatre, we gathered around the space selected for the *varde*. In silence each of us placed her or his stone, to which we added all those that had been sent. Kanichi Hanayagi danced with his fan. The Balinese ensemble, led by I Made Djimat, lit incense and prayed, and we of Odin Teatret sang. Many cried. Then we went for supper, to talk, make projects and discuss our daily activities.

The next day we started rehearsals for the new Theatrum Mundi performance, *Four Sonnets for Sanjukta*. In the final scene during which I could no longer hear the sound of steps or the bells tied to Sanjukta's ankles, I looked at the face of Mr Peanut, the character with a skull head, who rested on my lap like a baby. My heart ached with the awareness of how *everything* had changed irrevocably. The strongest pain, however, was to realise that, despite Sanjukta's absence, the performance was improving.

* * *

After the first festival in Cardiff in 1986, the following year I organised a second meeting of what by then was the Magdalena Project. I had invited thirty actresses of different nationalities to Odin Teatret. I wanted to build on the collaboration during the training. Each woman had the opportunity to lead the others and change the situation. It was like a theatre game that I called 'the marathon' despite it being more similar to a relay race. The first 'director' created a scene with all the other actresses; then the second 'director' elaborated this scene to a certain point that, in turn, was the starting point for the third 'director', and so on. On the last day, in groups of two or three, we occupied the whole theatre presenting many small performances: in rehearsal rooms, changing rooms, a cupboard, on the top of a tree . . .

Zofia Kalinska, the Polish actress who had collaborated with Tadeusz Kantor, was part of a group that presented its work in Odin Teatret's blue room. For a year she had directed *The Magic Circle*, a performance project with a group of six women. Zofia always used to say: 'You can do everything, but not today!' In the blue room, Zofia sat with a mirror in her hand, enveloped in a black coat that emphasised her blue eyes and her blonde and white hair. Her large figure was transfigured. She no longer looked like a nice round clumsy grandmother. She didn't do anything; she only looked at herself in the mirror and at times glanced around. I couldn't take my eyes off her. Zofia captured my attention as if I was bewitched. I had the feeling that I existed only while following each of her slight movements. I couldn't understand from where this immense presence came and how she emanated it. I wanted to solve the mystery, but the more I watched the less it was clear to me. Zofia had invaded the space and my mind. She was magical.

* * *

Buendía is the name of a theatre group in La Havana. They work in a deconsecrated orthodox church that they had saved from ruins and rebuilt. Flora Lauten, the founder of the group, is one of the most prominent figures in Cuban theatre of the last thirty years. The playwright and dramaturgical advisor Raquel Carrió joined her to form the group. Together they have developed a particular and original style that mixes popular Cuban *buffo* theatre, folklore of African origin, themes inherent in Cuba's political and social context and allusions to world classics.

Flora did her apprenticeship with Vicente Revuelta, the director who first introduced Brecht and Grotowski to Cuba. She worked for some years with Teatro Escambray, in a rural area, living with her two children in primitive conditions and taking theatre to the peasants of the region. Before the revolution, Flora had been the last Miss Cuba. One only hears about this when her mother interrupts her piano recitals to proudly display an album of photographs and newspaper cuttings. Flora and her mother live together in an apartment by the sea.

Teatro Buendía have performed at festivals, won prizes and toured throughout Europe, the Americas and Australia. As is usual in Cuba, the State guarantees them a salary, but takes all their earnings. They don't receive any subsidy. To pay for programmes, photographs or technical equipment for a new production, and to finance tours, they have to ask the Consejo Nacional de las Artes Escénicas for support. They earn the equivalent of about fifteen dollars a month each. Since a double economy exists in Cuba, survival has become difficult. The state money covers basic needs, while the *peso convertible*, which can be obtained only by changing foreign currency, is meant for everything else, such as, for example, petrol or beer. One of the consequences of the difficult economic situation is that many Cubans are tempted to emigrate.

Over the years, many members of Teatro Buendía have decided not to return home after their foreign tours. New generations succeed those who have surrendered, forced to earn dollars or euro for themselves and their families. This choice has never tempted Flora and Raquel. They could not live anywhere else but on their island. For each new production they grit their teeth and start again, replacing the actresses and actors now living in exile, mobilising an enormous energy. They don't give up.

Once, however, Flora also felt tired. Her sixtieth birthday was drawing near. She was alone asking herself if it was worthwhile to gather the group once more to start on a new performance. Perhaps it was better to give up and devote herself just to her family and to teaching.

There is no beach in the part of La Havana where Flora lives: the coast is rocky, uneven and sharp. From here hundreds of Cubans have left in improvised boats made of inflated tyres, in the hope of crossing the Gulf of Mexico and reaching the coast of Florida. Many have ended up as food for sharks. Walking along this coast, ensnared by doubts, Flora stopped in front of a dry, broken tree that had been brought to shore by the waves. She loaded it on her shoulders and, doubled up under its weight, she crossed roads and squares, until reaching Buendía's deconsecrated church. She held the tree up in the middle of the room and embraced it. She decided to start again.

Every time I visited Cuba between 2001 and 2002, I saw Buendía's performance of *The Bacchae*. Flora had directed it and Raquel had written the text, inspired by Euripides. Eight young students had joined some of the older actresses and actors who had returned. Once again the church rang with the vitality of voices singing.

In the last scene of *The Bacchae*, a woman in black embraces the dry tree. The woman, Agave, seems to be pregnant. Under her cape she hides the head of her son Pentheus whom she tore to pieces during a Dionysian ritual in the mountains. She is pregnant with death, holding on to the lifeless tree.

She vows: 'Here my ancestors are buried, here my children were born. Nobody will take me away from my land.' Sand runs through her fingers.

* * *

Melissa came to Holstebro with her group of Colombian rappers accompanied by Patricia Ariza. She was seventeen years old and seven months pregnant. She lied to Patricia in order to travel to Europe for the second Transit Festival with the theme Theatre – Women – Politics. With her big belly she hopped higher than anyone, sang with more decision, danced ceaselessly and taught with enthusiasm. She told us about her life and how she had started making theatre. She said that she wanted to help the young women of her country. She lived in the Crucecita, one of the poorest districts of Bogotá.

One afternoon Melissa, with all of Gotas de Rap, knocked on the door of the Teatro La Candelaria where Patricia works as actress and director. Patricia feared an assault from this threatening group of young people, but they only wanted to work with her. They had heard that Patricia had staged a *Hamlet* with a drug addict and they were convinced that she was the right person to lead them. They were right. Patricia has directed a performance with a group of young prostitutes, a concert with children from Urabá (the Colombian region on the border with Panama, devastated by civil war), a festival of *desechables* (garbage-people: this is what some sectors of society call beggars and children who live on the streets in Colombia), a project with *desplazados* (displaced people who have had to leave their homes and towns because of civil war), and she coordinates an association of artists for peace.

Patricia and her partner, Carlos Setizabal, have staged an opera with Gotas de Rap: the true story of a young man who was murdered. His friends exhumed his body and took him to the sea because this was his last wish. They carried the corpse as if he was drunk; they feasted, danced, drank and sang, and at the end took a bus to the coast. In the performance, Melissa played the murdered boy's girlfriend. She sang against the military, against machismo, against violence, dressed in a t-shirt and wide trousers that dragged on the floor.

I met the rappers and Patricia in Wuppertal in Germany in 1997 at a festival organised by Kordula Lobeck. I directed the festival's closing performance in Wuppertal's town hall. After an initial parade, the Colombian rappers 'assaulted' the building and went onto the roof to wave their enormous flag. The spectators were welcomed by unemployed youths from Marseilles who had become puppeteers, under the leadership of Marie-Josée Ordener. In the second room a choir of patients from local psychiatric hospitals was directed by Brigitte Cirla. In the third room, and along the staircases, prisoners and ex-prisoners from Milan's San Vittore jail performed led by Donatella Massimilla. The spectators were introduced into the town council room through a series of doors while the actors, as if they were jailers, made sounds with a ring of big keys. Inside were imposing tables belonging to the mayor and councillors. Everything was clean, severe and smelled of order and power. The rappers appeared suddenly from under these tables, jumping on top of them to sing and dance wildly around the figure of Mr Peanut who transformed from Death into a child. Melissa ran to the windows, opened them and raced down to the square inviting the spectators to follow her. She gathered messages from school children who smiled at her, put the messages into a paper boat, attached the boat to a balloon and let it fly off into the sky. Standing on a ladder in the middle of the square, surrounded by hundreds of people, she followed the boat disappearing into the blue with her glowing smile. The spectators accompanied her gaze full of hope for the future.

I dedicated the third Transit Festival on the theme Theatre – Women – Generations to Melissa. She was an example: she taught us to look at the distant horizon. She was pregnant again when she died in a car accident together with her first child.

* * *

In 2002, Brigitte Kaquet asked me to help her during the Festival Voix de Femmes that she organises every two years in Belgium. She wanted me to stage an intervention of mothers and relatives of 'disappeared' people. An international network had been created around the Festival with the theme of 'cultures in resistance'. Brigitte wanted to make this artistic and political encounter visible during the last concert in which all the artists presented one or more pieces from their repertoire. I chose Soha Bechara to read the declaration that the 'mothers' network had written during the week of the Festival. Soha has spent ten years confined in jail for having tried to kill a commander from the militias that collaborated with the Israelis during the occupation of her country, Lebanon. Soha, thirty years old, black eyes and dark hair, accepted.

The Argentinian actress Ana Woolf entered marching with an empty chair on her shoulders. Mothers and family members of the 'disappeared' followed her in single file in silence. The chair was placed on the stage in the middle of a semicircle formed by the women. A tiny Algerian 'mother', illiterate, a scarf covering her hair (she told me that she would take it off only when she saw her husband again), placed a big open book on the chair. After having shown it to the spectators, every woman inserted a page in the book with writings in her own language, sketches, words full of anger and pain.

Soha started to read the declaration. Her voice was resolute, warm, unwavering; she was aware of the meaning of every word. At the end, the youngest woman closed the book and held it up to her breast while a Berber woman started to sing in the audience. The singer and the group of women on stage joined in the song and danced. The rhythm of the song was happy, the singer was moved to tears, the women started to smile. Their message was one of sorrow certainly, but also an invitation to fight for life. They descended from the stage and mixed with the spectators.

The 'mother' from Plaza de Mayo had lost eight relatives counting sons and daughters-in-law; the Iranian 'mother' had six photographs hanging from her neck to remember her husband and children; the son of the Palestinian 'mother' had recently been killed while wearing the peace movement's green shirt; the husband of the taciturn Kurdish 'mother' was in jail; the Yugoslav 'mother' did not know where her brother and husband were; the daughter of the Belgian 'mother' had disappeared, killed by a paedophile who was still not convicted; and there were many more.

The silence seemed endless and then suddenly the spectators reacted with lengthy applause. Soha whispered to Ana: 'We'll do it, you'll see, we'll do it! We will change the world!'

* * *

I was giving a workshop in Mostar in an old gym. Children of all ages went there habitually from school to play ball and run about, but during the Alternative Academy and International Theatre Festival the room was used as a performance space. The offices of the local police were just outside. Men in uniform welcomed me in the morning. I worked with the participants on vocal actions, on the relationship between body and voice, text and movement. To save time, at the end of the workshop, I had prepared the props for my performance, *Doña Musica's Butterflies*, in one of the changing rooms. I had ironed my costume and the embroidered shawls that cover Doña Musica's table and chair. I had prepared the little black wooden box with its hidden flame and butterflies. I had taken out the lamps and placed around them the white flowers that form the performance's garden. Then I had gone for lunch and to present a work demonstration at the Puppet Theatre on the other side of town.

Mostar is full of small cemeteries. Christian and Muslim graves occupy what used to be parks. The date of birth on the graves varies, that of death is always the same: 1993. The inhabitants buried their dead in the middle of town because they could not move away from the built areas. During the war, my host, Sejo, had sent his wife, son and daughter to live in Vienna and Zagreb. I asked him why they had not returned. 'My house was bombed. We don't have a place to live.' All their clothes, photographs and books had been destroyed. He really wanted to get hold of a new copy of Stanislavski's *My Life in Art* that a friend had given him when he was young.

Sejo and his group had kept on making theatre during the war. They took off their uniforms and, armed with special authorisation, went out after curfew. They met in a cave to rehearse. Local inhabitants gathered around the rehearsals. The festival programme was all that was interrupted in that period. Now they had been able to reopen an office in a reconstructed building, in the quarters of the public baths. The theatre was under the swimming pool and the offices under the roof on the top floor. To see a performance and reach the telephone in the office I had to walk over planks of wood and plastic sheets. 'Is theatre a luxury?' I wondered while I looked out of the window: the main square had just been rebuilt with a modern fountain at the centre, bright new Italian buses were parked there and crowds of children were begging from the foreign soldiers sitting at the restaurants' tables. The soldiers wore the same blue UN uniforms and berets as those soldiers who just took photographs when Joha, an actor who works with Sejo, was captured and taken to a concentration camp with other men and women from his town.

The following morning Doña Musica's white artificial flowers had disappeared from the changing room. Thefts can happen on tour, but thieves usually take technical equipment rather than props. The room should have been secure: armed police guarded the entrance. I was surprised as well as worried. Why had they only taken the flowers? Was someone trying to boycott the Festival and the performances? Not understanding the language, I could not follow the discussions that arose after I announced the flowers' disappearance. Sejo was mortified and furious. He promised that he would solve the mystery and find the thirty flowers that were missing for the performance the following evening. I started leading the workshop again.

While I worked I peered at Sejo who appeared from time to time with a couple of flowers. The children who had come for their gymnastics lesson the previous evening had taken them. The soldiers and police officers had not thought it strange that they left with flowers in their hands. Some children had taken them home, others had hidden them, others had thrown them in the rubbish. In the ruined city they must have thought that artificial flowers were superfluous objects unworthy of any kind of consideration. Sejo visited the families of all the children on the gymnastics class list. Joha went to the nearby town to buy new white flowers, but they were not the same. I was sad. The flowers returned in a bad state, some cut up, others creased, stained, missing petals. Ten flowers were never found. They are still in Mostar.

* * *

In February 2001 I was invited by the American University of Cairo to perform and teach. I took advantage of the tour to travel on the Nile and visit the temples along the river. One day, halfway along the journey, I reached Luxor.

The warm and incredibly vibrant colours hidden in a hole beneath the desert in Nefertari's tomb had been painted to honour only the dead and the gods. But nowadays, for a maximum of ten minutes, ten people at a time are allowed inside, up to a total of one hundred and fifty visitors a day. I had already seen many other tombs of pharaohs, queens, nobles and their children in the Valleys of the Kings and Queens close to Luxor and been struck by the knowledge and artistic skill of our ancestors 3,000 or 4,000 years back. And yet – even though I had been warned that the tomb of Ramses II's wife was special – I was completely taken by surprise.

It must have been the contrast of descending the steps into the tomb accompanied by a group of Japanese and North American tourists, leaving behind the blinding sand and stone and sun of the desert and the cameras and postcards of the outside world. The density of the colours jumped off the walls and bewildered me; greens and oranges I had never seen before. I put my hand to my mouth and stood very still. Tears started falling. I had never had such a reaction before and was not aware that I could be moved to tears by looking at paintings. I was only in the first room. After some minutes I gathered my courage, and approached one of the columns to look into the next room while descending more steps. Never in my life had I seen anything so beautiful, I kept on repeating to myself. First I saw the colours and later the shapes, Nefertari in her white dress, the flowers, feathers, jaguar skins, the cows and bull. Nefertari stood proudly, stepping forwards, lovely. Every detail of her neat body and face was precise, her elongated black eyes shining with wisdom and curiosity.

Once all the temples were painted in colour. When a pharaoh died they were abandoned and slowly they filled with sand carried by the wind from the desert. Incredibly grateful for what I had experienced, I was aware how inadequate my thanks were to the guide – a man from Nubia, the region turned into a lake by the Aswan dam.

The guide could no longer visit the homes and tombs of his family, as they were now under water for ever. He had explained how the rhythm of life in Egypt changed when it was no longer regulated by the seasonal floods of the Nile, and how the temple of Abou Simbel was saved by moving it stone by stone to a higher hill to avoid it being submerged. All this happened only some fifty years ago. I was witnessing a thousand-year-old heritage and half a century of radical change.

Continuing my travels, I reflected upon what determines such drastic decline in countries so rich in culture and history, and why, when we can send people to the moon, we are no longer able to make colours of the quality made thousands of years ago. No scientist has been able to discover the secret of those colours. Does this mean that quality of that kind is no longer essential in our lives today?

* * *

I was in Salvador in Brazil to work with August Omolú and Eugenio Barba on the performance *Orô de Otelo*. In the evenings I attended some Candomblé ceremonies. Women were separated from men, so I always sat among strangers, too shy to ask questions about the meaning of the different passages of the ritual.

The first ceremony I saw was in a very small room in the back of a house. Like everyone else, I left my shoes outside and sat on a bench, with the three ceremonial drums on my left, in front of a barred window. At the end one of the drummers started dancing. He seemed to be in a trance even though I had been told that this was not possible for a drummer. He pulled up his trousers and put a white sash around his bare breast. At times he would stop dancing, place his hands behind his back and wait for one of the women to come and adjust his sash before starting to dance again.

The background for the next ceremony I witnessed was a sumptuous house surrounded by cars and taxis. Inside everything was white: marble floor, walls, chairs and clothes. Many women were dancing in a circle around a pillar all dressed in huge lace skirts, their hair hidden by long scarves. At the sound of their particular rhythms, the Orixá, the 'saints', descended upon the devotees who danced to 'ride' them and make them go into a trance. One by one they were taken out of the room, while the others kept on dancing in a circle. In front of me a woman, who appeared to be a normal visitor, started shaking from her shoulders; she fell off her chair and rolled on the floor. Nervously I asked myself if just anyone could fall into trance, as the woman was taken out of the room through the door where the others had disappeared. Then I heard fireworks in the garden announcing the entrance of the 'saints' dressed in their splendid costumes. One of them kept rushing from the centre to the four sides of the room. The observers moved away quickly as she arrived. Her eyes were closed, but she could see. She held a small silver sword and had a crown: she was Iansá, the warrior goddess of wind. I did not know this at the time as it was necessary for me to see many ceremonies before being able to recognise the variations of the different Orixá rhythms, dances and costumes.

During the ceremonies the dancers in trance would stop to have their jewellery and clothes adjusted. Their faces were serious, sometimes aggressive, their eyes vacant, but present in their bodies. They reminded me of the faces of Odin actresses and actors during training. With the trance, the casual movements and relaxed repetition of the dance acquired precision and life, just like those of an actress's actions. In trance, the body knowledge took a spectacular and extraordinary form, which could not be repeated in a state of normal consciousness. This capacity is inherent in the tradition. The same precision that an actress achieves through training and rehearsal is perceived in these bodies as knowledge induced by the movement of the dance and the rhythm of the drums.

The precise shape of the movements is achieved by modelling a particular quality of energy in action. The body exploits and goes beyond its limits to rediscover an archaic memory, to give life to what the dancers are not conscious of knowing and will not be able to remember afterwards. The modelled energy does not think of expressing anything, nevertheless it reverberates with the enigmatic atmosphere of the experience. I cannot say I understand the meanings and codes of the Candomblé ceremonies, but I will never forget having witnessed them.

* * *

In Bali a lot of time is dedicated to beauty. The decorations in the streets and homes, in markets and temples are exuberant and colourful. Nature helps with an abundance of water and flowers, and agriculture with the terraced rice fields. The women take hours every day to fulfil their duties towards the family shrine and the village temple. All offerings are handmade and all food for the ceremonies is prepared and cooked at home. The women dress in ceremonial costumes and walk for miles carrying trays with offerings on their heads. They learn to dance, sing and play music as a form of prayer.

Each time I visit Bali, I ask myself how women there can find so much time to carry out their customary rituals every day. In Europe, where eight hours are spent at work or school, it is usually only a few widows or great-grandmothers of the south who attend church services every morning, or nuns, who have chosen prayer as their profession. Time seems to be what I miss most. Time passes and I run after it.

* * *

Luckily I was giving a voice workshop: the theatre where I was working was dark. The electricity came back on only for the evening performance, and even then not always. I found out what *apagón* meant. I had read about *apagones* in newspaper articles on the economic crisis in Cuba and I had heard about them from Flora Lauten and Raquel Carrió: they were ways of 'saving' electricity in parts of the city.

Some cooked at night for the next day, some said the heat of the summer months prevented them from working, and some queued for hours to see a theatre performance. I was in Cuba during the so-called 'special' period, in 1994. The traffic was non-existent and the road lamps were turned off. Every day there would be accidents with the Chinese bicycles that had no lights or reflective glass, ridden by two or three people at a time. Apart from the accidents, people were afraid of assaults in the dark: to steal a bicycle in a country where there is no public transport is a good deal.

The theatre lobby had a large glass door. I gathered the workshop participants there to see their faces. There were many more than those on the original list. I asked them if they wanted to work six hours consecutively or have a break. It was difficult to reach an agreement. The main problem was water: how to get hold of it in the centre of town? I had to get the theatre's secretary to promise she would leave open the office in which there was some drinking water available.

They were all puzzled by the idea that it was possible to work for so long. They were even more confused when, as the first task, I made them clean the stage floor. Then, to teach them to 'give' their voice and make vocal actions, I asked the participants to speak a text while they 'played ball' throwing shoes at each other. It was not easy to find the shoes in the dark when they fell. I also made them do an exercise I called 'the Cuban car': to start the car you use a handle and when the motor fires the handle is thrown far away; while turning the handle vigorously you make the sound of an 'r' and when throwing it away you follow its flight with the sound of a vowel.

Raquel's car inspired the exercise: she borrowed her neighbour's battery to start it. The car was of Russian origin and it was impossible to get spare parts for it. With my foreign passport and dollars I could buy petrol at a filling station for diplomatic personnel, at any time and without queuing. I decided to fill Raquel's tank. Raquel looked at me with her eyes popping out of her head, but I insisted and she started filling up. The petrol poured out of a thousand holes in the tank and I ran to find a bucket to recover the precious fuel. The next time we only half filled it.

The special period has ended, but not the *apagones*. In recent years I have often been to Santa Clara, a Cuban town in the province, at the invitation of Roxana Pineda and Joel Saez of Teatro Estudio. I have the habit of always going to see the small statue of Che in front of the Party's Headquarters. Unlike the commemorative monument on the outskirts of town, this statue is small and humorous. A young, good-looking Che, with long wavy hair, takes a resolute step forwards. He has a little goat and a child on his shoulders, a crowd of people coming out of the buckle of his belt, some women hidden in different parts of his chest and a fake piggy-bank opening on his back. I saw the statue for the first time because of an *apagón*: I could not prepare my performance because there was no electricity. After waiting some hours, I had decided to be a tourist.

During the first Magdalena Sin Fronteras Festival, organised by Roxana in January 2005, an *apagón* provided me with an idea. We were gathered in the theatre to see a demonstration and talk and we had all entered with candles in the dark. The foreign artists were under the spell of Cuba: they had seen an old people's home for women who had portraits of Christ beside Fidel in their bedrooms, a school for art teachers still under construction frequented by girls and boys of every colour, a very poor orphanage full of children enjoying the masks and puppets being shown to them; and they had heard how members of an independent theatre group receive a salary – low, but still a salary – and a state venue, provided simply because it is a theatre. An international theatre festival for the first time outside the capital? Not many in Cuba believed it would succeed. Bravely Roxana had accepted the challenge of breaking frontiers and bringing the world to her town: there were many candles in the room and the heat went to our heads. I asked the young women present what the Magdalena 'grandmothers' should do at the next Transit Festival in Holstebro. The answer was unanimous: make a performance together. Luckily it was dark and they couldn't see my reaction to the idea of the amount of work such an idea implied.

* * *

An ant is rushing over my piece of white paper. At times it meets the nib of my pen, then it disappears. Every stem of grass under the blank page is different. The ant does not follow the shape of the words I write, but a path of its own, apparently just as chaotic and irregular. The wind flips the paper over, my eyes go along the lines but my mind is somewhere else. I must start again.

Now the ant is on my fingers moving towards where I hold my pen. I am left-handed. When I was small I wrote back to front. 'Like Leonardo!' said my mother proudly so that it should never be a problem. The ant is climbing up and down the grass stems beside the paper, and the paper is full of words. Is this a text? Do I mean the ant on the grass or the words on the page?

How quickly ants' legs move and how thin they are. The words on paper do not follow the scent of food, home or partners. Does a text smell? A yellow flower towers over the grass. A fly buzzes close to my ear, the sun is shining and the wind continues to create confusion among my papers.

The ant, once more on my pen, is following a trail I am not able to decipher, as if composing a secret alphabet, or preparing a labyrinth. It seduces and fascinates me. Last night the moon was almost full. It freed itself unexpectedly from the clouds sliding fast across the sky, shining on the rough sea between the rocks. The sky was a Magritte painting. The light suddenly came on and nature was imitating art. Outlined by the Mediterranean umbrella pines, the sky had the shape and colours of a Japanese print. Only the ideograms were missing to connect the moon with the waves.

Words are ants running to discover a path that only we understand and texts are clouds left in a blue sky as messages that only as yet unknown women in the future will be able to read. The words on paper remain inert until someone reads them and gives them life. Then they take a surprising direction, just as surprising as the direction the ant follows while carrying an enormously heavy piece of leaf towards a black hole in the grass.

I read what I have written again: 'Sometimes it is a real struggle to get up in the morning. The bed is warm and comfortable. The pillow has taken the shape of my head and the duvet covers me from top to toe. Outside it is dark and cold. I have to go to the theatre. Work needs to be done. I could telephone and say I am ill. I have never done that. I feel so tired; my body is heavy; my eyes don't want to open. The alarm clock has rung. If I don't get up I will fall asleep again. Denmark in the winter is not inviting at six in the morning. Training, meetings, rehearsals, performances, preparing props and costumes, packing, unpacking, opening emails, answering letters, making accounts and tour plans, archiving, cleaning, reading, being a spectator, teaching, directing, learning texts, moving piles of paper from one side of the table to the other, writing a book: a routine imbued with an energy that comes from discipline but still needs strong motivation every day. The others are expecting me. We all need me to be there. If I don't do what I have to do today, tomorrow will be worse. I close my eyes again. Faces I am fond of appear; I listen to their voices. I tear myself out of bed. The warmth of the travels in Brazil, Egypt, Cuba, Bali and Chile also helps me get up. Once the day has started there is no way of stopping it.'

188 *Faces, words, landscapes*

* * *

The same day I finished the first draft of this book, I read in a newspaper that on 23 July 2004 Mostar's restored bridge will be inaugurated. I want to go back to Bosnia and cross it. Doña Musica's ten white flowers are waiting for me on the other side of the river.

Mostar's bridge
Postcard: FORTUNATRADETOURS d.o.o. Mostar

For DVDs of Odin Teatret's
Performances, Work Demonstrations
and other material, go to:

shop.odinteatret.dk/shop/frontpage.html

Performances include:

- Doña Musica's Butterflies
- The Castle of Holstebro
- Kaosmos

Work Demonstrations include:

- The Dead Brother
- The Whispering Winds
- The Echo of Silence

Odin Teatret
Nordisk teaterlaboratorium

For Product Safety Concerns and Information please contact our EU
representative GPSR@taylorandfrancis.com
Taylor & Francis Verlag GmbH, Kaufingerstraße 24, 80331 München, Germany

www.ingramcontent.com/pod-product-compliance
Lightning Source LLC
Chambersburg PA
CBHW050535300426
44113CB00012B/2119